The Other Toscanini

THE OTHER TOSCANINI

Life and Works of Héctor Panizza

Sebastiano De Filippi
Daniel Varacalli Costas

North Texas Lives of Musicians Number 13

UNT PRESS

Denton, Texas

Permissions:
University of North Texas Press
1155 Union Circle #311336
Denton, TX 76203-5017

The paper used in this book meets the minimum requirements of the
American National Standard for Permanence of Paper for Printed Library
Materials, z39.48.1984. Binding materials have been chosen for durability.

The original edition of this book was made possible thanks to the support
of the Instituto Italiano de Cultura (Embassy of Italy in Argentina) and
received institutional support from the Teatro Colón in Buenos Aires.

Library of Congress Cataloging-in-Publication Data

Names: De Filippi, Sebastiano, 1977- author. | Varacalli Costas, Daniel,
author. | Sachs, Harvey, 1946- writer of foreword. | Sequeira, Jessica, translator.
Title: The other Toscanini : the life and works of Héctor Panizza / Sebastiano
De Filippi, Daniel Varacalli Costas ; translation by Jessica Sequeira.
Other titles: Alta en el cielo. English | North Texas lives of musicians series ; no. 13.
Description: Denton, Texas : University of North Texas Press, [2019] |
Series: North Texas lives of musicians series ; number
13 | Includes bibliographical references and index.
Identifiers: LCCN 2019030012 | ISBN 9781574417746 (cloth) | ISBN 9781574417845 (ebook)
Subjects: LCSH: Panizza, Ettore. | Conductors (Music)--
Argentina--Biography. | Composers--Argentina--Biography. |
Toscanini, Arturo, 1867-1957--Friends and associates.
Classification: LCC ML422.P23 D413 2019 | DDC 780.92 [B]--dc23
LC record available at https://lccn.loc.gov/2019030012

Translation by Jessica Sequeira

"Obra editada en el marco del Programa 'Sur' de Apoyo a las Traducciones del Ministerio
de Relaciones Exteriores, Comercio Internacional y Culto de la República Argentina"
"This work published within the framework of 'Sur' Translation Support Program of the
Ministry of Foreign Affairs, International Trade and Worship of the Argentine Republic."

The electronic edition of this book was made possible
by the support of the Vick Family Foundation.

The Other Toscanini: The Life and Works of Héctor Panizza
is Number 13 in the North Texas Lives of Musicians Series

*To Benito, Pablo and Juan, to Ciro
and Fernando, and to Eugenia.*
—Sebastiano
*To my Italian ancestors, maternal and
paternal, who emigrated to Argentina.
They worked hard so that today we can listen to this music.*
—Daniel
*This book appears fifty years
after the death of Héctor Panizza,
in his memory.*
—The Authors

TABLE OF CONTENTS

LIST OF IMAGES

Foreword

by Harvey Sachs

Ars longa, vita brevis—or so the saying goes. But when the art in question is that of an interpreter of classical music—a singer, an instrumentalist, a conductor—its lifespan is not very long. If, today, the names of the violin virtuoso Niccolò Paganini, the piano virtuoso Franz Liszt, and the great conductor Gustav Mahler are still before the public, it is because they composed music that is still widely performed; the names of their contemporary virtuosi, however outstanding, are unknown to most of today's music-lovers.

In the twentieth century, many interpretive artists fooled themselves into believing that their glory would last forever, thanks to audio and video recordings. But we now know that this is not true. Yes, the names of Enrico Caruso, Jascha Heifetz, and Arturo Toscanini are still familiar to people who are deeply interested in classical music, but how many of today's music-lovers actually watch or listen with any sort of frequency to the many filmed and/or recorded examples of those artists' performances? Or think of the conductor Herbert von Karajan: during the later decades of his life, Karajan had himself filmed and recorded over and over again, in rehearsals and performances—indeed, almost every time he coughed or sneezed! —with the assumption that he would be as adored posthumously as he was in his lifetime. But within a decade of his death, his "relics" had been consigned to the same bargain bin that awaits the work of all non-creative artists.

How much worse, then, is the situation for performers whose names were not "household words" in their own day! Whether they were brilliant and widely admired or merely serious and competent in their work— if, for whatever reason, their personalities did not have the sort of éclat that attracts publicity— they are nearly always doomed to posthumous oblivion. Unless someone undertakes to resurrect their reputations.

Such an act of scholarly archaeology has been carried out with mastery, dedication, and affection by Sebastiano De Filippi and Daniel Varacalli Costas in creating this much-needed book on the conductor Héctor Panizza. Panizza made a huge contribution to musical life not only in his native Argentina but also in Italy—the country of his roots— and in the United States and elsewhere. This book not only presents a detailed, fascinating account of Panizza's life and work: it also provides an overview of musical life in Argentina before and during Panizza's lifetime as well as essential background information about music and musicians in the other parts of the world in which the Argentine maestro carried out his activities.

The authors have also turned their attention to Panizza's considerable accomplishments as a composer. In Argentina, he is known for the patriotic "Canción de la Bandera"— which, by the way, is a setting of a text, originally in Italian, by Luigi Illica, one of Puccini's principal librettists. But Panizza also wrote other operas, orchestral works, chamber music, and songs, and even if this music has not entered the category of "immortal international masterpieces," in its day it was performed by important interpreters, and some of it is undoubtedly worthy of revival today.

As the biographer of Arturo Toscanini, whom Panizza esteemed and who, in turn, honored Panizza with his trust and confidence, I have learned much from this book, which makes an important contribution to the history of twentieth-century music in Argentina and beyond.

Harvey Sachs

Nueva York, July 2015

Harvey Sachs has published ten books, of which the most recent is the biography *Toscanini: Musician of Conscience*. He has written for the *New Yorker, New York Times, Times Literary Supplement* (London), and dozens of other publications worldwide. He teaches at the Curtis Institute of Music in Philadelphia and is a former artistic director of the Società del Quartetto in Milan. He has held fellowships with the John Simon Guggenheim Foundation, the New York Public Library's Cullman Center for Scholars and Writers, and the National Endowment for the Humanities.

The Other Toscanini

Introduction

Héctor Panizza was perhaps the most prominent orchestra conductor in all of Latin America, and he is certainly one of the most important musicians to come out of Argentina. These claims may seem bold, but they expand to the grander belief that Panizza stands among the most distinguished conductors in the history of musical interpretation.

If by way of hypothesis we accept the second statement as true, the reader may then ask why Panizza's legacy dwells in relative obscurity today. We felt compelled to research his life and works, and to write this book precisely because of that curious gap in critical awareness. We aim to rectify the inadequate recognition Héctor Panizza receives for his substantial contributions to the canon.

Maestro Panizza was a tireless worker. A quick glance at his biography (which spans ninety-two years) reveals a meteoric career seemingly more at home in the 21st century than the 19th century world he came from. Panizza signed contracts with the most preeminent opera houses in the world: La Scala in Milan, Covent Garden in London, the Metropolitan in New York, the Staatsoper in Vienna, the Deutsche Oper in Berlin, the Opéra Comique in Paris, and the Teatro Colón in Buenos Aires. At each of these venues, he conducted a vast repertoire for many years. He also performed in countless smaller theaters all while skillfully managing extensive symphonic repertoires.

Panizza knew a good deal of the royalty and aristocracy who controlled the sociocultural destinies of Europe and America from the end of the belle époque to the second postwar period. These social circles often elicited praise for Panizza from some of the main composers of his time, such as Giacomo Puccini and Richard Strauss, who admired his work and held him as a thoughtful interpreter.

He recorded a great deal, although only a portion of those recordings were preserved digitally alongside a certain number of radio broadcasts from his time at the New York Metropolitan.

Panizza was also a composer, though his intense career as a conductor significantly limited his time for musical creation. Despite this, almost everyone in Argentina (even those who could not identify him or remember his name) recognizes the aria "Canción de la Bandera" from his opera *Aurora*. Since the 1940s, generations of Argentine youth have sung this melody while watching their flag climb the school-yard banner pole. Today it seems curious that, though customary for the time, *Aurora* was composed around an Italian text bearing the signature of Luigi Illica, one of the librettists of Puccini's most famous operatic trilogy: *La bohème*, *Tosca*, and *Madama Butterfly*. So one of Argentina's patriotic school songs is an aria from an Italian opera, with verses written by one of Puccini's librettists? Well, yes. This is Argentina.

Despite his birth in Buenos Aires, those who do not understand Argentinian culture of the time will perhaps question whether Panizza was Argentine. Skeptics point to his Italian parents, his studies in Italy, the subsequent development of a great part of his career in that country, and to his death in Milan. But Latin American nationality begins with the *ius soli* or "right of the soil." The European mind seems to overlook those fruits of immigration, and how the transplantation of cultures from other lands underpinned the formation of Latin America.

Those who continue to think no one makes better German music than a German, or Italian music than an Italian perpetuate the same form of nationalism responsible for two world wars. They may also believe only an Argentine can successfully compose tango, or that any other form of indigenous music may only come from that place. Facts refute this fallacy at every turn.

"Is my name Héctor or Ettore?" This question haunted Panizza his entire life. At times he felt (or was made to feel) Argentine in Italy and Italian in Argentina. Whatever the case may have been, he was esteemed and envied, and he won both friends and enemies on each side of the Atlantic. He realized the lofty achievements expected of a brilliant Argentine on both shores while ceaselessly serving his country of origin.

The few available recordings of Panizza's orchestral work display his enormous capacity for artistic talent and professional excellence. On these tapes, we can hear the rigor of his analysis in addition to his ability to imbue the fire of his baton into the soundscapes his orchestras produced. He was thoughtful of his source material, and he was as forceful and incisive as he was expressive and lyrical. He had the expertise of a European maestro from the end of the 19th century and the modernity inherent to New World conductors during the initial decades of the 20th century.

Perhaps only the conductor Arturo Toscanini possessed a repertoire, creative process, prolific productivity, and career that was comparable to what Panizza achieved. As we will see, after the Teatro alla Scala in Milan reopened as an "autonomous entity" following the Great War, Toscanini and Panizza shared space on the *cartellone* and divided their responsibilities equally, conducting the same number of operas and concerts. Not even Toscanini, the great organizer of the self-governing Scala, could be considered in this instance superior to Panizza: he needed a partner and chose the Argentine.

This in itself should have been sufficient to secure Panizza's prominence in the history of musical interpretation, but his partnership with Toscanini was just the beginning of an even greater career. Over the years, Héctor performed compositions Arturo never took on. Panizza also conducted opera companies and symphony orchestras in locales his colleague never visited.

Still, Toscanini's fame and critical praise thoroughly surpassed the recognition Panizza received, and that is a phenomenon worthy of study.

Toscanini's committed opposition to Nazism and Fascism stands among the reasons for the enormous difference in how history regards the two conductors. With regard to politics, Panizza was comparatively naïve, inadequately informed, and simply indifferent. This lack of perspective was magnified during the Second World War when the United States elevated the explosively charismatic maestro from Parma to an emblematic banner man for ethics and freedom. Panizza was conversely frightened by the conflict and demurred from public comment. He was discretion personified.

No modern orchestra conductor could feasibly emulate Toscanini's rehearsal methods. The man was infamous for throwing tantrums during rehearsals and casting toxic aggression toward his musicians. It is not an exaggeration to suppose his career would not have flourished had he begun it after the Second World War. Instead, this era marked the end of his career, and despite their somewhat deficient sound, the performance recordings this octogenarian made for the National Broadcasting Corporation in New York allow us to appreciate the life and energy he brought to his craft.

Unlike Toscanini, Panizza did not have an American advertising and publicity machine to heighten his public profile. Though, he did model a professional disposition that has withstood the test of time. He was able to show his extraordinary talent without giving in to arrogance; he was a demanding conductor and artist but he never ceased to be a gentleman. He handled his authority with grace and dignity; he had no need of authoritarianism. He had a slim figure, premature baldness, measured gestures, and his ever-present pince-nez. Despite his comparable training and talent, Panizza's composure distanced him from his wilder, more renowned colleague.

Even so, Panizza's career is cause for vertigo, and Argentina deserves to know one of its most outstanding sons; it deserves the right to disseminate and understand his work, to cast off so many other careers, past and present, frequently based on media hyperbole. With very modest advertising support and no other foundation but the excellence of his work, he still had his day as an absolute "number one."

But with the passage of time, the faint material traces of the great conductor seem to have vanished, along with the memory of his musical feats. The bust his daughter Valeria donated to La Scala broke when a careless tourist knocked it over. The copy she donated to the Teatro Colón cannot be located. The dressing room for maestros, which bore his name at the Colón, disappeared after the official completion of the theater's restoration in 2010; nothing is known about the big photograph that hung from one of its walls.

These are some of the reasons that justify this work, which does not attempt in any way to be exhaustive but rather constitutes a starting point so that other experts can take up the torch and research more deeply. It is our hope that this book contributes to the recognition Héctor Panizza deserves as one of the great musicians to emerge from Latin America, and one of the main music performers of all time.

PART ONE

THE LIFE

CHAPTER 1

MUSIC IN 19TH CENTURY ARGENTINA

It is necessary to take a brief look at the historical evolution of music institutions in Argentina if we are to understand the familial, societal, and cultural influences that molded Héctor Panizza.

The nation's taste for opera was born when Gioachino Rossini's *Il barbiere di Siviglia* premiered on September 27, 1825, in Buenos Aires at the Coliseo Provisional.[1] Opera had been present in Argentina since the birth of the country itself. The nation's first governing body gathered to consolidate power after the capture of King Fernando VII by Napoleon Bonaparte. This fact left the viceroy alone: he represented nobody. Furthermore, the now-captured Spanish monarch was also responsible for the arrival of Mariano Pablo Rosquellas, the first promotor of Rossini's opera on these shores.[2]

Rosquellas was a singer, violinist, and composer who was born in Madrid in 1790 and trained in Italy. As a child, he became a victim of political persecution when his family became involved with revolutionary activity within Spanish territory. He left his home for stranger shores and after passing through Brazil, arrived in the city of Buenos Aires where he continued to develop and sharpen his musical skills.

The music scene at this time was ripe for a renaissance. The city's major performance venue, the Teatro de la Ranchería, burned down in 1792, only to be replaced by the previously mentioned Coliseo Provisional, which opened in 1804 at the corner of Reconquista and Cangallo (today Perón) streets, diagonally from the church of La Merced. What passed for opera at this time amounted to an assortment of theater plays, arias, opera scenes, and performances of popular songs. Rosquellas immediately took note of this cultural weakness and decided to introduce himself as a serious musician by singing arias written by the most famous composer of the time: Gioachino Antonio Rossini.

Following the successful local premiere of *Il barbiere di Siviglia*, Rosquellas' devotion to Rossini's work led to a torrent of productions. In 1826, he conducted *La Cenerentola* and *L'italiana in Algeri* for the first time. A year later, he put on the much-anticipated local debut of Mozart s *Don Giovanni*, along with Rossini's *Otello*. In the following season, he did *Tancredi* and *La gazza ladra*. The year 1829 marked the return of the more serious Rossini contemplations with *Aureliano in Palmira*.

In 1830, the governor of Buenos Aires, Juan Manuel de Rosas, having just assumed office, attended the performance of a work Rosquellas had debuted in his first season: *El califa de Bagdad*. It seems this was not the opera by Rossini or Manuel García, but a composition with text in Spanish by Rosquellas himself. Despite his attendance, the governor allied with the church on questions of public morality and was resistant to the genre as a whole. He did little or nothing to support it. During that same year, Rosquellas brought *Otello* to Montevideo and later moved to Bolivia, where he would later die in the capital city Sucre in 1859.[3]

Operatic activity entered into a predictable dark period until 1848, when the Italian *impresario* Antonio Pestalardo arrived to premiere the first titles of Bellini, Donizetti, and Verdi in this region. The renaissance took place in another venue: the Teatro de la Victoria, which had opened ten years before on the street of the same name (today Hipólito Yrigoyen), between Tacuarí and Buen Orden (today Bernardo de Irigoyen). For all practical purposes, it was the first theater hall dedicated to opera built in Argentina. Though this landmark event occurred during Rosas' rule, the political climate had to change —a constitution for the country had to be dictated— before opera could further develop. Thus just as knowledge of the Italian *bel canto* in the first half of the *Ottocento* came to Argentina thanks to Rosquellas, the first performances of the work of Giuseppe Verdi took place thanks to Pestalardo.

On September 7, 1848, Verdi's music was first heard in Buenos Aires, with the duet from the opera *I lombardi alla prima crociata* played on flute and clarinet. During the 1849 season, along with the local premiere of Bellini's *Norma*, Verdi's *Ernani* was also performed, but without its original orchestration. To coincide with one of the Argentine national holidays, as was tradition at the time, Pestalardo at last premiered *I due Foscari* at the Teatro de la Victoria on May 25, 1850. This was the first of Verdi's scores performed in Argentina with its original instrumentation.[4] *Nabucco* and *I lombardi alla prima crociata* (1851) would follow this title in the same season, alongside other operas by Bellini, Donizetti, Mercadante, and other less well-known composers.

After the Battle of Caseros sealed the fate of Rosas's government and marked the beginning of the constitutional era in Argentina, the Teatro de la Victoria came upon hard times. Despite the existence of other minor halls, such as Buen Orden and Federación, Buenos Aires still needed an artistic space reflective of its growing metropolis, the import of the works staged there, and the planned Europeanization of the new Argentina. Such was the proposal put forth by figures like Domingo Faustino Sarmiento and Bartolomé Mitre, who were both statesmen and opera enthusiasts.

In essence, Buenos Aires' high society encouraged the construction of what is today called the "old Teatro Colón." The venue was inaugurated on April 25, 1857, facing Plaza de Mayo and surrounded by Rivadavia, Reconquista, 25 de Mayo, and Bartolomé Mitre streets. The first opera

performed there was Verdi' s *La traviata*, with a cast headed by Sofia
Vera Lorini and Enrico Tamberlick, who sang the Argentine National
Anthem before the curtain opened.

At that time, the organization of the country had not yet been
completed. Although a National Constitution was approved in Santa Fe
in 1853, the province of Buenos Aires rejected it and instead became
an independent state with an eponymous capital city until the Battle
of Pavón in 1861. During this period, a council of public works took
on four projects considered to be fundamental to national progress: the
first railway in the country, a new dock for the port and corresponding
customs house, a gas company, and an opera house.[5]

Curiously, the same year a steam engine barrelled through the Argentine landscape for the first time, the old Teatro Colón opened. Despite the
prestige of the artists who would perform there and its considerable size,
the venue would only last thirty years. By a strange paradox, in 1887 this
Teatro Colón building —whose owners had never finished paying for
the land— had to be sold to the National Bank to enable the construction
of a new theater of the same name, using the profits from the sale. This
new theater was located precisely on the property of the Estación del
Parque, where the first Argentine train had set out three decades before.
The current Teatro Colón stands there to this day.

THE FORMATION OF A TASTE

The year of 1872 would prove to be crucial in the development of
opera in Buenos Aires. The Argentine capital was recovering from the
brutal epidemic of yellow fever it suffered the previous year, which
killed almost 10 percent of the population. Another opera house of great
importance was inaugurated, which was fated to lead musical life in the
capital during the twenty-year gap between the closing of the old Colón
in 1888 and the opening of the new one in 1908. On May 25, 1872, the
Teatro de la Ópera opened its doors on Corrientes Avenue with Verdi's

Il trovatore. From this year onward, there would be two opera houses in Buenos Aires that would be able to offer competing productions and casts, and seeking to improve.[6]

The taste for Italian culture, established with that primitive *Barbiere* in 1825, began to compete with the fashion for all things French, implemented by the rising Generation of the '80, who dreamed of using France as a model to make Argentina into a nation with a European profile.

From the reviews by Paul Groussac —a French expat and writer settled in Argentina who was both an influential music critic and eventual director of the National Library— one can infer that during these seasons, new titles were presented with hardly any delay with respect to their premieres in Europe, and that the passion for Verdi was equal to the interest in Meyerbeer or Gounod and at times even paled before the latter.[7]

Proof of this is that the Politeama Argentino, the third great theater to be added to the ranks of the old Colón and the Ópera, was inaugurated on June 16, 1879, with a work emblematic of the French repertoire: Meyerbeer's *Les Huguenots*.

The competition between these halls was marked. For example, in 1888 the old Colón closed its doors with Verdi's *Otello*, with no less than the role's creator Francesco Tamagno at the head of the cast, while at the same time the Politeama presented it with the well-known tenor Roberto Stagno.

By the last quarter of the 19th century, the passion for opera was fully in place in Buenos Aires' high society, and the companies and artists brought by impresarios for each season were of a rank similar to those of a European opera house of the first order. The evolution of the taste for symphonic music would take slightly longer to arrive, and would remain in the hands of Italians (mainly maestro Ferruccio Cattelani) and the prominent Argentine composer Alberto Williams.

The creation of a true operatic "market" led to the multiplication of theaters built and dedicated to opera, additionally supported by the growing wave of immigration —mostly Italian— which counted among its ranks artisans of the most varied professions. These skilled individuals were determined to work in a society that offered them a real chance of progress, though not the rapid enrichment many people had imagined. The immigrant deluge, however, began to change the local perception of Italian culture from that of a source of prestige and innovation to a wellspring of bad habits and destabilizing political ideas, principally anarchism.[8] With each passing year, conflict amongst differing nationalities would crescendo to ever-greater relevance in the public discourse, and would eventually balloon to excessive and pernicious significance.[9]

The Teatro Nacional opened amidst this context in 1882 on Florida street, between Bartolomé Mitre and Cangallo. In 1889, the Teatro Onrubia (later called Victoria after the neighboring venue of the same name closed before it was finally renamed Maravillas) opened on what is currently Hipólito Yrigoyen street, at the corner of San José; in 1891 the Teatro de la Comedia opened at what is currently Carlos Pellegrini 248; in 1892 the Teatro Odeón —shamefully demolished at the end of the 20th century— opened at the corner of Corrientes and Esmeralda, where from 1872 the Variedades were placed and the first film in Argentina was projected; the Teatro Apolo opened on Corrientes and Uruguay, and today still functions as a modern theater located within a commercial gallery; the Teatro de la Zarzuela (later called Argentino) opened on Bartolomé Mitre and Uruguay; in 1893 the Teatro Mayo opened on Avenida de Mayo and Lima, and the Teatro Rivadavia, today Liceo, opened facing the Plaza Lorea. This is the only 19th century theater that survives today in Buenos Aires, as all the rest were erased from the map. In general, these halls formed the circuit for performing Spanish companies.[10]

These were not the only spaces for musical theater: in a more popular style, but with opera performances, there was the Teatro de la Alegría (1870) on Chacabuco street between Alsina and Hipólito Yrigoyen; the Teatro Casino (1885) at Maipú 326; the old Teatro San Martín (1887, rebuilt in 1892) on Esmeralda between Sarmiento and Cangallo; the Edén Argentino (1890) on Callao between Sarmiento and Corrientes; the Politeama Sudamericano (1894) at San Juan 2023; and the Teatro Doria (1887, later rebuilt as the Marconi in 1903) on Rivadavia Avenue, in the middle of the district of Once, where until the 1960s opera singers could cut their teeth before an audience that was at once enthusiastic and easygoing.[11]

Meanwhile at the luxurious Ópera, in charge of the 1901, 1903, 1904, and 1906 seasons, there was the blazing presence of Arturo Toscanini, who conducted in Buenos Aires, along with the Italian and Wagnerian repertoire, works he would never again perform in his career, such as Mozart's *Don Giovanni* and Weber's *Der Freischütz*.[12]

In the first years of the 20th century a few more venues of great relevance to Argentine cultural life would be inaugurated: in 1907 the Teatro Coliseo was assembled in an old circus ring. It would come to be the site of the world premiere of Mascagni's *Isabeau* in 1911 in the presence of the composer, and the Argentine premiere of *Parsifal* in 1913, anticipating the Wagnerian veto on performances of the work outside Bayreuth by half a year. It was also the venue for the first national radio broadcast in 1920, with music from the same opera.[13] In 1908, two new theaters opened: the Teatro Avenida, later strongly associated with the Spanish community and particularly with zarzuela, and the current Teatro Colón, which would end up transforming into the monopolizing epicenter of operatic and musical activity in Argentina after the close of its competitor the Teatro de la Ópera in 1935 and its conversion into an *art deco* building also dedicated to cinema.

By that time, the world was still reeling in the aftermath of the First World War and the market for opera had changed irreversibly. Public support would fortunately rematerialize with the 1925 creation of the Teatro Colón's resident artistic bodies, and when its "municipalization" began to take effect at the start of the 1930s, any private initiative was supplanted.[14]

Chapter 2

The Panizza Family

Héctor Panizza's father Giovanni Grazioso was unable to resist his attraction to Argentina's flourishing musical scene. He arrived in Buenos Aires during the old Teatro Colón's 1872 season in order to join the orchestra as first cello under the baton of his countryman Nicola Bassi. A year before, he had visited the Indian city of Calcutta, then served as first cello for the orchestra that premiered Verdi's *Aïda* at the Cairo Opera House under the baton of the double bassist and composer Giovanni Bottesini.[15]

In Buenos Aires, Giovanni Grazioso would meet two colleagues, Pietro Melani and Tommaso Marenco (both great professionals, like Giovanni), who had already performed at the inaugural *Aïda*, and who would also leave their marks on Argentina.[16] The adventurous musician had studied with Franco Faccio, the composer and conductor responsible for the Italian premiere of *Aïda* in 1872 and, fifteen years later, the world premiere of *Otello*, both at La Scala in Milan.

Born in 1851 in Gazzuolo, near Cremona, Giovanni Grazioso arrived in Argentina when he was twenty-one years old, with a background that appeared more than promising. There is no evidence that he came from a family of musicians, however, though several professional colleagues shared his *cognome* at the time. The Panizza family has been referred to as a "musical dynasty," with comparisons to no less than the Puccini family. Clarifying the connection between this family and our subject, however, is far from a simple task.[17]

Although it is not possible to establish a genealogy, at least the extremes of the probable tree are clearly linked to music: the branch that begins with Giacomo Panizza culminates with the subject of this biography.

Giacomo Panizza was the first important musician to bear this surname, as far as we know. According to a contemporary source, he was born in 1803 near Alessandria and died in 1860.[18] During the 1830s and 1840s, he was a well-known conductor and "maestro al cembalo" of La Scala (where he was successor to maestro Vincenzo Lavigna, who was also one of Verdi's teachers) in addition to a lecturer and composer, particularly of ballets. In 1837 he prepared the vocal score of the final alternative aria composed by soprano María Malibrán for the role of Adina in *L'elisir d'amore* by Donizetti, which was published by Casa Ricordi in Milan.[19] The fact that in 1848 he left his position at La Scala to become musical director at Covent Garden in London, and later was also appointed by the Teatro Regio in Turin, suggests a fascinating symmetry: these were also highly significant places in the career of Ettore Panizza himself.[20]

Between the two of them, there are several professional musicians with this surname who are mentioned by different sources. Leaving aside Héctor's father Giovanni Grazioso and his siblings (who also have well-known careers, which we will discuss further on), three "Panizzas" are consistently given credit for having conducted the 1884 world premiere of *Le Villi*, Puccini's first opera. They are the virtually unknown Augusto, Arturo, and Achille Panizza.

Augusto Panizza, who died in 1919, conducted the local band in the city of Frascati for thirty years, but nothing indicates he had anything to do with the great composer from Lucca.[21] Arturo Panizza is the favorite among the most qualified Puccini researchers, who nevertheless do not seem to have any information about his biography.[22] Achille Panizza, though, creates a more serious problem. Several sources accuse him of being a notorious *scapigliato*, with compositions that have been preserved.[23] It happens that one of these scores has precisely the same title as one widely attributed to Giovanni Grazioso: *Il caporal Bastogio al campo d'istruzione*, which premiered at the Teatro Fossati in Milan in 1872.[24]

In this respect, the musicologist Aníbal Cetrangolo's hypothesis is as surprising as it is uncertain: Achille and Giovanni Grazioso are the same person. If this hypothesis is correct, Achille would be a pseudonym used by Panizza to sign vaudevillian works of musical theater, such as the previously mentioned *Bastogio* and others from his catalogue like *Le nozze per astuzie* (which premiered in Calcutta) and *I briganti*, which was in fact signed by Achille.[25] However the composer would have kept his real name for more serious works such as the operas *Clara*, *Cecilia*, and *Gianni da Calais*, which have since faded into obscurity.

This explanation is bolstered by the fact that the *scapigliati* did often create anagrams with their names. The most famous of these cases is Arrigo Boito, who signed a few essays and the libretto for Ponchielli's *La Gioconda* as Tobia Gorrio. Furthermore, Boito was not really called Arrigo either. The first author to use the term *scapigliatura*, Cletto Arrighi, was in reality named Carlo Righetti.[26]

However, nothing can be verified with respect to the presumed "alias" of Giovanni Grazioso, which seems more like an invention or slip of the pen. An explanation as to why Giovanni would have used a pseudonym to conduct the premiere of *Le Villi* has proven elusive, much less why his son did not record this in his memoirs, when he himself conducted Puccini's first opera on several occasions and paid generous attention to his father's less relevant professional activities.

The matter grows even more problematic if one takes into account the fact that "Panizza" refers directly or indirectly to the baker's profession, and is quite a common surname. It comes from Veneto and spread to

Lombardy (the region where Giovanni Grazioso was born); subsequently it spread throughout the world, particularly Argentina, where the Panizza name is shared by families and brands alike. Moreover, there are many trademarks and people named "Panizza," even in the musical sphere.[27]

To complicate the matter even further, Giovanni Grazioso Panizza sometimes introduced himself or was introduced as Giovanni Panizza-Pugnalini, in apparent homage to his mother.[28] According to Héctor's memoirs, however, his father was the second son of a tailor from Mantua named Aquilino, and of a mother named Giuditta Pasqualini.[29]

Giovanni had an older brother named Gisberto, the only one who did not dedicate himself to music, and three younger siblings: Annunziata, an esteemed dramatic soprano; Giuseppe, a similarly prominent cellist who joined orchestras in Europe and the United States; and Oreste, a music teacher and performer on the cello and piano.[30]

Of all his siblings, his sister was the most capable, and she was able to maintain an international career. She often introduced herself as Annunziata Stinco-Panizza (or vice versa), as she was married to baritone Enrico Stinco Palermini, her usual partenaire. Both participated, for instance, in the world premiere of *Loreley* by Alfredo Catalani in Turin, in 1890. It happened often that during a work like *Cavalleria rusticana* she assumed the role of Santuzza while he played Alfio, as it happened at the Teatro Solís in Montevideo.[31] After the death of a son at sea, Annunziata ended up settling down in Rio de Janeiro, where she died after having worked intensely throughout Europe and Latin America (particularly Argentine cities like Rosario and Córdoba).

The rest of the "Panizza clan" chose to settle in Argentina. The father Aquilino would die in Carnerillo, in the province of Córdoba, where he lived with Giuseppe; Gisberto would end up amidst friars in a monastery; and as we will see later on, Oreste came to provide important material support (through his income from public school teaching) to Panizza the father while he carried out his performances in Argentina. In fact, Oreste was widely known throughout the 1890s for regularly presenting collections of school songs for publication to the National Council of Education, such as *A la noche, El canto del cisne* and *Vals.*[32]

Giovanni Grazioso returned to Italy after his experience at the old Colón in 1872. Contractual hiring was typical of seasonal work. Since it took place in the southern hemisphere, the local seasons mainly developed between May and October with the most important events in the southern winter, a period then on break in Europe.

The impresario in charge of the Colón beginning in 1868 was Angelo Ferrari, who had been living in Buenos Aires for a decade. In his early years, Ferrari was a violinist at that theater, a highly regarded teacher, and Antonio Pestalardo's rival. It was Ferrari, through his frequent travels to Italy in search of outstanding artists, who hired Giovanni Grazioso at the old Colón.

The following year, once again at the request of Ferrari, Panizza the father returned to Buenos Aires to fulfill the double role of performer and teacher, and continued to do so until 1875, when weighty reasons forced him to permanently move to the city.

During one of his return trips to Milan, Giovanni met Eugenia Valdata, a singing student born in Grava, Alessandria. The young woman lodged at the house of the Panizza family, and before long she had struck up a formal courtship with Giovanni.

Immigration was often a traumatic moment in a person's life. The beginning of a new life tended to mark an abrupt break with the entire previous one. Too often, this meant parting ways with loved ones and significant others, though it was necessary if the immigrant wanted to find fortune and a quality of life that was impossible to achieve in Europe.

It was a cliche repeated among immigrants that of the son who emigrated and left his betrothed in his native land. Later, he forgets about her. On occasion, this would happen even when there was a marriage, a pregnancy, or even a child already born to link two people. In general, the women who were engaged or married did not allow these moments of forgetfulness to occur without taking further action. They set out on the journey in whatever manner they could— even without specific information regarding the location of their husbands or fiancés. Generally, they did so in the company of some "countryman," also an immigrant, and did not give up until they found their partner, who invariably honored his commitment in accordance with the very strict Italian culture of the 19th century.

This was the case of Eugenia Valdata and Giovanni Panizza. Eugenia embarked on her search in 1874 in the company of the Giustiniani family, and found Giovanni living with three friends in an atmosphere worthy of *La bohème*, which at least dissipated suspicions that the young man had "remade his life" with another woman.

The memoirs of Héctor Panizza do not record the celebration of matrimony between Eugenia and Giovanni —although such a ceremony is likely to have taken place either in Italy or in Buenos Aires, given the conventions of the time. A child was born from this union on Suipacha street on August 12, 1875. This child was Héctor Octavio José Panizza, later known worldwide as Ettore Panizza.

The Argentine laws adopted the *ius soli* in matters of nationality (a completely logical policy in a country with a population made up substantially by immigrants). Thus Héctor Panizza held Argentine nationality without losing the Italian nationality of his parents, like the millions of other children living under the same law. Despite Italian law's adherence to *ius sanguinis*, which guaranteed Italian citizenship to the children of Italian parents, the musician never renounced his Argentine nationality, and it was erased neither by the italianization of his name nor by his settlement in Italy.

The property on Suipacha Street where Héctor was born, with all the symbolic power this implies, later came to form part of the land belonging to the Teatro de la Ópera when it expanded. By then, the hall on Corrientes Avenue was the property of Antonio Pestalardo and connected with the private house of its owners. Ex-leaseholder of the land Robert Cano reacquired it in 1882 and added a French-styled façade as part of a larger building-renovation project in 1886.[33]

Héctor was baptized in the Catholic church of San Nicolás, then located exactly where the Obelisco was later raised at the intersection of the current Corrientes Avenue with Nueve de Julio Avenue. His family belonged to the parish, and they lived just a few hundred meters from their house of worship.

At four years old, the boy was brought to Italy for the first time. Only those who had progressed rapidly in Argentina could afford the luxury of a return trip to their place of origin. Ten years after Héctor was born, however, his father managed to earn enough to bring his brothers Giuseppe and Oreste to Buenos Aires. The first would move to Córdoba to teach cello while the second would take charge of Giovanni's classes during his travels to Italy. This kind of precaution suggests the Panizza family never wanted to cut personal and professional connections with their place of origin.

Giovanni's father Aquilino and his brother Gisberto arrived in Argentina months later, Gisberto as the "black sheep" in a family of musicians. As previously mentioned, only their sister Annunziata developed her life as a musical performer outside Argentina.[34]

Berlin-born pianist and composer Conrado (Konrad) Herzfeld was a rising figure during this period, in addition to his role as Héctor's first music teacher. Herzfeld had been living in the Argentine capital since 1868 and founded the music conservatory "La Capital" at 783 Artes street (today Carlos Pellegrini) in Buenos Aires. He was very close to the Panizza family, and he also played a significant role in Panizza's artistic development.[35]

Herzfeld's efforts yielded fruit quickly: at ten years old, the boy was already able to perform Auguste Durand's *Chaconne* on the piano. Two years later, in 1887, he would finish the composition of seven pieces for piano with the title *Flores primaverales* (in Italian, *Fiori primaverili*).

For his part, Giovanni was intensely connected with *porteño* (meaning "born in Buenos Aires") musical circles at the end of the 19th century. His appearances as a conductor at Florida Garden during the most popular cycle of concerts offered in Buenos Aires led him to join the ranks of other prominent musicians of the same nationality like Nicola Bassi and Riccardo Furlotti. This truly popular art cultivated a local public following, which extended beyond the opera scene. In 1882 his march *La Argentina* was performed during the South American Continental Exhibition, a great event of industry that took place in Buenos Aires and was inaugurated by President Roca.

Giovanni quickly scaled to higher positions in musical institutions of the time, such as La Lira, the Sociedad Orquestal Bonaerense, and the Sociedad del Cuarteto. He worked as a teacher and collaborated with magazines such as *El Mundo del Arte*. He also published two methods of music reading and music theory, in addition to a musical alphabet; all three were approved by the National Council of Education and promoted for use as such in the conservatory and in the cathedral of Milan. This fact alone indicates his prestige was much greater than posterity currently recognizes.[36]

In 1887 the Panizza family traveled once again to Italy. This was the first trip Héctor remembered, and it turned out to be musically significant to him. When he arrived in Milan, he enrolled at the royal conservatory, which had not been named after the still-living Giuseppe Verdi. In this institution headed by Antonio Bazzini, he studied harmony with Amintore Galli and counterpoint with Michele Saladino. Bazzini's masterful piece for violin, *La ronde des lutins*, is what he is known for now, but he was a prominent figure of the period and his students included Catalani, Mascagni, and Puccini.

The studies of composition and conducting were still not totally differentiated, and it was expected that a great performer would be able to compose. In fact, Panizza the father was a good model of this: the cellist-composer took advantage of his trip to produce his opera *Clara* at

Teatro Manzoni in September 1889. His own libretto was based on *Les Aventures du dernier Abencérage* by Chateaubriand. Annunziata Panizza sang the title role and stood at the head of a local cast, which included her husband Enrico.

Giovanni also practiced orchestra conducting while in Italy. It was no accident that Héctor gained experience in the profession at the same venues where his father showed his art. The boy of fourteen years old was able to watch his father conduct *Martha* by Flotow at the Teatro Chiabrera in Savona, and he even worked as a prompter in *Saffo* by Pacini at the Politeama in Genoa, where Giovanni also occupied the podium. Later, he conducted works like Auber's *Fra Diavolo* and Bellini's *I puritani* during two seasons at the Manzoni in Milan.

The father's double role as composer and conductor surely served as a tantalizing model for the son during his days as a young artist.

CRISIS AND UNCERTAINTY

The Panizzas settled in Italy after they accumulated good capital in Argentina. The family also expanded— the year of 1889 saw the birth of Mario Panizza and the removal of Héctor's seat of honor as Giovanni and Eugenia's only son.

However, the first major obstacle to the incessant progress of the agricultural export model designed by the Generation of '80 —the Argentine crisis of 1890— cost Miguel Juárez Celman his presidency, and on a more intimate scale, complicated the economic equation of the Panizza family. Giovanni sold his properties in Buenos Aires under poor advice and invested that money in shares of the Bank of the Province of Buenos Aires. The economic crash of 1890 drained the resources that would have guaranteed the Panizzas a calm existence in Italy. So the family was forced to return to Argentina despite the nationwide economic crisis. To do so Giovanni had to compromise his honor and accept a loan of money from his faithful Spanish servant Bernardo, a sort of dry nurse to Héctor.

In 1891, the Panizza family began a new stage in their lives marked by disappointment and uncertainty. They remained in Buenos Aires for a five-year stretch, time enough for feelings of affection for his native land to take root in Héctor. Between sixteen and twenty years old, Ettore would become known as Héctor; he would finish his personal development during a period of rebuilding for Argentina. Carlos Pellegrini was both president and the son of the engineer from Savoy who built the old Teatro Colón. With the creation of the Bank of the Argentine Nation, Pellegrini corrected the zigzagging path of the country so that it continued to cultivate its status as an international power.

Likewise, Héctor wanted to contribute money to his household given his family's sudden and unexpected impoverishment. His musical training enabled him to give piano lessons, which at the time were indispensable for any *porteña* girl from a well-off background. This occupation allowed him to launch himself into a rich musical life centered on opera. He followed in the footsteps of other great conductors like Erich Kleiber by working initially as a percussionist.[37]

Héctor found his place behind the timpani in vaudeville orchestras, such as the one presented at the brand-new Teatro Odeón. In a hall dedicated to French repertoire, Héctor gained experience as a musical assistant and then as a conductor of operetta. His talent enabled him to earn some additional money with a modest Italian season in Montevideo, during which young Panizza accompanied singers on the piano in a sort of "café concert."

The act of compostion continued to seduce Panizza the father as much as his son. The former finished his opera *Cecilia*, which years later he would refer to as "student" work due to its subject and purpose: it was a one-act children's opera that took place inside a school. The piece was performed with Héctor as conductor of the girls and young ladies of the educational establishment in the neighborhood of Belgrano where Giovanni was a teacher. Its success was such that in 1895 the illustrated libretto was published with photos of participating students, and the year after that the score itself was published.[38]

Meanwhile, Héctor continued climbing to new positions in *porteña* musical life. In 1892 he won first prize from the Symphonic Society of Buenos Aires with his suite for orchestra *Bodas campestres*, which premiered at the Teatro Nacional under his baton. His colleague and Giovanni's collaborator maestro Ismael Diepedaal performed Héctor's *Gavota para cuerdas* during one of the "musical matinées" put on by the Teatro de la Ópera. The staging ended with symphonic performances by Hércules (Ercole) Galvani at the Politeama. Instrumental music began to experience a growing popularity in Buenos Aires thanks to the fascination with Wagner, a composer who found one of his greatest local supporters in Alberto Williams, the beloved student of César Franck.

It was Williams who in 1892 founded the Ateneo de Buenos Aires, an institution that gathered artists of different kinds, among them musicians, authors, and painters. In 1893, the Ateneo organized its first contest for musical composition, which awarded two prizes. One went to Edmundo Pallemaerts, and the other to Héctor Panizza for a Suite made up of four sections: *Romance sans paroles*, *Étude impromptu*, *Barcarole*, and *Vals*. On November 13 of that year, the Suite was performed at the hall Operai Italiani.[39] This was the eighteen-year-old Panizza's first public recognition as a composer —he was given no less than a standing ovation at the request of the organizers.[40]

His scores began to be published in well-circulated magazines such as *El mundo del arte*, which in 1893 included a *Minuetto* for strings arranged for piano, strategically dedicated to Enrique Frexas, theater and music critic of *La Nación*.[41]

The previous year, the same magazine published Giovanni Grazioso's romanzetta *Quanti baci!*, which was dedicated to José Giustiniani and unmistakably suggests the father's efforts to direct his son along the same path he traveled.

In 1895, Paul Groussac confirmed the younger Panizza's meteoric ascent when he published an exclusive review of Panizza's first compositions in *Le Courrier Français*, under the title "The Panizza Audition" (the performance of which took place at the Teatro de la Ópera on June 28 that year). In it he states that "Mr. Panizza is a musician in the full extent of the word; for several years we have thought so, though he is still very young; it was enough to have heard him play an accompaniment, a performance as difficult as it was devoid of glitz, a true touchstone that distinguishes pure gold."[42]

According to the review, Panizza presented works he had written for two pianos (*Canto de octubre, Scherzo*, both entrusted to the young ladies Campodónico and Fortina, who received an *encore*) pieces for voice (an unusual *Ave Maria* for voice and cello, entrusted to Tamagno and Carlos Marchal), and orchestral excerpts (*Bodas campestres*). "A dangerous test for a beginner, which yesterday had nothing but happy consequences," Groussac noted in referrence to the heterogeneity of the repertoire.

The critic concluded the article with typical prose of the period that accurately portrays an aspect of Héctor's personality: "Mr. Panizza is young and modest, two rare qualities. Let us hope that the second lasts even longer than the first."[43]

At the same time, the new composer formed a chamber group with whom he put together a great range of activities. The two musicians he recruited graduated from the Conservatory of Brussels and moved to Argentina: Louis Gorin on flute and the previously mentioned Carlos Marchal on cello. Héctor, of course, contributed from the piano. He also composed two zarzuelas —*El autor del crimen* and *El último invento*— which were never performed.[44]

For the first time he focused on writing arrangements for orchestra. In his first youthful attempts, he wrote reductions for two very popular piecesat that time: Henry Ketten's *La Castagenette* and Louis Moreau Gottschalk's *Pasquinade*. This work would make him famous later, when he succesfully applied the lessons learned to Puccini's operas *Madama Butterfly, La fanciulla del West,* and *Il trittico.*[45]

One of the great maestros of music in Argentina, Edmundo Piazzini, entrusted to him the task of reducing Gottschalk's work. It was performed by Josefina Cano, the daughter of the owner of the Teatro de la Ópera, whose marriage to Piazzini would later yield another wellspring to the great musical family. The most recent living family member is the renowned Argentine pianist Carmen Piazzini, who has a brilliant international career, particularly in Germany.[46]

CHAPTER 3

FORMATIVE YEARS

On March 13, 1895, Héctor Panizza enlisted in the National Guard in order to complete his required military duties. At that time military service still did not exist, but inscription was compulsory and a rite of passage for every young man.[47]

In practice, the National Guard was a copy of the provincial militias, and anticipated both the influence of the Argentine army on 20th century local politics and the so-called "conscription," compulsory military service yet not created. The experience was a source of lasting friendships and was often recalled throughout one's life with fond anecdotes of sleepless mothers and furtive young love.

The official documentation of Héctor's enrollment states his place of residence as 560 Maipú Street (two blocks away from his place of birth in the center of Buenos Aires), his civil state as single, his age as nineteen years old, and his physical appearance as white complexion, blue eyes, medium-sized nose and mouth, brown hair, and height of 1m 70cm, without particular marks; as for his profession, it states "teacher and musician."[48]

Panizza evidently fulfilled the duties that the experience required of him, including some risky episodes due to turmoil in local politics, and that indispensable fleeting romance.

Having reached this point, however, his desire to return to Italy to complete his musical training was as ardent as it was essential. Due to historical disputes between Argentina and Chile, the first Conscription Act had just been passed in Argentina; it established the military mobilization of males born in 1875, a category to which Panizza belonged.[49]

Panizza found himself marvelously well-connected, so to avoid this problem he taught piano to the daughters of the influential general Luis María Campos, confidant to President Julio Argentino Roca and head of the first group of conscripts in the country.

With this political link and the economic assistance of Francisco Seeber —a wealthy landowner, businessman, military man, and politician who in time became mayor of the Argentine capital— Panizza was granted permission to return to Europe, to his longed-for Milan.

So it is that in the summer of 1895, we find Panizza in the Ambrosian city where a fundamental stage of his artistic and personal development took place. Panizza's teacher Saladino once again took on importance in his life with his classes in counterpoint, which increased to three per week with the aim of guaranteeing the re-admission of his student to the conservatory. Panizza also took piano lessons with Giuseppe Frugatta and composition with Vincenzo Ferroni. Ettore still did not live alone: he lived with his mother and brother at 14 Monforte street. His father arrived during Christmas that year to complete the family tableau. By February of the following year, however, all of them but Héctor had returned to Buenos Aires.

It was logical: he was then beginning a stage of very intense intellectual friendship, for example with the brothers Davide and Guido Campari, who provided him with the literary material to write his nine *Romanzas* upon poems by Paul Verlaine. Another relevant friendship was with

Romeo Carugati, a music critic who introduced him to the world of Strauss through his appreciation of *Salomé*, which Toscanini had recently performed at La Scala.

That same year 1896 he revealed himself as a conductor, albeit at a local scale and in an academic context. Continuing to display the skill he had shown in Buenos Aires, Héctor played the timpani in the conservatory orchestra, under the guidance of Antonio Bazzini. When faced with the challenge of conducting a passage, Panizza volunteered to do it, unlike his apathetic colleagues. When he heard the quality of the result, Bazzini said to his colleague Ferroni: "One can see he was born to be a conductor."

The preparations to occupy the podium were not simple, however. In that time whoever wanted to do so had to demonstrate a significant range of abilities, as much in the field of composition as in that of interpretation. Panizza already played the organ and had arranged some of Edvard Grieg's *Lyric Pieces* for orchestra. On March 10, 1897, the Norwegian composer sent him a friendly, witty letter in German about his work.

This encouragement yielded its fruits at the creative level: that year Héctor finished his first course of composition. For his final work, his friend Carugati wrote the libretto of what would become Panizza's first opera: *Il fidanzato del mare* (The Groom of the Sea).

The score had to overcome the difficulty created for him in February by the death of Bazzini, who had placed great hope in him. Happily his successor in the management of the conservatory, Giuseppe Gallignani, decided to conduct the score, which was premiered at the same conservatory to a warm welcome.

This "lyrical tale in one act" is essentially a poetic scene set to music. Panizza utilized his family relations to promote the work in Argentina. Fortunately, neither the simplicity of the plot nor the academic nature of the work proved to be obstacles in spreading the word about the performance across the Atlantic. This is how the work came to be performed at the Teatro de la Ópera in Buenos Aires on August 15, 1897,

at the close of the season, under the direction of Edoardo Mascheroni—
and in the same evening as Wagner´s *Tannhäuser*!

A CONDUCTOR IS BORN

Ettore (as he was known in Italy) Panizza completed his final year
of studies in Milan in 1898. In addition to joining a string quartet, he
graduated as both a pianist and a composer with the first prize in his
class, with the composition of his *Quartet in C minor.*

By that time the Panizza family had returned to Milan and, in view of
the excellent results of their son, Giovanni decided to pull strings to find
him employment in an opera company. He managed to do so, no less
than for the fall season of the Teatro Costanzi (today Teatro dell'Opera)
in Rome, exactly a year before the world premiere of Puccini's *Tosca*
took place there. The level of the company and the good reception of the
inexperienced maestro were additionally guaranteed by the presence of
an important conductor: Edoardo Mascheroni, who premiered *Il fidanzato
del mare* in Buenos Aires a few months before Panizza was received as
its composer in Rome at the Costanzi.

In that same context, Panizza met Pietro Mascagni, who was about to
premiere his opera *Iris.* The rivalry between Mascagni and Mascheroni
was well known: not only did the composer conduct the brand-new
score but, after a rebuff by Mascheroni, he assigned Panizza to both the
preparation and to the role of conductor for Verdi's *Rigoletto.* Additionally
he put Panizza on Massenet's *Le roi de Lahore* (sung in Italian), and the
oratorio *La risurrezione di Lazzaro* by Lorenzo Perosi, the priest-musician
who had been named music director of the Sistine Chapel by Pope Leo
XIII that same year.

The die was cast: Panizza would be a conductor, possibly in spite of
his aspirations to compose. The frantic pace of his intense activity on
the podium was already beginning to sweep him along and gradually
confine his musical creation to limited degree.

A COMPOSER'S ADVENTURES

Ricordi is not only the name of one of the most renowned musical publishing houses in the world. It is also the surname of a family who did a great deal for the promotion of music and in particular for Italian opera, thereby transcending the commercial interests that were naturally the primary driving force of their activity.

Though the property of a multinational company since 1994, its origins date back to a lone pioneer: the violinist Giovanni Ricordi, who founded it in 1808 and moved a large part of the archive to La Scala in 1825. This is the origin for that impressive collection of scores by Rossini, Bellini, Donizetti, Verdi, and Giacomo Puccini, the most successful opera composer of the 20th century. As the lightly comic film *Casa Ricordi* by Carmine Gallone recounts, the aging Giovanni was followed by Tito Ricordi, and then by a man with great genius in business and a fine artistic instinct: key figure Giulio Ricordi (1840-1912), who had dealings with Verdi as well as Puccini.[50]

In contrast, his older son Tito the second had a more arbitrary character and in general reaped less affection. [51]

Giulio was one of Panizza's first promoters in Italy. By 1899, after finishing his season in Rome, Héctor already had the profile and sufficient contacts to conduct Giordano´s *Fedora* in Florence. The opera had premiered under the composer's baton at the Teatro Lirico in Milan on November 17 the previous year, with Gemma Bellincioni and Enrico Caruso in the leading roles, but the publisher Sonzogno —a competitor of Ricordi— prevented the hiring of Panizza as he had not attended any of the previous performances.

"Sior Giuli" (as Giulio Ricordi was called) went to his aid while taking into account the rivalry between both publishing houses and the fact that Panizza was still not completely decided between turning fully to composition or orchestral conducting. He invited Ettore to write a new opera and promised him all the support necessary for its publication and performance. For this he introduced him to Luigi Illica, the librettist of *La bohème*—not to mention his contribution to the youthful *Manon Lescaut*—as well as *Tosca*, an opera that was then still cooking in the great Puccinian oven. All that without taking into account that Illica had also written the librettos for Catalani's *La Wally*, Franchetti's *Cristoforo Colombo*, Smareglia's *Nozze istriane*, Giordano's *Andrea Chénier* and Mascagni's *Iris*, among other operas of relative importance within the international repertoire. Thus we stand before a man who could contribute a good dose of experience to Panizza, who was at that time much less important and well known than he was. Héctor traveled from Rome to Milan to meet the "distinguished poet" (as he liked to call him) and among the many subjects he proposed, the musician chose the triptych that would be titled and originally announced as *Medio Evo latino* (to the detriment of the more correct Spanish version *Medioevo latino*). When he came to know of it, Tito Ricordi stubbornly opposed this opportunity presented to Panizza, then a young man of only twenty-three years old, while Giulio supported him to the end. While Illica was finishing the libretto, Panizza threw himself into composing a *Sonata for cello and piano*, which he sent to the competition of the Society of the Quartet in Bologna; there it won the second honorary mention. The composer would later withdraw this juvenile piece from his catalogue, though the same cannot be said for the nine *Romanzas* written that same year using the texts by Verlaine.

The circumstances surrounding Ricordi's publication of these last pieces are important for our biographical subject. Panizza was received one afternoon by Tito Ricordi at his Milan office on Omenoni street, where he was playing the romanzas on the piano. He suddenly saw the door of the studio open, and without previous notice, Giulio Ricordi appeared in the company of no less than Giacomo Puccini.

Panizza recalls in his memoirs how he felt intimidated and almost dumbstruck by the presence of the great composer who, though he had then only written one of the operas that established him (*La bohème*), was already for Héctor a kind of divine figure descended from Olympus.

The fact that he did not stop and was able to keep playing his music made him feel he had the stature necessary to measure himself against a colossus, and in some way to believe that he was also a respected artist. Panizza later reflected on his vision of the musician from Lucca: "I knew Giacomo Puccini by sight; I stopped in the street when I spotted him and watched him attentively as if he were a supernatural being. I still remember him on Vittorio Emanuele street, under the porticos, with the flap of his overcoat always lifted and the ever-present cigarette between his lips, smiling, out for a walk accompanied by two, three or four intimate friends. I followed them and my young mind harbored a great admiration as well as, I must confess, a certain envy. He was already the famous author of *Le Villi*, of *Manon*, of *Edgar*, and of *Bohème*... and to my inflamed fantasy it seemed impossible that this great man, blessed by God, could descend to walk amongst humble mortals...."[52]

According to the author, the romanzas distanced themselves from Italian songs in the style of Tosti, but they still received the approval of those present and, once published, seduced Madame Chappelle, an important personality in Milanese society at the time. Chappelle was an amateur singer who popularized the pieces in the city salons and, in addition, attempted to connect Panizza with Verdi.

Madame Chappelle had access to the intimate circle of the elderly composer at the Grand Hotel in Milan (even playing "quarto a scopone" with him). She arranged a meeting in January 1901, but Verdi died a few days before this. For Panizza, there only remained the memory of having once seen the author of *Rigoletto* leaving the offices of Ricordi on Borgonuovo street. But in any case the great maestro was not fond of giving advice and any new or foreign language seemed to him generally remote: not even Puccini— who decided to be a composer after listening to *Aïda*— could count on Verdi's advice or encouragement.

KEY YEAR

The year of 1899 was key for Panizza in both an artistic and personal regard. He managed to conduct at a hall in the provinces —the Teatro Chiabrera in Savona— Ponchielli's *La Gioconda,* which gave him many headaches, however.[53]

Apart from this, he spent the year almost completely immersed in the preparation of *Medio Evo latino.* As a result, he visited Illica where he met Alberto Franchetti, who was at the time focused on the composition of perhaps his most popular opera, *Germania* with text by the same librettist. Today Franchetti is unjustly relegated. He is a highly significant opera composer whose oblivion is due in part to 1938 fascist racial laws he could not escape despite his noble lineage. Much of his work was blackballed because of his Jewish heritage.[54]

That year, at Carnival ball, Panizza also met the woman who would become his first wife: Fulvia Tommasi. Overcoming the self-restraint and shyness of the musician, one of his best friends, Fortunato Biagi, dragged him toward the dance floor. At that moment, Panizza won the heart of the young woman as he played at the piano Chopin's *Nocturne in F sharp major.* That same night they separated themselves from the noise of the party and began a romance whose seriousness was confirmed the next morning by Biagi, who gave references about the honesty of the Tommasi family. This was the way in which an amorous link could end up in a wedding.

Fulvia enjoyed an education suitable to the middle-upper class, which was highly superior to what was usual for an Italian woman of the time. She was studying at the Accademia Scientifico Letteraria and loved music. Panizza was warmly welcomed into the family and soon, as was custom, the couple journeyed to the countryside on weekends, often to the lake of Lecco, accompanied by the brothers of the fiancée or, later, her parents themselves.

The day of Christmas Eve that same year, Giovanni Panizza arrived at the port of Genoa from Buenos Aires. He found his son enthusiastic about his new relationship and the progress of his opera, which he was able to play on the piano. He had worked intensely during those months— always in the morning, never at night— reciting the text out loud before setting it to music, and inspiring himself not in Nature or the solitude of his bedroom (environments which he detested) but in the midst of the people. He found strolls through the center of that Milanese metropolis capable of awakening in him the most varied musical ideas.

Héctor orchestrated the work dreaming that Arturo Toscanini would conduct it, a dream that, as we will see, would become reality, though not for the world premiere. This took place on November 17, 1900, at the Politeama Genovese under the baton of Edoardo Vitale, a reputable maestro, with a no less reputable cast made up of Lina Pasini-Vitale, Ernestina Cecchi, Amedeo Bassi, Giuseppe Camera, Amleto Galli, Attilio Pulcini, and Fernando Gianoli-Galletti. Panizza the father was present. The work was a success: the author, following the standards of the time, had to come out onstage after an acclaimed aria in the middle of the first act. Seven performances were offered, and these served as the close of the season.

The success was such that the organizer Camillo Bonetti decided to program it for the next year at the Teatro de la Ópera in Buenos Aires, for whose administration he was responsible. It was the first of five operatic seasons by Arturo Toscanini in Buenos Aires: four at the Ópera and one at the brand-new Colón. Fate would have it that the inexperienced composer's first opera was conducted by the eminent maestro who at that moment was thirty-four years old, and had already spent fifteen years as a professional conductor.

In May 1901, following in the footsteps of his family, Héctor Panizza set off for Buenos Aires on board the *Savoia*, the same steamship that would bring Giacomo Puccini on his visit to Argentina in 1905.[55]

His primary mission was to supervise the rehearsals of *Medio Evo latino* at the Teatro de la Ópera, which shared the season with the local premieres of Franchetti's *Asrael* and Wagner's *Tristan und Isolde* under Toscanini.[56] Faithful to his despotic character, Toscanini began to order cuts in the score; on one occasion during rehearsal, he asked Panizza to cut a section the author especially valued: the *Sirventese* for the tenor, in the second act, which had been acclaimed in Milan. Panizza resisted and, as was to be expected, Toscanini canceled the rehearsal, not without first hurling the sheets of music to the ground and uttering unrepeatable curses.

For all those who knew Toscanini well, this episode suggested that the performance was canceled. No one dared to contradict the mad genius who was responsible for the whole season and therefore its commercial success. Rumors that Toscanini's whims interfered with the composer's work did not spread; rather, the rumors concerned themselves with the supposedly poor quality of the score that inspired the maestro's rejection. But Panizza was lucky. A few days later, in the midst of his whole family's grief over the terrible affront, Toscanini decided to take up the work again in preparation for the concert.

The theater administration prohibited Panizza from attending rehearsals to avoid possible confrontations. Héctor, however, was not prepared to attend the premiere as just another spectator. Rewarding the ushers of the opera house with a few *pesos*, he slipped into the upper seats and, almost without breathing out of fear some sound would give him away, deeply moved, he listened to the rehearsals, which in his words did honor to a work he had always considered particularly inspired.

Panizza and family (father, mother, and little brother Mario) were finally invited to the dress rehearsal, at the end of which Toscanini effusively embraced Héctor in front of the orchestra, in one of his typically contradictory gestures of sincerity.[57]

Finally, on July 21, 1901, *Medio Evo latino* had its Argentine premiere at the Teatro de la Ópera. The local reception was important to such a degree that the most popular magazine of that time, *Caras y Caretas,* published a full-page caricature of Panizza signed by José María Cao (who years later would do the same on the occasion of Puccini's visit). The Argentine composer can be seen with a handlebar mustache as was the style that year and dressed in medieval attire; he is slender and carrying a lyre and laurels. The caricature is accompanied by an amusing epigram: "Since our audience suffers from madness / at times a great deal and at times just a little / when judging operas it can be extreme / Panizza said: 'I've already been warned' / and seeking the remedy for such manias / with his inspired *Medio Evo latino* / discovered the perfect means."

The magazine had already reported on the premiere of the opera in Genoa the previous year— it dedicated several photos and a long review that tells of *Medio Evo latino*'s "sensational success" amongst "the aristocratic audience of Corrientes avenue." In the review, there are a few reservations with regard to the coherence of the plot, which it considered suitable for "not one but several different operas," but it judges the undertaking by Panizza "already superior to the efforts of a mature musician in this kind of production."

With respect to his music: "Without attempting to present himself as innovative, he has proven his originality and the deep knowledge he possesses of multiple musical resources. None of those drawn upon by our praised compatriot are a servile copy of any procedure, and if they perhaps remind one of those employed by other maestros, one must recognize in Panizza an excellent taste in partly following given models. Knowing how to avoid modern manias —which in many cases means knowledge of the weakness of inventiveness itself —he has followed the pseudo-Teutonic composers so in fashion in the area where they truly deserve to be followed: in the orchestration."[58]

The opera also won the approval of Toscanini, who afterward recommended that Panizza set music to Goldoni's *La locandiera,* advice the composer never followed. President Roca himself (to whom the score is strategically dedicated) invited the author to the government offices to offer him management of the national conservatory, which was then at the planning stage. Panizza had already decided to continue his European career and not tie himself down to a bureaucratic organization, so he politely rejected the offer. He did request, however, through a note to the Congress of the Nation, a monthly subsidy of one hundred gold pesos for three years to continue working in Italy.

The note reads: "Buenos Aires, August 17 1901. / H. Congress of the Nation

/ Héctor Panizza before Your Honour I present and explain myself: / Since, finding myself without the means to continue my artistic career in Europe, I come to request from Y. H. that there be conceded to me a discretionary pension of one hundred gold pesos per month for the term of three years, a period of time I consider necessary to be able to perfect my musical knowledge. I am encouraged to embark on these new efforts due to the success obtained by my opera 'Medio evo latino', as much among my compatriots as in Italy, where it premiered. / In the hope that working to the best of my ability I will know how to compensate the protection I have received, honoring my country, it is gratifying to me to present to Y. H. the considerations of my deep respect and gratitude for his graciousness. / Signed: Héctor Panizza."[59]

According to the applicant, the pension was granted to him for only two years and finally was reduced to just one, upon being transferred to a "greatly favored" Argentine harpist, who wanted to perfect himself on the coast of Liguria. In truth, it was a general revision of these benefits ordered by law that determined Panizza's grant be prematurely interrupted.[60]

MARRIAGE AND GRIEF

Back in Italy again, Panizza found himself with a bleak outlook that had little to do with his recent successes. Tito Ricordi received him with a hostile attitude and let him know that for the moment his music did not interest the publishing house. His father— whom he met in Italy at the beginning of the winter of 1901—endeavored to offer *Medio Evo latino* at La Scala but the project collapsed. This was a more serious setback because the date of his marriage had already been set for January 6, 1902.[61]

The wedding between Ettore Panizza and Fulvia Tommasi was celebrated on the day as planned and was followed by a brief trip to the Ligurian coast. In the meantime, Héctor took the edge off the vice of composition with a *Trio for violin, cello and piano*, which he scheduled at the Patriotic Society in Milan. He also looked after his conjugal obligations: on October 22, 1902, his eldest daughter Valeria was born.[62]

Now with a family to maintain, the conductor had to confirm if the indifference of Ricordi was, as he suspected, only due to the attitude of the difficult Tito and not that of Giulio. A letter made things clear. Faced with a desperate request for work, "sior Giuli" arranged Panizza's first major contract as conductor: the fall season and Carnival of 1903 at the Politeama Genovese. At the same time, Panizza obtained a contract for the popular Carnival season at the Teatro Dal Verme in Milan, where he conducted Puccini's *Le Villi* in June of that same year, with hardly any repercussions. His father played in the orchestra and during a rehearsal Panizza had cause to regret criticizing the performance of the cellos, the section led by Giovanni Grazioso. That same night, father and son swiftly made peace, in a scene typical of the Italian behavior of the period: the son asking forgiveness amidst sobs and the father, falling silent, placing his hands upon him as a sign of blessing.

This critical episode seems logical in connection with the nerves due to the recent wedding and significant reduction of work that seemed to impede Panizza from his career as conductor and forced him to live in the family house in Milan. The importance of the position and the quality of his work at the Dal Verme earned him a contract at the Politeama Garibaldi in Palermo to conduct *Tosca*. But fate alternates between good and bad, and the day of the debut in that venue, on October 25, 1903, Héctor received an unexpected piece of news from Buenos Aires: his father had died there on October 8.[63] Giovanni was only fifty-two years

old, and his abrupt death found him alone, in a rented room. His funeral
was significant, since he was a musician and teacher highly appreciated
in the Río de la Plata. He was such an important figure that the Williams
family (whose greatest musical exponent was the previously mentioned
Alberto Williams) offered the Panizzas its family crypt. One year later,
the remains were transported to the Monumental cemetery in Milan,
where they still rest alongside his wife.

IN DEVELOPMENT

In November 1904, the Politeama Genovese entrusted to the Argentine conductor, among others, a brand-new work by Puccini: *Madama
Butterfly*, with no less than Salomea Kruscenisky in the title role, in what
was the first Italian revival following the second premiere of the opera
in Brescia under the baton of Cleofonte Campanini. Puccini himself was
at the performances, still feeling the echoes of the fiasco of his Milanese
premiere, which forced him to reformulate what would perhaps end
up being the most sensitive of his operas. In the middle of one of the
performances he scribbled an amusing poem on a slip of paper in which,
among other things, he affirms: *L'esecuzione è buona, / non manca mai
una croma, / non mi vien mai la stizza / perché ci abbiam Panizza* (The
interpretation is good, / it never misses even an eighth note, / rage never
strikes me / because we have Panizza).[64]

Ettore's career now found itself on the ascent, increased by the birth
of his second child Guido Grazioso on February 19, 1905. During this
time, he was hired by the Massimo in Palermo and achieved acclaim
with *Tosca* at both the Politeama Genovese and the Teatro di San Carlo
in Naples, where he came to conduct thirteen performances with that
title. In light of such a reception, this important company hired him
once again in 1906 to conduct *Madama Butterfly*, this time with soprano
Maria Farneti. In regard to the value of his interpretation, there exists
a letter which Puccini himself wrote to Panizza.[65] In this season and at
this theater Panizza also conducted *Tess,* an opera by Baron Frédéric

d'Erlanger. This nobleman, music lover, manager, patron, and composer was an essential factor in the ascendancy of the conductor's international career. So enchanted was the aristocrat with the art of Panizza that he offered him a contract to conduct starting the following year at the Royal Opera House, the famous Covent Garden in London, of whose board of directors he was a member.

The wind continued to blow in favor of our man. Escaping Naples due to an eruption of Mount Vesuvius, he spent the northern summer of 1906 in Milan, conducting his first season of symphonic concerts in the context of the Great Exhibition. The occasion was significant: the event brought together numerous political leaders for the inauguration of the Simplon, for many years the longest railway tunnel in the world, which permitted Milan to link directly with Paris.

Panizza's experience as a symphonic conductor would repeat after the 1908-1909 season at La Scala, when for the first time his artistic stature appeared on a level with that of Toscanini. The successor of Alfredo Catalani at the conservatory in Milan, Gaetano Coronaro, had just died, and the institution requested La Scala to include a work by him in one of the four scheduled concerts, two conducted by Giuseppe Martucci and two by Toscanini. But the latter refused, alleging the low quality of the works, and decided to sue the society of concerts to change his working conditions.[66]

Toscanini lost the lawsuit and Panizza conducted the scandalous concert, which included Coronaro's Intermezzo from *Il malacarne* and *Capriccio sinfonico*, Glazunov's suite *Of the Middle Age*, Catalani's Prologue to *La falce*, and Cherubini's *Anacreonte Overture*, in addition to Dvořák's newly written *Symphony "From the New World."*[67]

The winter of 1906-1907 found Panizza at the Teatro Carlo Felice in Genoa while the Casa Ricordi, dazzled by the brilliance of this star in full ascent, entrusted him to revise the *Great Treatise of Instrumentation* by his namesake Berlioz. Panizza took pains with the work and brought it up to date with an indispensable appendix. Giulio Ricordi, in praise, wrote the prologue to the edition.[68]

That same year Héctor Panizza completed the assignment for which he has come to be so widely known in his country of origin. This was *Aurora*, the opera that contains the "Canción de la bandera" (The Song of the Flag), for a long time sung by students at Argentine schools while raising and lowering the national flag at the start and end of school shifts ("morning" and "afternoon," respectively). The song spread through all of Argentina under titles like *Saludo a la bandera* or simply *Aurora*.[69]

After more than twenty years of stalled construction, the imminent opening of the new Teatro Colón was motive for the national government to commission an opera with an Argentine theme for the inaugural season, which finally took place in 1908. For Panizza, it was clear that this new opera house would end up substituting for his beloved Teatro de la Ópera, which had taken up the scepter of the Argentine operatic art after the disappearance of the old Colón, and which still competed with numerous theaters dedicated to vocal art.[70]

The new Colón, adorned with all the ostentation permitted by the most prosperous period the Argentine Republic enjoyed, deserved a corresponding homage on the eve of the centenary of its first national government. The commission came from Héctor Cipriano Quesada Casal, an Argentine politician, writer, and journalist whose son of the same name had been born the same year as Panizza and shared with him some experiences of youth.[71]

In 1906, Quesada the father was elected senator of the Legislature of the province of Buenos Aires. From his local seat, in the city of La Plata, he was able to guarantee that the government took on the assignment, consisting of "an opera dedicated to exalt the patriotic values of a young and thriving nation."[72]

The original idea for the plot belongs to him and this is why the credit for the libretto is often shared. However, once the theme was accepted by

Panizza, the opera's text was requested by the composer through Ricordi from the experienced Luigi Illica, after the happy experience with *Medio Evo latino*. Ricordi would have practically imposed this commission on Illica, who at that moment was finishing the first act of *L'austriaca*, one of the several operas discarded by Puccini, in this case based on the story of Marie Antoinette.[73]

Panizza composed *Aurora* in 1907 in Italy. His memoirs provide the specific details: it was in his small apartment at number 17 on the Fiori Oscuri street in Milan and in Moiana, in the lake district of Erba, where some distant family had a property. One morning in this latter place, as all his relatives had gone to mass, Panizza wrote the "Canción de la bandera." The orchestration was completed that same year in London, where Panizza developed a significant period of his career as opera conductor.[74] In that same city, according to a journalistic testimony, a first reading or private audition took place, which "numerous Argentines living there attended." Among the crowd could be "found Don Ernesto de la Cárcova, who came away with the most agreeable impressions and assures us that the work produced an excellent general effect."[75] The premiere at the brand-new Teatro Colón, on September 5, 1908, featured Panizza himself as conductor along with a top-notch group of performers headed by Maria Farneti, Amedeo Bassi, and Titta Ruffo. Prominent Argentine painter Pio Collivadino designed the set, and later that same year assumed the presidency of the National Academy of Fine Arts. In the playbill, one could read the words "Great artistic event. National solemnity."

A critic for *La Nación* utilized quite a curious prose to describe the event: "The performance in the hall of the Colón last night makes us believe that Verdi himself would have considered it a worthy context for the unforgettable debut of his *Otello*. It was no less dazzling, nor did a less dense atmosphere of charm predominate quivering with interest, when the magnificent *grand opéra* was offered before the eyes of the glorious Italian maestro... A complete success."[76]

Journalistic exaggeration aside, the evening was truly a success. The "Canción de la bandera" earned an "encore" for the tenor Bassi during all the performances, requiring consent from the mayor of the city or the theater manager, since local regulations prohibited the repetition of arias or opera highlights during performances except with the express permission of an authority, which could be awarded at that very moment.

Panizza the composer still seemed to eclipse Panizza the conductor; so much was this so that *Caras y Caretas* magazine, giving wide coverage to the rehearsals of the work, had to clarify the following: "In Europe not only has he been applauded as a composer, but great praise has been given to him also as a *maestro concertatore* and conductor."[77]

A certain hostility from part of the press, especially those who aligned with the rising tide of musical nationalism that would reach its zenith later during the 1930s, criticized Panizza for a lack of local color and excessive Europeanism. The text sung in Italian for an "Argentine opera" endorsed this criticism, though as was known, Italian in the emerging Buenos Aires was just as much the official language for every operatic work —be it French, German or Russian— as it was the native language for the majority of the city's population. One way or another, in the balance, it is true that "it was decreed by the press that *Aurora* was not an Argentine but an Italian opera" and that "Panizza for the Argentines, who are more Papists than the Pope, was too Italian."[78]

The article quoted from *La Nación*, however, is ambiguous in that on the one hand it remarked on this lack of local color, and on the other it recognized this aspect made the opera cosmopolitan and gave it aspirations to form part of an international repertoire.

The first target of the criticism was the librettist, despite the immense prestige of his background: "The little of Córdoba there was in the theme proposed to his ability as a librettist has blurred and disappeared into Italian verses. In *Aurora* Mr. Illica has had to improvise for himself a province in the pampas and an 1810 with an exclusively arithmetical value, so that the following has resulted for those of us who know it more closely: neither pampa, nor 1810. Argentine modesty will know how to forgive this charming fantasy of the distinguished and beloved co-author of *Bohème*."[79]

Aníbal Cetrangolo, summarizing the local elements that according to this review were missing in *Aurora*, draws up a list that might seem humorous: "the wind amidst the tall grasses, the forest of trees, the immensity of silence, the infinite expansion of the horizon, the land creaking in the midsummer heat."[80]

With respect to the ambiguity indicated, the critic in Bartolomé Mitre's newspaper balanced his negative remarks about the text and music with reflections on the future predicted by the work: "Of course, we do not consider this absence of national characters in the work to be a flaw, as this is an author whose education permits him, if not invites him, to develop very diverse sorts of ideals in his art [...]. *Aurora* is, in short, an Italian opera and, as an Italian opera, we must straight away add that it can well aspire to a distinguished position in the contemporary repertoire."[81]

The barbs that hurt the author most were those from *La Razón*, which remarked, "maestro Panizza has composed musical pages of value, which we recognize as not always suitable to the moment of the subject treated by the plot [...]. He has composed music with motifs and Italian passages in which there prevail the reminiscences of well-known operas. But we fundamentally believe that he does not lack inspiration, and that he has demonstrated this in his *Aurora*, which undoubtedly is not a paragon of musical beauty in the full extent of the word, but is an opera that has no fewer merits than others we hear and applaud frequently in our theaters and can perfectly figure in contemporary repertoires."[82]

El Diario went for the same line: "The critics have many provisos to make, but the audience has applauded the music of the Argentine composer with delirious enthusiasm and affection, an opinion of its own. *Aurora* is Italian music, 'Puccinian,' that is to say simple and melodious. In the first act, and in the second, there are several agreeable and elegant romanzas. Mr. Illica has not paid attention to the plan don Héctor Quesada sent him from here, and has written a ridiculous libretto. The third act begins on a *tramonto* and ends at dawn [...]. And there are other things of the same sort. The distinguished librettist has this time written *pour l'exportation....*"[83] In defense of one whom it considered a compatriot, *La Patria degli Italiani* noted the presence and approval of President Figueroa Alcorta himself the day of the premiere: "the President of the Republic applauded in his official box seat, the gentlemen applauded, and from the upper circles came prodigious rounds of admiring effervescence [...]. *Aurora* obtained the success it deserved."[84]

Another one of the most important reactions in defense of *Aurora* and its author was that of the magazine *Nosotros*, the preeminent literary publication of Alfredo Bianchi and Roberto Giusti. In one of its typical gestures —as it would do years later with Borges and a large number of cultural characters whom they favored— it organized a banquet of reparation in honor of Panizza, with the usual apologetic speeches and well-known libations.[85]

Beyond the above remarks, the critics did not sully the ideal with which the theater included this opera in its first season. To highlight the satisfaction received from this Argentine musician, the City Council of Buenos Aires —owner of the Teatro Colón— publicly presented him with five thousand gold pesos in a silver chest, in front of numerous artistic personalities and a large part of the theater staff.

Chapter 4

An International Career

Panizza's international career, what made him known as a conductor beyond Italian borders, began in 1907. From then until the outbreak of the Great War, life rewarded Héctor an enjoyment of the closing notes of the *belle époque*, the final caresses of a lost world in which elegance, manners, fine dining, and aesthetic beauty were the principal concerns for a society which beneath this patina simultaneously incubated its darkest features.

The admiration that Panizza's work in Naples awoke in Baron d'Erlanger led the maestro to be hired by the Royal Opera House in London; this relationship would continue for eight consecutive seasons. Panizza' life was thus organized in accordance with the London season, which essentially extended from May to August, encompassing part of the summer and allowing him to conduct in Italy, and other places in Europe, during the eventful months of the northern fall and winter.

Soon the conductor acquired enormous prestige in Great Britain, not only as a maestro of the Italian and even French opera repertoire, but also as an interpreter and proponent of English orchestral music, which at the time was approaching its high point. It is enough to mention how a contemporary referential music companion described Panizza's activities in 1910: "It is interesting to note that Elgar's *Introduction and Allegro for Strings* was presented through him to the Italian public, an act that if widely imitated by foreign conductors could prove and stimulate the existence of what the critics often have denied us: an English school of music."[86]

Panizza's legacy at Covent Garden was of enormous relevance. In addition to his constant work with the Italian repertoire, he debuted in London Massenet's *Thaïs*, Wolf-Ferrari's *I gioielli della Madonna*, Camussi's *La Dubarry*, Zandonai's *Francesca da Rimini* and *Conchita* (whose world premieres in Italy were also entrusted to him) and, of course, *Tess*, the opera by his mentor, which was offered in two seasons.[87]

In London, Panizza crossed paths with some artists he had already worked with in Italy. Perhaps the most notable was Luisa Tetrazzini, whom he had directed at the Carlo Felice in Genoa. The singer had not yet found acceptance in Italy, but Panizza decided to support her during a performance of *La traviata* in London and featured her in *Il barbiere di Siviglia*. Her success in these performances launched the international career of this great soprano— later confirmed during her long period in the United States— due no doubt to Héctor's artistic instinct.

The British activity of our biographical subject began with *Rigoletto*, with a cast headed by Mario Sammarco, Selma Kurz, and Amedeo Bassi. The singers whom he met at Covent Garden— and whom he would make quiver with his baton— are countless and of the first rank. A few examples are Nellie Melba, Emmy Destinn, Enrico Caruso, Alessandro Bonci, and Antonio Scotti.

Among the conductors in the house, of whom Panizza was already considered to be at the same level, were no less than Arthur Nikisch and Hans Richter, the eminent and robust maestro who spread Wagnerian art in England with help from George Bernard Shaw's writings, who then signed his musical criticism as "Corno di Bassetto." The relationship with Richter transformed into an artistic friendship, which led Panizza to travel with him three times to the Bayreuth Festival, where he watched him conduct *Die Meistersinger von Nürnberg* with unusual success. There he was also moved for the first time by *Parsifal*, a title that until then could only be appreciated when it was performed in Bayreuth (which until 1914 defended exclusivity over it, by express mandate of Wagner).

One of the obligatory stops on those trips was Munich, where Héctor sought out the possibility of listening to music by Mozart to steep himself in the Classical German style, which was not initially one of his specialties.

During his stays in London, Panizza was able to enter society with notable success, even coming to know royalty. He met Edward VII in his final years, by express invitation of Windsor Castle; after the death of the monarch, at the coronation gala of his son George V in 1910, he conducted the second act of *Il barbiere di Siviglia* while sharing the podium with Richter, Cleofonte Campanini, and Percy Pitt, today a forgotten musician who nevertheless was the first Englishman to conduct *Der Ring des Nibelungen* in Great Britain.

The gala turned out to be an exceptional event: the structure of the Covent Garden box seating was modified to receive dignitaries from all over the world, and for the Argentine conductor the occasion signified an acceptance into the heart of a country which was then the indisputable first world power. George V was scarcely interested in opera; in fact it supremely bored him. Fortunately his level of engagement did not hinder the prosperity the operatic art enjoyed throughout England.

An imperial whim joined two great rivals on *La bohème*: the equally whimsical Melba and the Mediterranean Caruso, whom Panizza had the chance to conduct. Melba was offended by the king's favoritism toward Caruso and refused to attend rehearsals. Panizza was so confident in her reputation that he decided not to participate in the fuss. Melba even asked him if he knew the opera! Panizza, it is clear, was not the irritable Toscanini; on the contrary, his bourgeois profile, strategic mentality, and fine elegance permitted him to triumph even in hostile situations, and thus gradually ascend as a brilliant and reliable star.

HAPPY YEARS

During this time, at the beginning of every fall, Panizza moved with his family to Italy, where he already had guaranteed contracts in several theaters. Between 1906 and 1909 he conducted at the Carlo Felice in Genoa; later, beginning in 1912, he was "municipal" conductor— that is, hired directly by the commune— at the Teatro Regio in Turin, and for two seasons he resided at the Casino de San Remo to take charge of its musical season.

In the city that later would become famous for its festivals of popular music, an intense operatic and symphonic activity was then developing, in a milieu of natural beauty and high society that would be remembered by Héctor as one of the most pleasing experiences in his life. This was so to such an extent that he considered making San Remo his place of permanent residence. His contract permitted him to live in the casino itself with his rapidly growing family: his wife Fulvia and two small children, Valeria and Guido. He was given a private room and a study, which were decorated daily with fresh flowers.

Visitors from the upper social classes flowed toward the place, coming from the beaches of Liguria or the French Riviera, interested in music, improving their health, or exercising what today we call tourism. The presence of the casino added interest to this grand life though Panizza, naturally averse to games of chance, never risked even a chip. All that attracted him were boccie balls and croquet; tennis also interested him, but conducting obliged him to look after the muscular tension in his right arm.

An interesting circle of friendships gathered around Panizza, who was fond of social life and hostile toward solitude, which for him was synonymous with tedium or "spleen." One of his friends at that time was Franco Alfano, the composer who years later had the honor of completing Puccini's *Turandot*, the task for which he is best known and unjustly criticized by posterity. The talented composer of the opera *Risurrezione*, among others, offered Panizza the premiere of his *First Symphony*, which is dedicated to him.

This fact is not unimportant: in San Remo, Héctor could not only conduct opera, but also for the first time in his life take charge of a complete symphonic season. His interest in the new music was evident: his programs featured works by Debussy, Ravel, Scriabin, Glazunov, Prokofiev, Elgar, and Richard Strauss, in a time when these composers represented the current state of music (the idea of the avant-garde had still not spread with dodecaphonism). It was possible to program this repertoire thanks to the quality of the orchestra. Panizza was responsible for choosing its members, many of whom, due to their artistic qualities, would go on to form the orchestra of the Teatro alla Scala in Milan in 1921, when this was constituted as an "autonomous entity" under the aegis of Toscanini; some musicians even had access to the orchestra of the New York Metropolitan Opera, where Panizza would meet with them again at a later stage of his career.

Still in this happy prewar period, he was also able to conduct at the regional and international fairs organized in Italy, which added to their commercial aims the organization of brief high-quality opera seasons, as occurred in Verona or Treviso. In these years Panizza also began a solid relationship with the Teatro Dal Verme in Milan (where he had conducted for the first time in the 1902-1903 season), beginning with his presentation of Rossini' s *Guglielmo Tell* in 1910. The flipside of these more popular activities were the elegant seasons in San Remo, which were soon extended to the casino in Nice.

Panizza spent four fall seasons at the Teatro Dal Verme— where in 1884 Puccini debuted his first opera, *Le Villi*, and in 1892 Leoncavallo presented his *Pagliacci*— that paved the way for his entrance to La Scala. In fact, a large number of the musicians and chorus members who performed in the theater on San Giovanni sul Muro street (which before the war had a capacity much greater than today and lacked, as was usual then, an orchestra pit), would later go on to play in the first season of the

Milanese opera house. It was at the Dal Verme that Héctor conducted the world premiere of Zandonai's *Conchita* and for the first time in Milan, Wagnerian titles like *Die Walküre* and *Tristan und Isolde*. There were eleven performances before a full auditorium, each with positive critical response.

In prewar Milan, opera was one of the main entertainments of society, in a manner that is unimaginable in today's global society, and Héctor was part of this milieu. It was also a hive of friendships and contacts, of which he took good advantage. To mention just one case, Arturo Toscanini and Arrigo Boito attended the rehearsals of *Conchita*, by invitation of Tito Ricordi, who was in charge of staging the title.

Panizza came to have a friendship that endured over time with the composer of *Mefistofele,* Arrigo Boito. The opportunity arrived when he had the chance to conduct this opera at the Dal Verme, but Boito did not then attend the performances of his work. His brother, instead, did go. This was the architect and writer Camillo Boito, who had designed the Casa di Riposo per Musicisti for Verdi. Camillo became so enthusiastic about Héctor's conducting that he set up a meeting with him at his brother's house. Panizza never forgot the elegance of the composer, his personal refinement, his fondness for new appliances (he welcomed them with an electric tea kettle) and the request he put to him to play highlights from his *Mefistofele* on the piano. A few days later Panizza received a portrait autographed by Boito, which he kept forever in his study.[88]

Héctor also gained access to the Teatro Regio in Turin, where he had been preceded by no less than Toscanini himself. The works programmed there were of high caliber: it is enough to mention *Don Carlo, Die Götterdämmerung* (sung in Italian) and the recent *Isabeau* whose world premiere had taken place at the Teatro Coliseo in Buenos Aires in 1911.[89]

Panizza triumphed with *Il crepuscolo degli dei*— achieving the approval of the knight-commander Giuseppe Depanis, a harsh music critic— as well as with a Wagnerian symphonic-vocal concert. Later came one of the great artistic events in Turin: the premiere of *Parsifal* in the city, the veto on the composer now lifted. To prepare himself, Héctor traveled to Bayreuth and also to Zurich, where he was impressed by an abstract set design from the opera. Contrary to what might be assumed, Panizza preferred this setting to the one in Italy, which had attempted to be historically faithful, inspired by the interior of the Siena cathedral, yet he was not able to impose his wishes on the stage director.

Parsifal was offered in important opera houses across the Italian peninsula: the first performance was in Bologna, followed by La Fenice, the Costanzi in Rome, and the Regio in Turin, modeled by Panizza's hands beginning on March 8, 1914, over the course of twelve performances in Italian translation by Angelo Zanardini. The great event gave rise to well-known banquets, in particular that of the Princess Letizia di Savoia (the great-niece of Napoleon), who invited him for dinner at the castle of Moncalieri. Panizza took on several new important works during these years in Turin, for example Zandonai's *Francesca da Rimini*, with a libretto by Gabriele D'Annunzio, and Giordano's *Madame Sans-Gêne*, (premiered at the Metropolitan Opera in New York) with a setting Héctor managed to impose, pushing aside the staging director Gustavo Macchi in favor of elements appropriate to the theater. Afterward Panizza arranged *Die Walküre* and *Siegfried*, as well as a work forgotten today by Alfredo Catalani, *Dejanice*, which drew Toscanini as a spectator, as he was a great friend of the composer who had prematurely passed away. The voices Héctor worked with in Turin would be shining stars a few years later, such as Claudia Muzio and Toti Dal Monte.

Between England and Italy, Héctor lived quite far away from his country of birth during this time. The exception was a visit in 1908 to conduct his *Aurora* at the Teatro Colón; an invitation to conduct *Parsifal* at the Coliseo, was rejected due to the alleged demand that the performance not last longer than three and a half hours.[90]

This life plan would be interrupted in 1914. The 1913-1914 season was the last of Panizza's continuous London period (he would go back to working in London only in 1924) and also the first in which Panizza participated in a company's tour: in this case, that of Covent Garden, the first in 1913 at the Opéra Comique in Paris with *La bohème*, and later at the brand new Théâtre des Champs Élysées in Paris, where between May and July 1914 he conducted the German repertoire along with Felix Weingartner, while he shared the Italian repertoire with Roberto Moranzoni, featuring works like *Un ballo in maschera*, *Il segreto di Susanna*, and *Manon Lescaut*.

Critics, who considered it brazen to present this "juvenile" work in the land that had brought to light Massenet's *Manon*, condemned Puccini's work. One understands this position which today would seem like unacceptable chauvinism: nationalism was at its maximum boiling point on the eve of the Great War. Héctor returned with the company to London in August, the month that the war would break out. He barely had time to cross the English Channel before he found himself, now on the continent, facing trains jammed with soldiers and cannons. The *belle époque* had definitively come to an end.

ON THE EVE OF THE FIRST WORLD WAR

The northern winter of 1914-1915 held little activity for Panizza. However, the next winter he benefited from the propagandistic needs of Italy, which awarded him a contract to conduct in Spanish cities like Barcelona, Valencia, Bilbao, and San Sebastián. By the winter of that year, the impresario Ercole Casali had already assumed control of the management of the Teatro Real in Madrid and brought Panizza with him. In 1916 he would conduct *Tristan und Isolde* and *Thaïs*, with Geneviève Vix and Mattia Battistini. While there Héctor also struck up new friendships, such as the one that linked him to the great Spanish violinist and conductor Enrique Fernández Arbós.

He also took up his Italian activities once again at a place now dear to him, the Teatro Regio in Turin, where he was responsible for the seasons until 1915, and would continue after the end of the war. In 1916 he was invited to conduct at the Teatro alla Scala in Milan by the duke Visconti di Modrone and by Vittorio Mingardi, the artistic director since 1908, replacing Giulio Gatti-Casazza who had gone on to rule over the destinies of the Metropolitan Opera in New York.[91]

At La Scala, Panizza was inspired once more to perform works as dissimilar as Gaspare Spontini's *Fernando Cortez* (curiously, an American theme for what was virtually his debut), Umberto Giordano's *Siberia*, and Victor de Sabata's *Il macigno*. The next year, the quality of his work earned him a renewal of his contract, but to no avail: the military conflict resulted in the close of the house. His final activity there during the war was in April 1917, with a "symphonic-operatic concert" in which he shared the podium with a child prodigy, Willy Ferrero. The evening opened, significantly, with the performance of the national anthems of France and the United States.

Shortly afterward Gatti-Casazza invited him to the Metropolitan, but the journey by sea was very dangerous. Fresh in the memory of the musicians was the tragic death, on March 24, 1916, of Enrique Granados onboard the torpedoed *HMS Sussex*.

But even at the height of war and without moving about too much, operatic posts opened up one after another for Panizza: in Bologna, where he conducted Donizetti's *Lucrezia Borgia* and Puccini's *La rondine*, in its premiere for Italy, with Toti Dal Monte and Aureliano Pertile, following its premiere in Montecarlo; and once again in Rome at the Costanzi, in a great season that in 1918 seemed distant from the human bloodbath of the first world war.

The year the war ended, the impresario Walter Mocchi invited Panizza to conduct at the Colón, but the maestro's fears of the risks implied by the maritime journey remained valid. It is also very probable that Panizza's decision to refuse the invitation was influenced by Toscanini's negative opinion regarding Mocchi's administration.[92]

Already by June 1919, however, the Arena di Verona, which had been closed for the duration of the war, reopened and Ettore was invited to conduct there. The Arena had two complete companies and drew around 20,000 viewers to each show. In works like Ponchielli's *Il figliuol prodigo* (of which he conducted fourteen performances), Panizza fervently recalled an image that today we could associate with a rock concert: the audience lighting matches at the end of the opera's second act. The longed-for peace had arrived and the town, which surely had lost many of its sons, could dedicate itself to enjoying one of the most popular arts. Panizza would return to the Arena only in 1923, to conduct Massenet's *Le roi de Lahore* and Bellini's *Norma*, a performance that was perhaps the peak of his popularity in that very particular milieu.

For the 1919-1920 season the Regio in Turin would once again invite him to conduct Catalani's *Dejanice* and Puccini's *Il trittico* in their local premiere, with the presence of the composer and one of the librettists, the talented Giovacchino Forzano. This production then went on to the Teatro Grande in Brescia, in the context of an important fair.

Another post that opened itself to Panizza's talents was the Teatro Donizetti in Bergamo, a place he found, like every small city, rather dull. There he made an incursion into directing a peculiar work, *Il carillon magico*. The piece was a "mimo-symphonic comedy," but in reality was a ballet whose music was composed by Riccardo Pick-Mangiagalli, which had recently premiered at La Scala. Riccardo was a composer with whom Panizza was united by a warm friendship and who would come, years later, to succeed Ildebrando Pizzetti as director of the Conservatory in Milan, where both had trained in composition with maestro Ferroni.

In Panizza's career, friendship was always a sort of magnet that attracted him to specific cities. In Florence he had spent the first summer of the postwar period lodged at the residence of tenor Amedeo Bassi, whom he prepared for *Tristan und Isolde*. The stately Turin contained numerous friends after several seasons spent there and so became a strong point of attraction for a man who hated solitude. But as 1920 approached, he was faced with a lack of offers by the opera house to which he hoped anxiously to return. Instead Héctor accepted a contract in Trieste, where he conducted and brought on tour works like *Tristan, Sanson et Dalila, Falstaff,* and *I quatro rusteghi.*

The relationship between Panizza and the poet Gabriele D'Annunzio, one of the most singular characters in Italian culture, began during thistime. In musical terms, the relationship would bear fruits in 1923, when the writer invited Panizza to conduct *Orfeo ed Euridice* in the open air in Brescia, a production in which D'Annunzio would serve as staging director and that Toscanini would attend as spectator.[93]

As an active participant in the First World War —even in the bombing of Vienna— and holding pure nationalistic tendencies, the poet and soldier took control of the city of Fiume (today Rijeka, in Croatia) at the end of the war, after the area was ceded by Italy in the Paris Conference. There D'Annunzio established a personal regency, with a profile anticipating that of the *duce* Benito Mussolini himself, though the Constitution he implemented was in advance of the ideology reigning in Italy at the time. His limitless boldness —he organized irregular forces and attempted to set up a new Society of "Oppressed" Nations— clashed with the military failure, but also earned him personal glory and even a noble title from the king of Italy, Vittorio Emanuele III.

The help Toscanini had offered in 1919 to conduct at the Teatro Verdi in Trieste in solidarity with the writer —a daring gesture that would merit decorations of war—, was far in the past now. D'Annunzio called the ensemble of musicians gathered his "Orphic legion" and transferred to Panizza the honor given to him by Toscanini, also calling him an *ardito* (brave one) in that legion of "symphoniacs."[94] On the local level, D'Annunzio's military adventure had provoked the temporary close of the Teatro Verdi to avoid further stirring up spirits. The break allowed Panizza to rehearse *I quatro rusteghi* and work alongside the stage director Delfino Menotti, in a proof that during this time the "*maestro concertatore* and orchestra conductor" was the principal figure of the show. Sixteen opera performances were scheduled and Ettore was given the new title of "specialist" in this work by Ermanno Wolf-Ferrari, based on Goldoni.

At the Verdi, during a gala performance of *Aïda*, Panizza had the opportunity to directly greet Vittorio Emanuele III and Princess Elena, and play for them *La campana di san Giusto*, one of the Italian songs of the First World War that would transform into Trieste's liberation anthem, when national troops entered to recover the city.

Panizza also met there the Neopolitan pianist Antonino Votto, for whom he would later be able to find a place at La Scala. The great temple of music in Milan would give a key turn to the consolidation of Héctor Panizza's career as orchestra conductor.

CHAPTER 5

FROM LA SCALA TO THE METROPOLITAN

At the end of the Great War, the mayor of Milan, Emilio Caldara, along with Arturo Toscanini, conceived reopening the Teatro alla Scala as an autonomous non-profit organization dedicated to artistic excellence, divested of political interference, and economically sustainable.[95] The idea was totally new in the Italian theater scene. "Every idea of speculation and benefit was banished from the intentions of the managers," Panizza recalled.[96] The project proposed a model of morality for the culture of the peninsula. Toscanini was a fierce organizer who not only displayed artistic severity and a concentration of power— as much musical as theatrical—as a *maestro concertatore*, but who was also determined to change what he considered historical shortcomings or ingrained bad habits. As a result, he established a few nonnegotiable rules: punctuality, the placement of the orchestra in a pit, the darkening of the hall during performances to avoid social distraction, the prohibition of encores for singers, and a reverential silence before the artistic act. Panizza was co-protagonist of this revolution that guaranteed high standards for the

form of making opera during the 20th century, with effects that continue
to this day.

The offer to participate in the project came to the Argentine director
through the engineer (and ex-baritone) Angelo Scandiani, while Héctor
was directing a single 1921 season at the Colón. The former had made
contact in New York with Toscanini, who among other things had
requested that Panizza be his primary musical collaborator and decided
to assign him *Parsifal* for his appearance on the new stage.[97]

Today it seems just short of incredible to see the posters for the opening
of the Teatro alla Scala in its 1921-1922 season and observe that, in
rigorous compliance with alphabetical order, the name of Ettore Panizza
appears in the same font and size as that of Arturo Toscanini alongside
it, since they were then the two music directors of this opera house.
Between them are divided in equal parts the ten operas that finally formed
part of the *stagione*: Toscanini conducted *Falstaff, Die Meistersinger von
Nürnberg, Boris Godunov, Mefistofele,* and *Rigoletto,* while Panizza took on
Parsifal, Il trittico (making its premiere at La Scala), *Il barbiere di Siviglia,
La Wally,* and *I quatro rusteghi.*[98]

This balance, however, was not fully acceptable to everyone. In a
letter concerning the *scaligero* debut of his *Trittico,* Giacomo Puccini,
inexplicably contradicting previous missives, for the first time showed a
clear preference for Toscanini. The composer wrote: "As for the direction
of the opera, I firmly maintain that if the opera is not conducted by
Toscanini I shall be damaged by it— not only materially (that is, in
the performance) but morally. I know Milan (remember *Butterfly*). [...]
Without Toscanini, the opera would be presented in an inferior light."[99]

It is difficult to understand this note, given the regard and sympathy
that for some time Puccini had professed for Panizza, beginning from
the 1904 performances of *Madama Butterfly* in Genoa and the 1906
performances in Naples, also documented by the warm letter from January
of that year, previously quoted.

Perhaps Puccini's note can be understood as one of the many tortuous curves of an artistic relationship crossed through by encounters and disagreements of all kinds. The turmoil only settled when Toscanini reluctantly agreed to conduct Puccini's operas, although he became increasingly less convinced of Puccini's importance, due to his eminently nineteenth-century point of view. What is certain is that the dispute with Puccini appears commercially concerned, and on the margins of that dispute, Panizza and Toscanini seemed to mutually consider each other peers.

The forces of the city contributed everything necessary for the opera house to reach the peak of its history. To take one case, *Il Corriere della Sera*— the main newspaper of Milan and one of the most important in Italy— launched a subscription sales model to fund a stage remodeling project. The general manager of the theater was Scandiani, who counted on full support from mayor Caldara.[100]

The reopening of La Scala took place on December 26, 1921, with *Falstaff* under Toscanini's baton, followed by Panizza in *Parsifal*, beginning January 5, 1922. The Argentine conductor emotionally recalled his debut at the autonomous entity with Wagner's final work. Toscanini "advised him until he came down to the podium and after two years asked him to conduct it, in exchange for *Lohengrin*."[101]

Toscanini's commitment to the autonomous La Scala was complete and his ideal of developing theatrical activity according to his artistic principles was finally free from all compromise. "This was a motive for sacred respect as well as fear," recalls Panizza, who was Toscanini's greatest collaborator. "To put it this way, there wasn't a day that we did not remain for several hours together."[102]

They often went to lunch with Scandiani at Savini, a well-known restaurant in the galleria Vittorio Emanuele, where they were stalked as celebrities by the local press, who took notes on every one of their movements, took pictures, and even caricatured them. The friendship between Toscanini and Panizza reached its highest point at that time: the native of Parma invited the Argentine to eat at his house after debuts, along with friends, artists, and other distinguished personalities of the city. In this intimate context, Panizza remembers that Toscanini would transform into "a calm and joyful conversationalist who was bursting with sympathy and never attempted to impose himself on the rest of those present."[103]

Apart from this, the relevance of the reopening of La Scala was such that the king of Italy decorated Panizza with the order of knight commander.[104]

In an interview given in Argentina on the occasion of his visit in 1921, Panizza exhibited his brand new *scaligera* position with pride and gave information about the financial base of the project: "I have been hired for five years to conduct, in the company of Arturo Toscanini, at La Scala in Milan, whose seasons take place annually from December to the end of April. From Buenos Aires I will go directly to Italy to prepare the performances for the next season. Through the contribution of wealthy Milanese opera aficionados, the sum of ten million liras was gathered; four were used on important reforms, which put La Scala amongst the best theaters in the world, six remained as funds for the theater; in addition, to cover the 12 percent tax on operatic, dramatic and cinematographic performances in Milan, 1,200,000 annual liras will be collected. This signifies the economic independence of La Scala, as now it will be able to make art without greater financial concerns. Works will be premiered by young people and foreigners, the *mise en scène* will be looked after, as well as the costumes; in a word, we will make culture. It is a pride and a satisfaction for me, as I hope it is pleasing for my country, to be the first foreign conductor to serve permanently in an opera house with the prestige and tradition of La Scala. I was responsible for the last season of this theater, and as you can imagine it gratifies me to return to it in such favorable conditions, alongside Arturo Toscanini."[105]

It was an honor to conduct at the musical temple of Milan by the side of Toscanini, but the Panizza family also aspired to a higher level of life: they left a modest apartment and went on to acquire a much larger one on Ruggero Settimo Street in the area of Plaza Piamonte in the western outskirts of Milan.

For the two seasons following, however, the Argentine maestro would cease to work exclusively for La Scala, so as to be able to undertake his first North American adventure, which would have, as we will later see, a painful end.

THE NORTH AMERICAN TEMPTATION

Panizza found himself attracted by a juicy offer from the Auditorium Theater in Chicago for the 1922-1923 season. With supreme tact— and a certain boldness— he declined part of the *scaligere* productions for the following season, for which he was primarily replaced by Antonio Guarnieri.

Opened in 1889, the Auditorium Theater had been the site of the debut of the Chicago Symphony Orchestra in 1891 and the beginnings of the Chicago Opera Company in 1910. Its founder, no less than Cleofonte Campanini, had died in 1919 and the wake was held on the stage of the Auditorium itself.

While the company set out on the search for a great Italian conductor to replace Campanini, a year before Panizza' s arrival, it had wagered on contracting the Venetian maestro Giorgio Polacco. Polacco's high profile was set by his tenure as principal conductor at the Met. The first live radio broadcast in the city was carried out with him conducting a performance of *Madama Butterfly*.[106]

But Polacco did not end up taking the new position; instead he set off on travels to France, Cuba, and South America, only coming back when called by the singer Mary Garden, who was in charge of managing the company. Polacco and Garden sent a letter to Toscanini offering him the "co-direction" of the company, but the conductors had argued when they worked together at the Met and Toscanini was not willing to repeat the experience. La Scala had been made to his image and likeness; "he had no intention of ever working again in a traditionally run theatre like that of Chicago or the Metropolitan."[107]

Polacco and Garden thus sought an alternative within the same artistic environment and this is how they decided on Héctor Panizza, at least for the Italian repertoire, which formed the main part. It should be added that Polacco and Panizza had also met in Buenos Aires during the southern winter of 1921, more precisely at the Teatro Colón, where in addition they had conducted a concert together.

With these precedents in view, Héctor set sail with his wife Fulvia from Le Havre on the *Rotterdam*; they left their children in Milan, now already adults, and headed toward a society whose prosperity they knew about through the direct testimony of Toscanini and were resolved to win over, though they still did not speak a word of English.

They disembarked in New York on October 25, 1922, along with another conductor invited for the same reasons— the Dutchman Richard Hageman— and traveled by train to Chicago. There they met with an unforeseen circumstance: the complicated Polacco, who had taken the initiative to share his seat of honor with Panizza, now had doubts about the convenience of this working arrangement. The problem finally found a peaceful solution and Héctor conducted *La bohème, Parsifal* (with German artists), *La fanciulla del West,* and other Italian titles, with a success that earned him a contract for the following season, to which Panizza agreed mainly for its significant payment.[108]

The authorities of La Scala were far from offended by his distance, and offered him an opportunity to conduct *I quatro rusteghi* on his return to the theater. There Panizza replaced a conductor who had not finished deciding whether to take on the work. During the spring he gave symphonic concerts in that hall— where he programmed his *Nocturno*— and at the Regio in Turin, where he included in his program the "Canción de la bandera" from *Aurora* (in its original Italian, naturally). The summer brought in the longed-for vacation. The following winter, the Panizzas returned to Chicago for his second season, which this time included a tour ranging from Boston to Salt Lake City and New Orleans: a journey that took them two months of intense activity, always aboard a special train that carried the orchestra, the choir, and the ballet. The breadth of the repertoire was considerable: Halévy, Massenet (*Cleopatra*, *Thaïs*, *Manon*), a great deal of Meyerbeer (*Dinorah*, *L' Africaine*), Saint-Saëns, von Flotow and, among others, Verdi's *Otello*. The critics often emphasized the opportunity Panizza always granted the singers to be able to display their abilities.[109]

Panizza enjoyed this American experience in part because he could insist on presenting his own works. Indeed, this was a highpoint of the season for him and during the course of a few weeks, he managed to present two titles from his catalogue before audiences in the United States.

These were, however, works that had been composed the previous decade, some quite a few years before. *Tema y variaciones (Theme and Variations)* had won the Certani competition in Bologna in 1916 and *Il Rè e la foresta (The King and the Forest)* was practically finished in 1920. In fact, that year, in the course of an interview with *Caras y Caretas* magazine during his visit to Buenos Aires, Panizza had followed a custom among composers of that time and presented the journalist with a handwritten and dedicated excerpt from this last score, whose original title (quickly left aside) was *Dal re e la foresta*.[110]

This work for vocal soloists, choir, and orchestra was offered as a world premiere, with a choir of some fifty people and symphonic orchestra, under Nathaniel Finston's baton, on December 30, 1923. The context was peculiar: a concert of one hour, on Sunday at noon, organized by the Chicago Theater Orchestra, a company— more than a simple orchestra — whose object was to spread opera in the English language.

A review says: "The world debut of the symphonic poem by Ettore Panizza *Il rè e la foresta* was presented as a high-quality event, in care of the orchestra, choir, a baritone, and a soprano. Hundreds of prominent figures from the musical circles of Chicago congratulated Mr. Finston and the organization Balaban & Katz after the concert. The music of Panizza once again reflects the work of the profound musician and cultivated scholar, and is masterfully orchestrated. The work is poetic, colorful and original, even when here and there one must admit that the popular Italian conductor of the Chicago Civic Opera has worshipped at the Wagnerian shrine and felt admiration for Février's *Monna Vanna*, insofar as the first theme recalls that of the tent scene from that opera. Even so, the work is extraordinary and establishes Panizza as one of the most refined modern composers. The score should be presented once again in Chicago, as well as other cities of the United States, for it can be heard everywhere with interest."[111]

For its part, *Theme and Variations* has been the composer's orchestral score most played to this day, especially in his native Argentina, which, at this time, was less generous in its allowance of space for the composer's instrumental literature. The work had already been performed in Buenos Aires in 1920, thanks to conductor Ferruccio Cattelani and his cycle at the Associazione Italiana di Concerti.[112] For his first North American audition on January 25, 1924, Panizza himself stood at the podium of the Chicago Symphony Orchestra. This concert was special because the legendary conductor Frederick Stock was in charge of the program, while Panizza only conducted his own score.[113] This moment signified the culmination of Panizza's career as an orchestral composer, probably forced by his enormous prestige as a performer. With time, he would lose his ability to influence programs, and would write music only for the Argentine milieu.

It is clear that for Panizza, not only was it quite complicated to sustain a career in composing along with one in conducting at the same level, but there was also an aesthetic question to consider: he could not even approach the idea of being a cutting-edge artist. In an interview at the start of the '20s, after confessing to have written "three acts of an opera about Napoleon, which I later abandoned at the danger of making the great emperor sing," he pronounced: "A musician must choose, when he begins its career, between the virtuosity of conducting or of composing, for there is not enough time, in our age, to simultaneously dedicate oneself to both."[114] Shortly afterward he would say, with sincerity as unequivocal as it was unusual: "I was born in the '80s; I am still a romantic and my style would not now be modern. Therefore I no longer compose."[115]

TRAGEDY ON THE HIGH SEAS

The year was 1924 and the communications were flying: from Milan, Toscanini sent him the part of Asteria from Arrigo Boito's opera *Nerone*, so he could teach it to soprano Rosa Raisa on his return from the United States. The Panizzas set sail from New York on the steamship *Duilio* but they had hardly spent time at sea before Fulvia began to experience intense fevers, which until that moment had been concealed by aspirins; it was eventually diagnosed as pneumonia. A few days after setting out, she died onboard the ship. Fulvia Tommasi had been for Panizza not only the faithful wife and mother of his children, but also his permanent companion on artistic journeys. "In Milan we have our 'refuge'" —she had declared during his visit to Buenos Aires in 1921, injecting herself into an interview with her husband— "but very rarely can we rest, when we are returning from London or preparing the departure for Rome or Spain."[116]

During a time when antibiotics still did not exist, all those travels exposed the woman to contagion, even when she appeared to be physically and intellectually at the same level as her husband, and with emotional reserves to enjoy and organize the honors he was reaping.

Panizza, broken by the pain, was able to arrange for her body to remain in the hold of the ship until his landing in Italy, where his two children were given the unfortunate news. Luckily, these two already had life plans that allowed them to compensate for the sorrow of the unexpected death. Valeria, dedicated to sculpture, was about to marry an engineer named Ambrogio Colombo. Guido, for his part, had already begun a career in engineering with the consent of his mother. Despite having learned to play the cello, he rejected a musician's career in the face of his father's influence.[117]

Héctor was absolutely devastated by the loss of his wife. He fell into a deep depression and swiftly received the help of Toscanini, who proposed that he move from his apartment on Ruggero Settimo Street to the Hotel Regina. He lived there with only the company of his son, for Valeria had already begun her new life as a married woman. Although Panizza was not a practicing Catholic, he enormously appreciated the spiritual assistance of Father Pompeo Mainini, who managed little by little to pull him from his grief and inactivity.

REIGNING IN ITALY

There were also strictly professional motives that forced Panizza to shelve his depression. He received invitations to conduct once again at Covent Garden, at the Regio in Turin, and of course at La Scala. The Auditorium in Chicago once again invited him but was met with Héctor's rejection, as he could not stop associating the place with the death of his wife.

He counted on Toscanini's esteem. Now Toscanini was the one who had commitments in the United States, more precisely at Carnegie Hall in New York, and he needed his reliable maestro at the autonomous theater in Milan. When Toscanini returned from his first season with the New York Philharmonic, he awarded his colleague a key-ring as a symbol of the respect and the affinity he felt for Panizza. The key-ring bore a gold plaque, which read: "Ettore Panizza. Teatro Scala. Milano." The Argentine would keep it forever.[118]

La Scala grew notably in those years. Now some fifteen operas were scheduled there each season, a number that would increase every year. The conductors' staff was as numerous as it was interesting: Vittorio Gui, Gabriele Santini, and Franco Ghione; two composers who were taking responsibility for their own operas: Richard Strauss (who was also conducting Mozart) and Ildebrando Pizzetti; and two new valuable newcomers, to whom Toscanini entrusted the substitutions: Ferruccio Calusio —an Argentine born in the city of La Plata— and Antonino Votto, the most direct of Panizza's epigones. For the 1925-1926 season, Héctor took on one of the peaks of his career: conducting Wagner's *Ring*, which was performed in its complete form for the first time at La Scala under the stage direction of Ernesto (Ernst) Lert. Starting in 1927, the cycle was carried out in its entirety three times in three weeks and repeated in successive seasons.

With regard to the music, the team at La Scala took supreme care: with firsthand knowledge of Bayreuth, Panizza attempted to transfer Wagner's idea of the "mystic gulf" to the *scaligero* temple. The design in Bayreuth, by order of Wagner himself, includes a pit covered by a sort of curved platform to make the orchestra invisible, and submits musicians and conductor to an inhumane heat. As compensation, the orchestral sound seems to emerge from unknown depths and never covers the singing; the spectator is confronted by pure sound without the interference of seeing its material source: the orchestra.

Panizza managed the height of the piston on which the orchestra sat to be adjusted according to the part of the *Ring* it was playing, lowering the level from the second act of *Die Walküre* until the end of *Götterdämmerung*. He had a "hood" installed to muffle some stridencies and brought a new instrumental arsenal from Germany: Wagner tubas, to which six harps were added. A fact that today seems curious: *Der Ring des Nibelungen* had to be sung in Italian, just like the rest of the foreign repertoire; this was local tradition and house policy, sanctioned by Toscanini himself.

The singers, generally speaking, were of the first rank: some who would soon be stars were consecrated there, like Gina Cigna, who debuted at La Scala as Freia; others were shining stars but then fell into oblivion, like Spanish tenor Isidoro Fagoaga, the Siegfried in that saga.

At the end of the opera seasons, Panizza was given a taste of conducting symphonic concerts, both at La Scala as well as in other halls in Milan such as the Conservatorio and Teatro del Popolo, along with the Tonhalle in Zurich. An example of Panizza's symphonic program —taken from a Milanese performance in those years— is the following: the overture of Rossini's *L' italiana in Algeri*, one of Bach's violin concertos, Rabaud's symphonic poem *The Night Procession*, Holst's *The Planets*, Sibelius' *Concerto for violin* and Victor de Sabata's symphonic poem *Juventus*. It was without a doubt a truly versatile and eclectic selection of works.

These rich seasons in the middle of the '20s also made their organizers dream of going on tour: in fact Panizza planned to participate in a *tournée* through Paris with the *troupes* of La Scala to conduct *Falstaff* (Toscanini's specialty), but did not manage to pull it off; in contrast, he did offer his own specialty in Zurich: Wolf-Ferrary's *I quatro rusteghi*.

The same decade was also marked by the sad death of Puccini in Brussels (November 29, 1924), the commission to Franco Alfano to complete *Turandot* —the last opera by the maestro from Lucca— and its polemical premiere at La Scala conducted by Toscanini, who not only ordered the closing scene prepared by Alfano to be reduced, but in the first performance —on April 25, 1926— did without it, leaving the podium after the final measures written by Puccini.

Panizza was connected to this event of world resonance: it was he who would succeed Toscanini after the title's premiere. While some sources point out that it would have been Panizza responsible for the debut of the version of *Turandot* completed by Alfano (due to the partial desertion of Toscanini at the first performance), in reality Toscanini conducted two performances of the completed *Turandot* (on April 27 and 29) and left the following five, beginning from May 8, in the hands of Panizza.[119]

In this way, though he cannot be assigned credit for the absolute premiere of the complete title, the Argentine was an active part of the world creation of this great opera, which he could not conduct at the Colón, where Gino Marinuzzi premiered it on June 25, 1926, two months after his *prima scaligera*. For Panizza, the inability to premiere *Turandot* in Buenos Aires was a disappointment on par with missing the opportunity to conduct Richard Strauss' *Elektra* at the most important theater in his native country, despite a direct recommendation from the composer himself.

But the glories of La Scala did not elude him: even if he did not take charge of *Turandot*'s world premiere for those two performances, Panizza debuted Puccini's *Trittico* in Milan. Even non-Italian repertoires were entrusted to him, beginning with Wagner and following with Richard Strauss (*Elektra, Der Rosenkavalier*), the French repertoire (Charpentier's *Louise*) and the Russian repertoire (Rimsky-Korsakov's *The Tale of Tsar Saltan*). This would continue to be the case at least until the '30s, a five-year period when there was little doubt Héctor had achieved artistic maturity.

IN THE RECORDING STUDIO

As a good product of the 19th century, Panizza maintained a dual relationship with technological improvements: on the one hand, he distrusted them; on the other, he was tempted to take advantage, especially if they tended to spread his fame.

Panizza's first recording experience is linked to one of his mentors from the first part of his career: the Baron Frédéric d'Erlanger, who, as has been pointed out, was the one who had brought him to Covent Garden. At the dawn of recorded music, more precisely in 1904, d'Erlanger had founded the pioneering Italian recording label: Dischi Fonotipia, dedicated to capturing the great voices and the most prominent violinists of the moment, who were then much more popular than any orchestra conductor. The firm distributed and published in Italy the recordings of His Master's Voice.

In the age of acoustic recordings, it was impossible to record a complete opera with such limited means. The brief duration of the 78-rpm discs, added to the limitations of frequency in the taking of sound, only worked for short pieces and a small number of instruments, and even so the quality was very poor. Logically, Panizza knew of the two recordings made through the acoustic system of his "Canción de la bandera," sung by Amedeo Bassi and Florencio Constantino, respectively, in the years 1908 and 1910.

In 1925, the era of "electrical recording" began— a bouquet of microphones and not-quite-mechanical recording equipment. A year later, the new technology came to Italy, associated with the firm Fonotipia, which to win new investments immediately merged with the German label Odeon.

For these first experiences with electric recording, d'Erlanger invited his admired Panizza along with the orchestra of the Teatro alla Scala or, alternatively, the so-called "Great Symphonic Orchestra of Milan," predominantly consisting of musicians from La Scala itself.

Panizza knew about Toscanini's negative opinion of the old recording system, which his colleague had tried with the ensemble of La Scala in Camden, New Jersey, at the beginning of that same decade. But this time the technology was different. In May 1926, the engineers of His Master's Voice brought their team to Covent Garden to record Fiodor Chaliapin's voice in *Mefistofele*. Given the good results of this experience, plans were made to record *Turandot* at La Scala, in the second series of performances with Panizza as conductor.However, what few proofs they managed to produce were accidentally lost.[120]

In compensation, the Argentine director submitted himself with the musicians of La Scala to the first sessions in which highlights from operas of the Italian repertoire were recorded: *Turandot, Il trovatore, Aïda, Otello, La Gioconda, Mefistofele, Madama Butterfly, La bohème, Andrea Chénier,* along with other titles from foreign repertoires also sung in Italian, such as *Lohengrin* and *Carmen*. The albums were finally released in 1928, the year in which electric recordings caused a frenzy in Italy, the majority under the Fonotipia and Odeon labels. Panizza was at the center of this enthusiasm, while Toscanini recorded his own albums with the New York Philharmonic, in the United States.

In April 1928, Panizza began to leave recorded testimony of his expertise in the symphonic repertoire with Mendelssohn's *Hebrids Overture*, to which other brief pieces by Bizet and Berlioz were added. These records were subsequently released by La Voce del Padrone, which became the name of Fonotipia starting in 1931. This firm merged the same year with the Società Nazionale del Grammofono, a tributary of Columbia, following the same operation accomplished in England by His Master's Voice (known in Italy as La Voce del Padrone) and Columbia Records, giving life to EMI. By means of these corporate intricacies, Panizza's albums appeared in the catalogues of different labels, which ultimately all derived from the originating label Victor.

In his visit to Argentina in 1929, and on the occasion of the premiere of the nationalist opera *El matrero* by Felipe Boero, Panizza was invited to make a recording in Buenos Aires by the Victor label (a subsidiary of the old Victor Talking Machine in the United States, which that year had been absorbed by RCA). In August that same year, contemporary to his opera performances in his native city at the Teatro Colón, Panizza recorded the most important excerpts from the three acts of *El matrero*, with a reduced orchestra made up of musicians from the Colón's Resident Orchestra. The commercial interest of the recordings, aside from Panizza's reputation, was to promote Apollo Granforte, the great Italian-Argentine baritone who played the role of Liborio, and shared the sessions with two local singers: the tenor Pedro Mirassou and the mezzosoprano Nena Juárez.[121]

A curious anecdote occurred during one of the first sessions, when "El canto del hornero" from the first act was recorded, sung by Granforte. According to the score, toward the end the aria is interrupted by a brief spoken interjection by the mezzosoprano, who was absent at the session. It was thus Panizza who had to recite it, a pleasing bit of chance that permitted his voice to be recorded for the first time. The episode has a curious implication: what Panizza had to say is the phrase "that's not gaucho," with the disdainful meaning in Argentina of "that's not creole" or "that's not national." Considering that the greatest objection to his *Aurora* was its Italianness and that *El matrero* ended up being the only Argentine opera that surpassed *Aurora* in its number of performances, the phrase on Panizza's lips takes on a historical dimension and rare symbolism.[122]

Apart from this, Panizza's previous recordings were already actively circulating in Argentina: an advertisement in *Caras y Caretas* magazine put his recordings of *Lohengrin*'s "Mercè, mercè, cigno gentil" by Fernando Ciniselli and the chorus of the shepherdesses in *Andrea Chénier* alongside albums featuring tango stars like Gardel, Firpo, Canaro, and Corsini.[123]

Panizza's romance with the recording studio was extended upon his return to Italy. In 1930 and 1931, an intense series of recordings of the symphonic repertoire were made, which came to be a unique testimony to his activity in this field. The session in Milan on January 5, 1931, has a special importance: with the Orchestra of La Scala he recorded Mendelssohn's *"Italian" Symphony* for La Voce del Padrone / Grammofono. In addition to its own merits, it is probably the first complete recording of this work in the world, a fact generally overlooked due to its limited distribution.[124]

SECOND WEDDING

In the personal sphere, it is clear that Panizza had emotional reserves to spare. His placid image did not detract from his sociability and stability, or his reasonably optimistic spirit. After the death of his wife, he lived first at the previously mentioned Hotel Regina, then at the Savoy. He spent Sundays at the house of "Dottore Rizzini," the correspondent for *Il Corriere della Sera* who would soon become his friend and a nexus with one of the most powerful newspapers in Italy.

His son Guido continued to live with him, and in March 1925, Valeria gave him news that returned his lost spirits to him: the birth of his first granddaughter Fulvia (named in memory of her grandmother). Panizza came to know of this while he was conducting *La Wally* at a *matinée* performance; it made such an impact on him that in his memoirs he recalled the exact moment: between the third and fourth acts (never had that last act passed so quickly, he amusingly noted in his memoirs).

Valeria decided to pull his father away from his life in hotels and convince him to move into an apartment in the same building as the new Colombo family. Guido, for his part, continued to actively study engineering. After his graduation from the Milanese Polytechnic, he traveled to Germany and then to England for further studies.

Panizza did not stop either: he married again in early 1926 after less than two years of widowhood. In Milan, he received a visit from Amelia Valdata, a cousin whom he had known in Rome, when he conducted at the Costanzi. She possessed many similarities to him, and Panizza appreciated that. In addition to bearing the same last name as his mother, Amelia played the piano, painted (in order of preference, in addition to his passion for music, Héctor enjoyed the visual arts in second place; reading was further behind), she was domestic and discreet, and his sons and friends accepted her. All except Arturo Toscanini, who despite having countless lovers and even one or two extramarital siblings, was not only against divorce but also the idea that someone could marry for a second time as a widow.[125] Héctor Panizza and Amelia Valdata married in Rome on June 28, 1926. They spent a long honeymoon in Naples, on the island of Ischia and in Valsesia, Piamonte, and finally settled into Cappuccini street in Milan, a residence they kept their whole life. For Panizza, a wife mainly represented company, social reinsertion, and the solution of practical problems. His great career could continue, established on a marriage that would accompany it for the rest of his existence.

ART AND POLITICS

The relationship artists have with politics is always complex and frequently threatening to the free development of art. Its cultivators often find themselves used by the establishment in power. One had to travel a mined path to develop a career in an Italy that had been moving steadily toward fascism since the beginning of the 1920s. The majority of the men who exercised composition, music performance or teaching were in greater or lesser measure affected by Mussolini's regime and in general ended up giving way to it, more out of convenience than conviction.[126]

The case of Toscanini was exemplary. After an initial approach to fascism —he was sympathetic for it when its political platform seemed to approach socialism— he transformed into a persona who objects to all totalitarianism, even if it were only because he himself was a totalitarian in his profession and could not admit external interference. But to linger on this aspect of Arturo's personality would be unfair to his commitment sustained over time, which led him to suffer physical violence after his refusal to play the fascist hymn *Giovinezza* in Bologna. He rejected even trivial meddling no matter the cost. Some time afterward, while based in the United States, he collaborated widely with the brand-new orchestra of Palestine. He did so during a time in which Nazism had forced countless Jewish musicians of the first and second rank to emigrate if they did not wish to perish.

Panizza was witness to these dangers and his personality, diplomatic and discreet, played in his favor. He could not be ignorant of the obvious support for the regime of public figures like Pietro Mascagni or Alfredo Casella, the persecution of the work of Alberto Franchetti, or the distancing of Vittore Veneziani from his role as chorus master at the Teatro alla Scala due to his Jewish origins. To this were added the temptations submitted to by the greatest Italian operatic composer of the moment, Giacomo Puccini, whose death barely two years after the March on Rome no doubt saved him heartaches, manipulations, and probably an irreparable stain on a biography in which personal nostalgia predominates over public gesture.

The highest point of the relationship of Panizza with Italian fascism occurred in 1934, when he had a personal meeting with Mussolini. The project he offered him seems today —at a distance— absurd: he requested the support of the state for the creation of a school of liturgical music in Buenos Aires. What motivated Panizza was that Germans were about to embark on a similar undertaking faced with the decline of music in the churches.[127]

It was a critical moment of nationalism extending from Europe to Argentina. The International Eucharistic Congress in Buenos Aires was celebrated in 1934, perhaps the most important and massive demonstration of power by the Catholic church in all of Argentine history. A demonstration in which music —supported by the most advanced technologies of the time— was transformed into a fundamental tool of propagation of religious doctrine and social control.[128]

In the Argentine capital, with epicenters at the Spanish Monument and the Avenida de Mayo (appropriate to the parallel revindication of Hispanic-Christian culture), the celebration of the Congress was presided over by the Italian cardinal Eugenio Pacelli —future Pope Pio XII— and seemed like a demonstration of images of a fascist army, which included scenes of public conversion. This was the *Zeitgeist,* and in this context Panizza apparently saw himself induced to bring to Mussolini a proposal that, strictly speaking, hardly corresponded with the official Italian policy to reduce the power of the church on behalf of the absolute supremacy of the state.

The driving force behind this initiative was Monsignor Licinio Refice and probably Héctor's own wife, faithful to the model of the time by which every wife of a historically important man must seek her own importance by engaging in pious activities, thus making herself worthy of social recognition. Refice was, in addition to a bishop, a traveler more dedicated to female company than to liturgy, and a composer not lacking in inspiration. His most famous opera, *Cecilia*, was performed at the Teatro Colón that same year of 1934, with the composer conducting and Claudia Muzio in the leading role. As the bishop was in the spotlight, it was not strange that Panizza proposed before the fascist leader himself that Refice head this school in the nation of exiled Italians.

Mussolini promised state support that never materialized, despite the diplomatic monikers of "Excellency" and "Maestro" the personalities exchanged, in a dialogue Panizza referred to in his memoirs in a form no less succinct than naïve.

The truth is that one of the motives that most kept Panizza awake and led him to present himself before Mussolini was that of his nationality. As has been mentioned, the law of the Argentine republic —a country whose population is in its majority made up by immigrants— adopts the *ius soli*, so that those born on Argentine soil are Argentines. Generally speaking, European countries —stamped by marked emigration and a descending demographic curve from the end of the 19th century (exacerbated by the wars)— maintains the *ius sanguinis*, which means that the children of European natives are Europeans, whatever the land where they were born, so long as they have not explicitly renounced their citizenship of origin.

To this day there are not a few musicians, dancers, and artists in general who display their double nationality in their biographies, often at the expense of their Argentine origin. Panizza suffered a great deal due to this double status, since he considered himself as Argentine as he was Italian and never renounced his nationality of origin. Due to the many prejudices in the world of music —which identify nationality with artistic ability to take on specific repertoires— Panizza suffered blatant discrimination during his time, in particular in Argentina but also in Italy. Curiously this was not so in the German countries, who trusted him to interpret Wagner without giving way to a false chauvinism.

Panizza admitted to have posed to Mussolini the professional problem this created for him, something that today can seem exaggerated in the light of his extremely far-reaching career, but that can be understood in the context of the intense nationalisms that marked the first decades of the 20th century and determined the armed massacres that laid waste to Europe.

During the brief meeting, Mussolini hinted at a conciliatory position, alleging that Argentina as much as Italy had the right to its own laws, therefore revalidating him as an artist on both sides of the Atlantic.[129]

The topic would not have gone further had it not been that three years later, now with the fascist regime on the brink of war, Héctor was invited to the auditorium of the radio in Rome to conduct Umberto Giordano's *Siberia*. It is clear that the relevance of Panizza's professional career would prevent him sooner or later from looking the other way in political matters. He could flirt with the officials of the regime, perhaps without knowing what the model of corporative state populism they proposed would soon turn into, but he could not allow interferences from the very highest spheres to tarnish his artistic achievement. At least in this sense, he shared with Toscanini a 19th century morality, and was uncompromising toward mediocrity.

In 1931, political interference at La Scala marked the decline of that autonomous entity, which for ten years had reached an undisputed level of excellence and shaped an entire generation of new conductors, instrumentalists, singers, and even stage directors. The death of general director Angelo Scandianigave way to the brief *interregno* of Anita Colombo, who had been secretary to Scandiani since the Toscanini period. She knew the internal threads of the opera house well, but her friendship with the rebellious maestro and her condition as a woman —unusual for a position of such significance at that time —earned her a distancing from the post after that first season.[131]

Finally, without finding a strong candidate for the general direction of La Scala, the Senate left the house in the care of the composer Erardo Trentinaglia, a member of a high-ranking family who possessed a *villa* in the Stresa valley that had been visited by Stendhal and Wagner, as well as his contemporaries Toscanini, de Sabata, and Giordano. This new figure opened the doors to upcoming composers and welcomed a political element on the board of directors, in this case the maximum authority of the Ambrosian province: Jenner Mataloni.

These events marked the paradoxical end of a cycle for Panizza. Trentinaglia set up a board of directors with Umberto Giordano, Riccardo Pick-Mangiagalli, Tito Ricordi, and Héctor Panizza, "one of the few survivors of the Toscanini era."[132]

In Argentina the news was spread in a distorted manner that Panizza had simply been designated "director at La Scala in Milan" by the "Italian government," to occupy the "executive music desk" of Toscanini, and glossed with the recurring refrain —encouraged by Panizza himself— that the Argentine maestro had never rose to such an honor at the Teatro Colón in his native land.[133] The role of member of the board of directors of La Scala —strictly speaking, a council formed at a moment of great confusion and institutional instability for the opera house— was short-lived for Panizza: in April 1932, the minutes of a meeting by the board of directors gives an account of the difficulties of the season that had just finished. La Scala ended up abandoning its Toscaninian model of high productivity and artistic independence. Mataloni blamed the members of the board for "lack of compatibility" amongst themselves, and before Mussolini's silence he himself took the reins of the theater in place of Trentinaglia.[134]

The angry protests of those displaced— essentially de Giordano and Pick— no comments by Ettore appear— were not heard by the *duce*.

Thus, 1931-1932 was Panizza's final continuous season at La Scala, crowning ten intense years of labor. After a return to the Colón for the final season entrusted to a private company —that of his friend Emilio Ferone— he returned to the Milanese opera house to conduct on a famous occasion: the centenary of *L'elisir d'amore* with Tito Schipa, Isabel Marengo, Salvatore Baccaloni, and Piero Biasini.[135] It also fell to him to conduct challenging works such as Wolf- Ferrari's *La vita nova* (in its concert version) and *Elektra*; Richard Strauss attended the dress rehearsal and at the end embraced him in front of the orchestra. By then he had already become his friend and Panizza was one of his favorite conductors. He dined with him and his son at the Hotel Cavour, gave him the score of *Salomé*, and agreed to later coordinate a meeting in Austria, a country Panizza looked toward in search of new horizons. He would not return to conduct at La Scala until after the war.

THE WIDE (AND DIFFICULT) WORLD

Panizza's departure from La Scala opened new doors for him. On the one hand, the new positions he took on reveal the very high prestige he already enjoyed. It is astonishing that an Italo-Argentine triumphed in Europe as performer of the German repertoire during that period of heightened nationalism. On the other hand, if one takes into account that the entrance of Panizza into the German opera market was in 1931, one can see him as an advance of what some years later would be the fluid Rome-Berlin exchange of musicians, one of the cultural flanks of the axis.[136]

Not only was he invited to conduct works like *La bohème* and *Simon Boccanegra*, along with the *Tannhäuser,* at the Staatsoper in Vienna alternating with Felix Weingartner; but the next year he was also proposed to be music director at the opera house, which Panizza rejected due to the meagerness of the fee. In the Viennese environment he was evidently respected and admired: even the severe critic Julius Korngold — father of the composer Erich Wolfgang Korngold— passed positive judgment on his *Tannhaüser* and met him personally.

In 1933, the year of Adolf Hitler's election as chancellor, Héctor Panizza was contracted by the Städtische Oper (later Deutsche Oper) of Berlin, located in the neighborhood of Charlottenburg. The theater was also in the care of the impresario Ferone, who the year before had brought Panizza to the Colón. His debut in Charlottenburg was on October 8,

1933; it was attended by the brand-new minister Joseph Goebbels —
who had begun to control the Deutsche Oper, in rivalry with Hermann
Göring, in charge of the Staatsoper— and the ambassador of Italy, Vittorio
Cerruti, who invited Panizza to his box seat and warmly congratulated
him during the interval.[137]

Having come to this point, it seems impossible to think that the
friendship between Toscanini and Panizza could have survived. Toscanini
had refused to conduct in Bayreuth beginning in 1933; during the 1920s
he had shielded himself at La Scala with his own people (among whom
Panizza stood out) to keep himself independent from fascism, even when
the project of the autonomous entity was born shortly before the March
on Rome. But the growing political interference was represented by a
seemingly trivial whim of the regime —to force Toscanini to play the
fascist hymn *Giovinezza* before a performance. When the maestro refused,
he received a beating at the door of the Teatro Comunal of Bologna in
1931, followed by clumsy harassment or "public shaming" at his own
hotel, tracking by intelligence services of the regime, and finally the
temporary retirement of his passport.

Toscanini, in accordance with his personality, was no longer prepared
to forgive anybody who supported, or even merely condescended or
tolerated, Mussolini. And Panizza, while individually in solidarity with
his colleague, never took a public stance on the matter; he continued
to work and take advantage of opportunities so long as they did not
interfere with his artistic achievements. We know that Panizza learned of
the attack on Toscanini when he was with Umberto Giordano. Unusually,
in his old age he would remember timidly that both were "embittered
by an episode of such vulgarity." He evidently maintained this lack of a
clear declaration about the kind of events that involved political violence
throughout his life.[138]

It is clear that one cannot evaluate Panizza's political attitude without
considering his personality. What Gianandrea Gavazzeni expressed about
several of his contemporary colleagues applies to Panizza: "Do you want

to know in what way Casella was a fascist? Simply that he wasn't an active anti-fascist. Above all, he was fundamentally uninterested in politics. (...) He existed outside that dimension and apart from historical or political culture. Look at De Sabata, for instance... He was so possessed by his musical demon that nothing else existed. He lived in his circumscribed, stupendous world, born of his exceptional musical nature (...) he once conducted for some German cabinet minister or other who had come to La Scala with Mussolini because he was the most important conductor in Italy at that time. To refuse would not only have been an open act of hostility: it never would have entered his mind. It would have been futile to ask him who Mussolini, Göring, Göbbels really were or what they did. He was completely out of this world, in that sense. Even Toscanini, whose opposition to the regime was fully justified, was not basically a person with whom one could have a concrete political discussion. He had his moral standards, sometimes very just but other times not so just (...) These are things that in a certain sense constitute part of a person's greatness —these negative limitations, this blindness towards the continuously changing reality of individual lives, of a society, of a culture. That may be why they were so great —De Sabata with his characteristics, Toscanini with his: they didn't understand life or reality. We who are infinitely smaller can, on the other hand, keep an eye on reality, on what goes on around us."[139]

It is probable that after the Bolognese episodes of 1931 Toscanini's relationship with Panizza weakened until it disappeared, as was the case with the countless majority of his colleagues who did not adopt a clear position when faced with fascism. But the return of Héctor to the Berlinese Städtische (Deutsche) Oper in 1937 and 1938 was the drop that made the cup runneth over.

The proof of the evident rupture is found in a letter from 1939, the only one published to date in which Toscanini mentions Panizza. In the missive, which the maestro addresses to his lover Ada Mainardi, he says: "You were losing yourself in the company of people whom I despise as men of no faith or moral principles, like the Pizzettis, Molinaris, Panizzas, and the whole mob of bad and good artists who infest Italy and the world. Artists who don't deserve to be counted as men, but rather as slaves."[140]

It is true that Panizza did not count on carrying out a career only in Austria or Germany (in fact, he rejected offers to conduct there). His fame also meant that he was invited in 1934 to work in cities as diverse as Budapest and Naples.

He could not answer the first call: the death of his brother Mario, fourteen years younger than him, practically left him responsible for his niece and nephew: Gianni and Geny. Panizza placed the boy and girl in excellent Milanese schools. Mario had been a lawyer also dedicated to journalism, beleaguered by respiratory problems that were exacerbated by his participation in the Great War, causing his death at the early age of forty-two years old.

As far as the San Carlo of Naples, the theater to which Ferone called him again, the organization and artistic level were deficient, especially for one already accustomed to working in the best venues. Héctor accepted the challenge and made a decision to raise the level with works of great difficulty: Verdi's *Otello*, Zandonai's *Francesca da Rimini*, Cilea's *Adriana Lecouvreur*, and the premiere of Pietri's *Maristella*.

"I am extremely happy with Naples," Panizza declared on one occasion to the Argentine consul of the Parthenopean city. "Despite my harshness, the masses at the San Carlos loved me. The audience could not have been more enthusiastic and the critics have outdone themselves... in their praise. The glorious maestro Cilea has not missed the opportunity to show me his gratitude for the success we achieved with *Adriana Lecouvreur*."[141]

The season ended with a successful symphonic concert at the Conservatorio di San Pietro a Majella with works by Wagner, in which *Parsifal*'s *Good Friday Music* had to be performed twice. The last opera performance was offered in his honor; the grateful musicians gave him a gold feather with their names engraved, which Panizza would jealously keep until it was stolen from the desk at what would be his next post: the New York Metropolitan Opera.

DISEMBARKING AT THE MET

Today one can say that Panizza's career was crowned by the successful seasons he spent at the Metropolitan Opera House in New York. To this day he is one of the six Argentine conductors —along with Ferruccio Calusio, Carlos Félix Cillario, Miguel Ángel Veltri, Daniel Barenboim and, on a single occasion, Dante Anzolini— to have achieved this goal. The Met's current status as the pinnacle of achievement for singers and *maestri concertatori* shows that Héctor possessed a career comparable to that of any great international artist of the 21st century.[142]

If one likes, to these mere six *Rioplatense* names linked to the Met in New York we can add that of the famous Carlos Kleiber, who —like his father Erich— lived in Buenos Aires and for many years held an Argentine passport.[143]

Panizza himself understood things this way in his memoirs, when he recognized: "I felt that after my long career (Scala, Colón, Covent Garden, Deutsche Opernhaus, Paris and Vienna opera houses) it was necessary, as a culminating point, to reach the Metropolitan so it would be complete."[144]

The conductor's New York stage began in 1934, after his previous commitments at the Colón during the northern summer. This circuit — Europe, Argentina, the United States— would be of vital importance for the artist when the Second World War broke out.

The impresario Ferone was key to this whole stage in Panizza's career, insofar as his power extended through a good part of Europe, the United States, and the Teatro Colón, until the latter was taken over by the city council. It was in Buenos Aires that Panizza came to know of the confirmation of his contract through a radio announcement made by Giulio Gatti-Casazza, the Italian who was the Met's boss for almost twenty-five years and with whom Panizza would spend just a single complete season. The news was publicized in June 1934 with the explanation from the press that this was a "prominent Argentine conductor."[145]

The mention of Panizza's nationality seems curious, for all that it was correct, if one takes into account that in general Panizza was better known as an Italian and that he was arriving as the one responsible for the peninsular repertoire, replacing his colleague Tullio Serafin.[146] The life and career of the conductor were once again on an upward path. His son Guido, now graduated and working as an engineer, had married an Italian, Laura Pozzi. In November 1934, Ettore set off with his wife on a luxury ship, the *Rex*, toward New York where he was received by Gatti-Casazza himself, who was preparing for his final season as manager. He had chosen *Aïda* as the start of the season, since it had been the first opera with which he had begun his "reign" twenty-seven years earlier. The conductor Giuseppe Sturani accompanied him as music coordinator of the Met.

This *Aïda* was the first challenge for the Italian-Argentine at the New York opera house and the work brought him good luck, in this as in other moments of his career. Visits by the public as well as journalists were allowed at the dress rehearsal, and the results were highly praised. This marked the beginning of a long working relationship. Panizza's first performance at the Met took place on December 22, 1934, and was acclaimed.

In the critical piece by Arthur Walter Kramer titled, "Aïda opens Gatti's final season at Metropolitan," he writes: "Panizza, New Italian Opera Conductor, Enthusiastically Received in Debut by Capacity Audience [...]. Musically the opening took on especial interest because of the debut of Ettore Panizza, who takes the place of Tullio Serafin. Like his predecessor, Maestro Panizza has won for himself a splendid reputation in Italy, where he has conducted at La Scala and other leading theatres. From the opening measures of the formless, but strangely potent Prelude, he made me feel that he can master his forces. He has an eloquent beat, a well-defined rhythmic sense, knows how to build his climaxes with gradual and certain effect and manages his choral groups with great precision. From the orchestra he brought forth a warmth and sumptuousness of tone that spoke volumes for his ability to dominate a group of players to whom he was new. There were times when the fortissimi were too great for the solo voices to come through, but they will doubtless be tamed, when the conductor is more familiar with the acoustics of the house; and some tempi were decidedly on the quick side. But he showed definitely in this `Aida´ performance that he is a conductor of distinguished attainment. On his first entrance he was given a rousing reception and after the second act came before the curtain with the principals, who after several recalls insisted on his coming out alone to receive the plaudits of an audience which showered him with the heartiest kind of applause."[147]

Elisabeth Rethberg, Giovanni Martinelli, Maria Olszewska, Lawrence Tibbett, and Ezio Pinza headed the cast. Argentine journalism gave an account of this memorable debut and aptly pointed out that Panizza was "the first conductor from the southern hemisphere to take up the baton at the Metropolitan Opera House."[148]

Having just arrived, Panizza lost no time in expressing himself on institutional issues, such as rejecting the proposed merger of the then Symphony Society of New York (today New York Philharmonic) with the Met Orchestra, aligning himself with Bruno Walter and Toscanini himself.[149]

If those statements were a specific reaction to a particular event, others did not achieve larger results: his demonstrations of surprise at the resignation of Giulio Gatti-Casazza, which interrupted a budding professional relationship, did not prevent the distancing of his compatriot.[150] Panizza's work continued with titles as diverse as John Laurence Seymour's *In the Pasha's Garden*, in its world debut, and Mozart's *Don Giovanni*. Rose Bampton deemed Panizza a "marvelous conductor" of the latter work, after having learned valuable lessons under him that later permitted her to successfully sing that title under Bruno Walter's baton.[151]

Other singers at his command are legendary today, such as those named above as well as Rosa Ponselle (the very close companion, in addition, of a mutual friend: Tullio Serafin) with whom Panizza soon got along well.

After this distinguished first season, his contract was confirmed for the following season. His itinerary continued to be the same: he returned to Italy, then set off to Buenos Aires in April aboard the *Neptunia* —where he coincided with the Hungarian maestro Roberto (Robert) Kinsky, the fondly remembered leader of maestros at the Colón— and then returned to the theater on Broadway and 39th Street. By that time the management of Gatti-Casazza had come to its end, and he was succeeded by the Canadian Edward Johnson (who came to have a career as a tenor in Italy under the name of Edoardo Di Giovanni). Among the conductors who shared the podium with Panizza were the Italian Vincenzo Bellezza and the Austrian Artur Bodanzky.

During the 1935-1936 season Panizza engaged in a slightly different scheme: Colón, Italy, then New York, where Johnson was now fully settled in as general manager of the Metropolitan Opera.

The work beginning from that year was intense and included one of his favorite operas, *La traviata*, starring soprano Lucrezia Bori, with whom Panizza successfully opened the new season.[152]

It also included the careful preparation of a new title for the Met repertoire: *Le nozze di Figaro,* for which he could count on Bidu Sayão (they worked together for two months) as Susanna, and Ezio Pinza as Figaro; the staging was done by Herbert Graf. The success was such that the production was requested by several opera houses —in Baltimore, Boston, Cleveland, Dallas, and Richmond— with sights on the annual tours the Met carried out during its New York recess.

Panizza served as a permanent guest conductor during his fourth season of successes. He also became fundamental to the renovation of the artistic bodies of the Met. His voice was heard at the moment that singers, directors, even prompters were chosen (for this task he brought on Otello Ceroni). Panizza's predilection for Italian and Latin artists in general was evident: he promoted singers like Alessio De Paolis (whom he considered perfect in his vocal technique), Salvatore Baccaloni, Gina Cigna, Licia Albanese, Stella Roman. and Fausto Cleva as a choral trainer. In addition, he renewed the orchestra, choosing new members after auditions.

Panizza valued his social life, and his profession began to afford him some luxury. During the first three years Panizza lived with his wife Amelia in New York, they stayed in one of the most lavish hotels in the city: the Ansonia. This fact speaks to the higher quality of life New York offered to its cultural elite. The Ansonia was one of the largest hotels in the world at the time; it had restaurants on every floor, dolphins in a fountain installed in the lobby, a cupola-viewing tower, Turkish baths, and even an elevator for cattle on the terrace, which supplied fresh milk to guests daily.[153]

In the fourth consecutive year of work in the Big Apple, the Panizzas decided to rent a house in a building west of Central Park, a place previously chosen by the tenor Giovanni Zenatello and his partner Maria Gay, a Catalan mezzosoprano who had been previously married to the composer Joan Gay, and with whom Zenatello enjoyed marital life until the end of his days. Both were very famous and chose to live in New York at the same time as Héctor.

The house was in reality a "penthouse" on 50th Avenue west of Central Park, a furnished triplex with ten rooms and four bathrooms, much closer to the old building of the Met.[154]

The place soon transformed into an obligatory stop-off for the singers closest to the Panizza couple, such as De Paolis and Baccaloni, and for the representative of Ricordi in New York, Renato Tasselli. Social commitments in a prosperous community like this overflowed every which way, obliging the Panizzas on occasions to reject them. Panizza and his wife best remembered the fête offered by the tenor Giovanni

Martinelli upon his arrival at the premises of the Beethoven Association; the party also included Geraldine Farrar, Rosa and Carmela Ponselle, Elisabeth Rethberg, Lawrence Tibbett, and Giulio Gatti-Casazza.[155]

Also, it is worth remembering the reception hosted by the peninsular journalist Italo Carlo Falbo, who was a collaborator with Luigi Pirandello and a national deputy. Falbo was also working as a director of the Società "Dante Alighieri" in New York. On that occasion, Giovanni Martinelli sang "Canción de la bandera."[156]

Panizza would often formulate certain journalistic statements of interest for the purpose of evenings like this. He liked to have a well-crafted justification to help the public understand his artistic standpoint. For example, with respect to the opera *In the Pasha's Garden*, he wrote: "It is very dramatic and very modern, full of dissonances, but a very good work," and even brought himself to give his opinion on jazz, which he qualified as "true art, very varied and interesting."[157]

Panizza's opera repertoire widened considerably during these years, if one takes into account that in 1935 he only conducted at the Colón operas by Rameau, Dukas, and Rabaud, while at the Met he proposed to prepare a new opera every year, following the success of *Le nozze di Figaro*. So he did with *Boris Godunov*, offering Pinza the leading role. Panizza took on later works of significance, such as *Otello* and *Falstaff*. Also, given the friendship and preference that Richard Strauss felt for him, he studied *Salomé* so the Met could once again program this title, which had not been staged there since 1907.

Among the glorious days of this period is included one during which he conducted from noon until midnight: first *Don Giovanni*, with Tito Schipa, then *Aïda*, before a continuous and overflowing audience.[158]

Another discovery was the repeat of Charpentier's *Louise*, with soprano Grace Moore as the protagonist. From then *Louise* became the favorite work of the "Tennessee Nightingale," who often brought amulets and souvenirs to Panizza when she returned from a journey. Moore recorded a performance of *Louise* with Panizza in its entirety and carried the albums to Charpentier himself, who was then distant from this score written early in the century and worked as a music teacher amongst the low classes in the outskirts of Paris. Shortly before dying in an airplane accident near Copenhagen, Moore, also a film actress, starred in a film about the opera advised by the composer —given the changes to the libretto he had introduced— and directed by no less than Abel Gance.

Lucrezia Bori was another singer whom Héctor admired: he conducted her farewell performance in Puccini's *La rondine* and later helped the soprano set up the Metropolitan Opera Guild, an association of friends of the Met.

For their part, the premieres at the Met of *Amelia al ballo* and *The Island God* (the Italian original was called *Ilo e Zeus*) by the young Italian-American Giancarlo Menotti certainly did not go unnoticed.[159]

These New York interpretations, which mark the most contemporary limit of the repertoire Panizza took on in the United States, aroused the interest of the recently arrived Igor Stravinsky.[160]

ALTERNATIONS

By 1937, the Nazis had seized power, and yet Panizza conducted in Berlin for two years at the Städtische (Deutsche) Oper. The alternation between Buenos Aires, Rome, and the United States continued, with a few changes. On the eve of war, while he was returning to Italy by ship from New York, he managed to arrange while onboard his first and only appearance at the festival of the Maggio Musicale Fiorentino, which would be his late debut in the city of Florence. The work chosen was *Turandot*, produced at the Teatro Comunale in the form of a lively and massive show. Panizza conducted four times in the capital of Tuscany, the last Italian city that would have him as conductor before the Second World War, whose main consequence for Panizza was to bring him more often to his native country and continent.

Perhaps it was this new approach toward the land of his youth that aroused Héctor's desire to be a composer once more. It was in this moment he refloated an opera that had been delayed a long time, which he had been composing in bits and pieces between his commitments as a conductor and that he would finally present under the title *Bizancio* (in Italian, *Bisanzio*). Its source was the novel *Théodore et Byzance* by Auguste Bailly and the libretto was by a friend, Gustavo Macchi. This project had been among his drafts for so long that some of them had even come to be seen by his father. In his memoirs, Héctor came to attribute the choice of theme to Giovanni Grazioso, who might have selected it immediately after the success of *Medio Evo latino*.[161]

By 1937 the structure of the opera had been reduced from its four original acts to three, through the fusion of the second with part of the third. After the orchestration was finished toward the end of the following year, *Bizancio* was premiered at the Teatro Colón on July 25, 1939, with striking success. It was then performed on three occasions; a fourth occasion was planned for a gala during the visit of the Uruguayan president, but the performance was canceled by the Colón's management, with whom Panizza maintained a mainly formal relationship.

The composer realized that the times had changed. Casa Ricordi could not publish the score due to difficulties linked to the war. Héctor managed for it to be printed instead by the publishing house Edizioni Suvini & Zerboni in Milan, by decision of its general manager, the lawyer Paolo Giordani, with whom he had friends in common. Panizza, while on board the *Neptunia*, a ship that set sail from Buenos Aires and was detained at the port of Montevideo by order of the Italian government, conscientiously prepared the edition of *Bizancio*. Héctor had just had his nasal septum operated on in his city of origin and had foreseen less social life for that trip, but never did he imagine spending fifteen days stranded. The time helped to complete the work, which he continued on the high seas until, when he arrived in Gibraltar, the *Neptunia* was held up once again, this time by the English.

Héctor did not stop: he arrived in Italy and saw his family, but set sail again shortly afterward for New York. Later he returned in the summer to Italy to spend the vacation with his in-laws.

In August 1940, the conductor had to face a true odyssey to travel to the United States in order to honor his annual contract at the Met. It was impossible for him to return to North America on an Italian ship. Absolutely opposed to trips by air —which furthermore were still not very common before the end of the Second World War— the Panizzas had to undertake the following journey: first they traveled to Switzerland, where with the help of Carlos Bobbio, the Argentine consul in Geneva, they achieved a letter of safe-passage to France; from there they passed to Spain and finally to Lisbon, where they managed to take the *Excalibur*, a North American warship that had been junked in 1931 and thanks to which the duke and duchess of Windsor were evacuated that same year to take refuge in Bermuda.

Panizza, from his particular situation, described the *Excalibur* as a boat of mixed goods and passengers, full of "fugitives," very far from the comforts to which he and his wife were accustomed. However, the vessel would become famous in music history: onboard was also Béla Bartók, on the way toward his final destination in the United States. Bartók and Panizza had very different backgrounds but their journeys both included a sense of desperation to arrive safe and sound and flee from an aberrant war. The Hungarian composer, contrary to the support of his country for Nazism, saw the nature of the war much more clearly than the Italian-Argentine musician.

What Panizza did see clearly was the artistic stature of the person with whom chance had made him share the journey. From his already somewhat antiquated way of regarding music, he describes Bartók thus in his memoirs: "Speaking with this man of a sweet, gentle character, with nothing authoritarian in it, you would certainly not have believed yourself to be speaking with one of the most advanced subverters of the universal musical language."[162]

HINTS OF RETURN

In New York, Panizza met with the composer Floro Ugarte, who in his role of general manager of the Teatro Colón had traveled especially to contract Ferruccio Calusio and Arturo Toscanini; the latter had just passed through Buenos Aires after nearly three decades of absolute absence, on a tour with the NBC Symphony (its last season in Buenos Aires had been in 1912, at the Colón). Ugarte managed to negotiate the terms that would bring Toscanini to Argentina for the last time in 1941 to conduct the Colón's Resident Orchestra, a visit that would result in a distinguished recording of Beethoven's *Ninth Symphony*. Panizza believed that the presence of Ugarte in New York was also responsible for the malicious dissemination of a poor opinion of *Bizancio*, which led to the opera not being programmed in the Big Apple, as had been his desire.

To top it off, Panizza was not hired for that season of the Colón either, by a management that was evidently averse to him. It is also probable that the presence of Toscanini was considered incompatible with that of Panizza, which in the light of Arturo's critical opinion of Héctor beginning with his letter of 1939, would likely have been the case.

In the northern summer of 1941 the Panizzas traveled to Buenos Aires and lived at the Hotel Alvear (as they would later make a habit). There they shared the majestic milieu with Ferruccio Calusio, Adolf Busch, and Albert Wolff. On this somewhat melancholy visit, the director dedicated himself to looking for backing from the local critics, especially his friend Gastón Talamón, an influential critic for *La Prensa*, then the most important newspaper in Argentina and the only one that reached the Library of Congress in Washington, D.C. His arrangements resulted in a project of nationalization for the Teatro Colón and an album with signatures of support.

That year he also dedicated himself to listening to Argentine singers in Buenos Aires: in this way he discovered a student of Rosalina Crocco whom he heard at the Teatro Politeama. He was so dazzled that he made her study the role of Maria in *Simon Boccanegra*, an opera in which he featured her along with Leonard Warren, alternating with Zinka Milanov. This was Delia Rigal, to this day the Argentine singer with the longest career at the New York Metropolitan. It is said that Panizza exclaimed after listening to her in "Porgi, amor" from *Le nozze di Figaro* and "Ritorna vincitor" from *Aïda*, "Questa ragazza è una voce!" and to later promise her: "If I return next year, you can be sure you will sing at the Colón."[163]

Panizza thus began his task of looking out for new local talent, which would extend to other valuable acquisitions like Carlos Guichandut. A year later, Héctor would insist, with his characteristic instinct and the agreement of maestro Roberto Kinsky, on placing Rigal in *La traviata* at the Colón (1943), later at La Scala, and finally in 1944 giving her the leading role in the revival of *Bizancio*.

The beginning of the following season at the Met (1941-1942) coincided with the Japanese bombing of Pearl Harbor, which occurred in December. Panizza's plans were partly frustrated by two absurdities comprehensible only in the context of war: his *Madama Butterfly* met with objections due to its Japanese theme and his *Salomé* was refuted due to its German composer.

Another absurdity, but this time personal, was the death at fifty-five years old of maestro Gennaro Papi, one of the Met conductors who had worked with Toscanini during his brief tenure at the house on Broadway (and also during his season at the Teatro Colón in 1912) and who at that time collaborated with Panizza as one of the main conductors. On November 29, 1941, Papi was found dead in his apartment, hours before conducting a *Traviata* that would mark the debut of Jan Peerce at the New York venue. Panizza had to jump in the bullring and attempt, it is said in vain, that the performers not hear the news until the end of the performance, so as not to affect the artistic quality. Days later Panizza, the manager of the Metropolitan Opera, and colleagues like Erich Leinsdorf and Giorgio Polacco wove through a crowd of more than 1,500 mourners to attend the memorial service at Saint Patrick's Cathedral.[164]

RADIO ON SATURDAYS

A relationship between the Argentine conductor and the recording market flourished for a five-year honeymoon between 1926 and 1931. And again between 1934 and 1942 the Met allowed his famous radio broadacasts to become records (which were commercially released on more than twenty occasions featuring the Argentine conductor). These dates speak to the fact that Panizza continued to arrange for his work to be continuously recorded during his career, from practically the beginning of electrical recording technology.

Just as with the electrical recordings, Panizza was an absolute pioneer of radio broadcasts, which were consolidated during his tenure at the Met and today are exhibited with pride as the oldest uninterrupted radio program dedicated to classical music in the world. Although with some isolated precedents, the first broadcast from the Metropolitan Opera house was produced on Christmas in 1931 with *Hänsel und Gretel*, but the tradition of broadcasts on Saturday afternoons, which continues to this day, began in the 1933-1934 season, when authority was transferred from Giulio Gatti-Casazza to Edward Johnson, precisely at the same time Panizza arrived at the Metropolitan.

The famous matinée is remembered with nostalgia by a musician with a good memory: "'Ah, there go off the house lights, which means that our conductor, Ettore Panizza, is on his way into the pit'— such was the refrain heard many a Saturday afternoon from 1934 to 1942 as the Metropolitan Opera's beloved radio host Milton Cross, announced the rise of the curtain on the performance of the day. Lucky were the Met subscribers and the vast radio audience in the U.S., Canada, among other countries, who knew that the pack of Italian operas assigned to Panizza — or operas in Italian, we should say, because these included Mozart's *Nozze di Figaro* as well as Moussorgsky's *Boris Godunov* (neither Russian nor English being deemed logistically feasible for that one) — would be in excellent hands."[165]

From box seat 44 of the Grand Tier of the old Met, especially prepared for the purpose, Milton Cross served as a host for forty-three seasons at NBC, which employed him and took charge of the broadcasts.

Panizza was also at the podium during the first broadcast funded by Texaco, which contributed so the cycle would not be interrupted during the Great Depression of the 1930s. This was the performance on December 7, 1940, of *Le nozze di Figaro*, with a cast headed by Pinza, Albanese, Brownlee, Rethberg, Novotná, and Baccaloni.

Additionally, during the Panizza period the broadcasts began to be transmitted by short wave to Latin America through NBC's White Net, and records were made from the audio transcriptions of performances by the same radio station between 1935 and 1943. These were sent so that local radios could broadcast them pre-recorded, with a superior technical quality; presentations and commentaries were even inserted in Spanish and Portuguese, according to whether they were sent to Argentina, Uruguay, or Brazil, respectively. In other words, the art of Panizza could be appreciated in multiple forms in his native land before it could be heard in faraway and belligerent Italy.

ANTICIPATED END

In those days Panizza reaped the fruits of his previous visit to Buenos Aires: he was called by the Teatro Colón for the 1942 season, after two years of not conducting at the main venue of his country. (These were precisely the two years that Toscanini conducted at the Colón.)

The trip once again transformed into an adventure. He departed in a Chilean steamship, the *Aconcagua*, which sailed from New York until crossing the Panama Canal, to dock successively in Lima and Valparaíso. From there he left to board the trans-Andean railway that, after crossing the mountains of the *cordillera*, left him in the Argentine town of Río Blanco. From there he continued by automobile to Mendoza and again took a train, this time to Buenos Aires. The tortuous journey —full of

discomforts to which the Panizzas were not in the least accustomed—
culminated at the Retiro station of the General San Martín Line, where
the couple was received by the Colón's authorities. There Panizza would
be given the luxury, once again, to conduct great works with prestigious
international singers.

With the war at full boiling point and after the break of diplomatic
relations with the Axis on the part of Chile, Panizza —who had chosen the
route of the Pacific to travel to New York— decided to resign his contract
in the United States for the 1942-1943 season. He would not return to
conduct in that country, which he bid farewell to with a performance
of *Tosca* in Cleveland, on April 11, 1942.[166]

The news of this resignation was received with astonishment in
September of that same year, when Panizza announced it from Buenos
Aires, with the (doubtful) justification that he would receive an important
appointment at the Teatro Colón.[167]

At a distance, it seems clear that Panizza's resignation from his seat
of honor at the Metropolitan Opera was premature and prevented his
inclusion into the canon of great orchestra conductors, among whom
he no doubt formed part. One must keep in mind, in the first place, that
this was a resignation: no one at that moment of his career suggested
any disapproval of his work; what is more, he was at the peak of his
prestige and fame.

The parallel with Toscanini, who was only eight years older, is of
interest here. Panizza and Toscanini lived in the Big Apple at the same
time between 1937 and 1942, without their old friendship reviving at any
time. If Toscanini could count on an extraordinary *ad hoc* orchestra —
that of NBC— to spread his mastery as a director of the great symphonic
classics, Panizza was for his part the star of the most important opera
house in the United States, which would seem an opportunity for display
even greater than what a radio orchestra could guarantee. Toscanini's
concerts with the NBC orchestra, just like the operas Panizza conducted
at the Met, were disseminated over radio by the same broadcaster, and

registered in both an official way by their respective organizations and in a personal way by music lovers.

The fact is that the recordings that made Toscanini famous belong to the final decade of his active life, when he was around eighty years of age. The previous recordings, even if they are valuable, are scarce, in particular those of opera, and number far fewer than Panizza's opera recordings of Panizza if his broadcasts are taken into account.

Did Panizza commit a strategic mistake for his career by leaving the United States in 1942? The answer can only be "yes." This point is when the fame of Toscanini acquires a disproportionate size compared to that of the Argentine. To abandon an opera house that had given Panizza everything to which he aspired —excellent pay, prestigious social life, the possibility to conduct a not exclusively Italian repertoire, wide radio dissemination, tours through the whole country— did not seem reasonable. It is very likely that the specter of war, in which the United States had just entered, intimidated the maestro, but this was the moment to take sides and Panizza was on the wrong one.

To return to a country like Argentina, then governed by an almost fascist president like Ramón Castillo (whom the government of the United States accused of favoring the Germans), followed by the military coup of 1943 of the same tendency, was very likely not read positively by the great country of the north. Furthermore, Panizza added Italian citizenship to his Argentine one, had been on good terms with Mussolini, had worked in Austria and Germany toward the end of the '30s, and neglected to offer any public criticism of the Axis. At most, he was against war in the abstract and the degree to which it implicated the destruction of the cultural and social medium in which he worked, but nothing more.

In comparison, Toscanini was active at organizing concerts to raise funds for war, competed successfully with Stokowski for the premiere of Shostakovich's *"Leningrad" Symphony*, exhibited a forceful opposition to the fascism of his native Italy —from which he was exiled— and brandished a flamboyant anti-Nazi discourse, leaving him beyond competition.

At the margin of the significant differences of personality —it is clear that Panizza had neither the artistic charisma nor the arbitrary temper of Toscanini— there is no doubt that if he had adopted another attitude when faced with the Second World War, and remained in the United States until he was eighty years old, the careers of Panizza and Toscanini would have converged on a similar point. While Toscanini would have been established as the great symphonic director he was during his final years, Panizza would have been remembered as the undisputed maestro of the Italian opera.

Whether due to fear of war, lack of public conviction, sympathy, or tolerance toward anti-liberal nationalist thought, or mere fatigue, Panizza's anticipated retirement from the world stage and his almost exclusive reclusion in Argentina played against him at the moment of consolidating his posthumous fame.

CHAPTER 6

ONCE AGAIN IN ARGENTINA

In the meantime, worry overwhelmed the Panizza marriage. The couple's children and house stayed behind in an Italy that felt increasingly remote. They would not be able to attend those concerns on this particular transatlantic journey from Argentina. In the meantime the integrity of their musical library in Milan kept them awake —a library that included *Aurora*'s original score, among other works. A friend, Italian soprano Elvira Colonnese, learned of their anxiety and brought them a copy of the score she had kept from previous performances in Argentina.

This fact seemed both providential and framed within the political context implied by the Argentine coup d'état of June 1943— an event promoted by a group of nationalist officers of strong Germanophile affiliation. *Aurora* had always been sung in Italian. The new political tendencies encouraged a translation into Spanish and entrusted the task to Josué Quesada, a son of Héctor Quesada —the creator of the original plot—. Ángel (Angelo) Petitta, an Italian living in Argentina, would be at his side.

The ideology of Quesada Jr. is a proof of the nationalist "fumes" that surrounded this cultural operation: he was secretary of the Argentine

Patriotic League, founded by the xenophobe Manuel Carlés, and an open supporter of the Franco regime.[168]

This was the version that won out in Spanish and ended up being the obligatory song in Argentine schools, despite it being riddled with imperfections and errors, even in the "Canción de la bandera" itself.[169]

With his conducting activity momentarily reduced, Panizza returned to his old love for composition and again picked up one of his most accomplished works: *Theme and Variations.* With the aim of facilitating the knowledge of this score, Panizza created, as an analogy to Brahms' *Variations on a Theme by Haydn,* a version for two pianos that would find a valid translation in the hands of Roberto Locatelli, who performed it with Luis La Via and later with Carmen Scalcione.

The southern summer of 1942-1943 found the Panizzas in Mar del Plata, the most important tourist seaside city in Argentina, which at that time was concluding an important renovation on the coast, with the replacement of its beautiful *art nouveau* boardwalk by a building complex in a more rationalist style, an initiative led by architect Alejandro Bustillo.

In this context, Panizza lodged at the Hotel Sasso and threw himself into fully revising *Aurora.* He adjusted the Spanish translation to the existing music and retouched the orchestration, in which he found traces of a juvenile artist who now felt far away.

The 1943 season at the Colón permitted him to discover a great artist: Rudolf Firkusny —a favorite of the *porteño* public in those years—, whom he directed in Beethoven's *"Emperor" Concerto.* He was also able to offer the entire symphonic version of *Theme and Variations,* a work that had been performed with cuts during its European concerts and at Chicago. The score generated interest, to such a point that Fritz Busch included it in his symphonic programs in Montevideo. From then on it would be his most-played orchestral work, and the one with which he would later take his leave as a director.

The war continued and Amelia received news of the death of a nephew of hers on the Russian front. At the end of 1943, with the season at the Colón ended, the couple went on board the *Cabo de Buena Esperanza* toward Lisbon. The Panizza family got to know the Portuguese capital, visited the Teatro Nacional in São Carlos —where Héctor received a promise of work— and then moved to Madrid to spend four months preparing the necessary documentation for travel to Switzerland. During the trip, Panizza read *La santa virreina* by the ultra-conservative nationalist José María Pemán; in Cádiz he met the Spanish writer and became enthusiastic about adapting the subject for a future opera he would never write. This was added to the other discarded projects Panizza had spoken about at some time, such as the previously mentioned opera about Napoleon.

The Spanish visit continued in Barcelona, where Panizza conducted three operas and a symphonic concert at the Liceo, and struck up a friendship with a maestro who would become known for his inspired compositions: Fernando Obradors.

At that time, the Panizzas received with relief the news that their family members as well as the house in Milan were safe. The English exercised a strict control over the entrance to the Mediterranean via Gibraltar as well as over ships in general. Panizza brought from Argentina a special passport granted to him by the *de facto* government of General Pedro Pablo Ramírez. The political naïveté of Héctor led him to make immediate contact with the provisional authorities— ultimately, he felt as Italian as he did Argentine and at that moment both governments seemed to be headed in the same direction. This was not only to receive diplomatic protection on his travels, but also to make artistic plans. He had given a project for the nationalization of the Teatro Colón to Ramírez, which will be analyzed further on.

Already in Europe, Héctor was proposed to be general manager of the Colón, an invitation which would never be made concrete. It would be his friend Ferruccio Calusio who took the artistic reins of the *porteño* opera house and scheduled the revival of *Bizancio*.

In the meantime, Héctor finished *Aurora's* new orchestral arrangement and faced his obligation to return to Argentina. Terror that the manuscript would be confiscated took hold of the Panizzas. Amelia decided to divide up the infolio into several parts and distribute it amongst the suitcases; their fear that the English would suspect that there was a coded message amongst the eighth notes was thus dissipated. The return on the *Cabo de Hornos* from Bilbao was as successful as it was uncharacteristically slow: their arrival in the Río de la Plata was delayed fifty-one days. Once there, a new season that included his *Bizancio* with a setting by Otto Erhardt awaited the composer at the Teatro Colón.

The Panizzas, now experienced travelers, once again faced a trip to Chile on the trans-Andean train, with all its complicated transfers. Héctor conducted works such as *Otello, La traviata*, and *La bohème* at the Teatro Municipal in Santiago.

NEW MILIEUS

Upon his return from Chile, Carlos Aparicio, the director of the Asociación del Profesorado Orquestal (A.P.O.), one of the most important musical institutions in the spread of the symphonic repertoire in Argentina, invited Panizza to conduct at the brand-new casino in Mar del Plata. The national government claimed the new boardwalk signed by architect Bustillo, the Provincial Hotel and Casino (the largest in the world at that moment), and the Brutalist buildings of the Italian-Argentine Francisco (Francesco) Salamone as points of pride.

The casino was inaugurated in 1938, and included a space originally dedicated to *boite* or dancing, destined for the elegant high society that at that time —and until the imminent advent of Peronism— had made Mar del Plata an exclusive Biarritz of the Atlantic.

In 1944, the Direction of Propaganda and Culture decided to convert the dancehall into a theater hall with a capacity for 1,500 people, named the Auditorium, today the Ástor Piazzolla Hall of the Teatro Auditorium.

On January 20, 1945, during the middle of the summer vacation, Héctor Panizza inaugurated the hall with the the A.P.O orchestra in a symphonic program that included works by Mozart, Beethoven, Aguirre, Ansermet, Wagner, and Rossini. He was personally accompanied by Ferruccio Calusio and Albert Wolff, among others, who later formed part of the cycle of concerts, along with piano soloists who are still very much remembered today. The success earned Panizza an invitation from the mayor of the city to return the following summer, for which he proposed programs of a high caliber, including works such as Richard Strauss' *Death and Transfiguration*.

A significant role fell to Panizza during this inauguration: he was given the power to both suggest acoustic improvements and demand that in place of a restaurant the surroundings of the auditorium be dedicated to the exhibition of paintings and sculptures. This created a forceful contrast between the spiritual and the casino's worldly life; they were two clashing aesthetics. Both initiatives survive to this day with small differences.

The year of 1945 was significant for both Héctor's personal and professional life. This was the year he publicly celebrated his "golden anniversary" with music, considering that initial moment of approval as a conductor Antonio Bazzini gave him at the conservatory in Milan.

For the world, 1945 was the year the Allies defeated the Axis, and the Second World War came to a close. The Argentine military government had broken its diplomatic relations at a very late date, and thereby revealed its true affiliation. For Argentina in particular it was the year of the emergence of Peronism, with which Panizza did not have particular issues. In fact, Peronism gave continuity to many ideas from the previous regime, including the not unimportant fact that Juan Domingo Perón had come to be vice president of the *de facto* government, and that this preceded his terms as constitutional president. Another significant fact is that Panizza's career at the Colón ended in 1955, exactly one month before the so-called Revolución Libertadora toppled Peronism from power, although one cannot attribute this conclusion to political reasons, but to his own physical decline and decision to professionally retire at eighty years old.

Panizza premiered his Spanish version of *Aurora* in 1945 at a complicated political moment, with Perón in full emergence and the people in the street. In fact, the de facto military authorities attended the performance on July 9, 1945: the president Edelmiro Farrell and the vice president Juan Perón.

The season did not end well: the general director of the Colón, Julio V. Ochoa, rudely ordered Panizza to withdraw his belongings from his dressing room with the term of his contract hardly ended, which generated a condemnation from the Asociación del Profesorado Orquestal with hints of scandal, as this was considered a lack of respect for a consecrated maestro.[170]

The account of a clarinettist from the Resident Orchestra, Juan Daniel Skoczdopole, is eloquent in describing the indignation aroused by the fact: "Maestro Héctor Panizza had conducted six titles in the season together with the ballet company at *Armide, La traviata,* and *Khovanchina,* precisely as his last performance at the end of August, ending his contract. He then requested that for a couple of days he leave his personal items in the dressing room, so that he could withdraw them when he was setting off on his trip to Europe. Ochoa, a rude man supported in his position by the Catholic Church, did not permit this and, since maestro Panizza insisted, sent for the police to be called to remove him by force— an unusual fact. The next day the commentary appeared in the newspapers, defending Panizza of course, as an Argentine musician who had premiered his opera *Aurora* during the inaugural season of the Colón in 1908!"[171]

It was also a complicated personal moment for the conductor-composer. Amelia was operated on for appendicitis two days after the opera premiere, which reawoke in Panizza the phantom of the unforeseen death of his first wife. He was on the point of renouncing the podium but, supported by friends and his own vocation, could endure the long convalescence of his wife, which extended over three months.

By the following summer the Panizza couple had already recovered: before traveling to Mar del Plata for the second edition of the concerts at the casino, they visited Colonia Suiza, in Uruguay, where to "take the edge off his vice" the maestro prepared Uruguayan tenor José Soler for *Il Trovatore*. It was one more display of his impartial generosity in the recognition and promotion of the artistic talents who crossed his path.[172]

The relief that came with the end of war allowed Panizza to travel in 1946 to his beloved Italy. He set off in a Swedish steamship with Calusio, Soler, and a new young man in his care: the Uruguayan Jorge Algorta, who made a good career as a bass singer at La Scala. In Geneva his children and grandchildren, already grown up, were waiting for him. It was a moment longed for by the maestro who had already reached seventy years, though his level of activity concealed it.

In Milan he met with Tullio Serafin, his classmate from the conservatory, who at the head of La Scala invited him to return to conduct in that beloved house. In 1947 he was responsible for *Lucia di Lammermoor* and *Der Rosenkavalier*. The experience was emotional, for he had not occupied the Ambrosian podium since 1931. The meeting with an old friend also moved him: on the *scaligero* board of directors were Umberto Giordano and Riccardo Pick-Mangiagalli, and conducting the chorus, Vittore Veneziani was there once again, all survivors of fascism. It was the rebirth of an old temple.

CINEMATOGRAPHIC EXPERIENCE

A peculiar experience in Panizza's career also occurred in 1947. He moved from Milan to Rome to take charge of the soundtrack of the film *La signora delle camelie* (The Lady of the Camellias), directed by Carmine Gallone. Gallone is currently considered one of the most important directors of Italian cinema in the first half of the 20th century, with a half century of uninterrupted work—120 films, among them many linked with Italian opera. At that time he was before anything else a popular director, whose fame would be based on the saga of *Don Camillo.*

Panizza was invited by the Teatro dell'Opera in Rome to direct an ensemble called, somewhat awkwardly, "Grande Opera Roma," which was nothing but the orchestra and chorus of the opera house of the Italian capital. In the film, the opera was summarized and novelized: in the prologue appeared Alexandre Dumas the son and Verdi; the main characters, played by actors, were dubbed by singers like Onelia Fineschi, Francesco Albanese, and Tito Gobbi. An important and beautiful actress, who was also a singer, sang the role of Violetta: Nelly Corradi. The film, in 35 millimeters, was distributed beginning the following year in the United States, Germany, the United Kingdom and France, with different editions.[173]

Unlike the *locandina* of the Italian debut, in which Panizza is not mentioned, Columbia put the name of Héctor Panizza on the poster (curiously it did not use "Ettore," by which he was known in the United States, but the original name in Spanish).

The conductor did not assign a special importance to this new facet of his activity: he continued to be a man of the 19th century in the very heart of the 20th, with his out-of-date *pince-nez*, his implacable aversion to airplanes and his impossibility of appreciating how by then the cinema had already assumed the central role that until then opera had held as the art of entertainment and opportunity for socialization par excellence.

ARGENTINE STRETCH

During the years following the war, Panizza began to confront a growing deafness and his own old age. He was trapped by constant maritime crossings and artistic triangulations between Europe, the United States, and Argentina. Panizza experienced the same kind of inner vertigo artists feel today when they travel by air and then perform in a new continent every other day.

Some symptoms linked to his peculiarities intensified in this stage of his life. The main one was the complaint of his own insufficient recognition as a composer in his native country. He repeatedly deplored the inappropriate frequency with which his operas were revived. Of course he failed to consider that he had only composed four, and one of them was more the work of a student than a mature artist. The other mitigating factor was the rising tide of nationalism in Argentina. In Buenos Aires, the impossible was done to ensure Panizza could not conduct the Russian, French, and above all German opera repertoire, which he frequented in the rest of the world,, though some exceptions were allowed.

Héctor continued with his philosophy of discovering, forming and launching youths with a talent for singing, and in 1948 traveled to Montevideo to conduct at the S.O.D.R.E. (Official Service of Diffusion, Radiotelevision and Performances), offering the Teatro Solís a *Trovatore* which was described as exceptional.[174]

After that happy experience he returned to Italy in the *Toscanelli* and made an express decision to extend his periods of rest. Serafin became in these years one of his closest friends; he traveled with him back to Argentina in 1949, on the *Andrea C.* His interest in the new repertoires did not let up— that year for the first time he conducted an opera he had never studied: Gluck's *Iphigénie en Áulide*.

Another important institutional task was entrusted to Panizza that same year. In November 1948 the State Symphony Orchestra (today the National Symphony Orchestra) was created in Argentina. A jury was set up made up of personalities like Ferruccio Calusio and José María Castro, which selected the ninety-two musicians who would make up the new ensemble. In September 1949 a new jury was formed to designate the principal director of the body, to which Héctor Panizza was invited, along with other figures like the composers Athos Palma and Gilardo

Gilardi. The selection went to Roberto Kinsky, the great maestro of the Teatro Colón, with whom Héctor had a relationship of great esteem.[175]

In the second concert of the ensemble, which took place in the recently inaugurated space of the Assembly Hall at the School of Law of the University of Buenos Aires under Kinsky's baton, Panizza managed to include his *Nocturno* in its first Argentine performance.

The passage of time was evident in 1950, when two anniversaries drew attention to it: half a century had passed since the world premiere of *Medio Evo latino* and Panizza himself had completed seventy-five years of age. That year he did not work at the Colón, in a season whose greatest guest conductor was Karl Böhm with his Wagnerian *Ring* and in which several younger colleagues, such as Antonino Votto and Calusio himself, occupied the podium Panizza considered was destined by right to him alone.

Compensation came from the State Symphony Orchestra. Panizza was responsible for a fall cycle on Mondays at the Teatro Metropolitan, where he programmed two of his own works: *Theme and Variations* and *The King and the Forest*. For this latter, given the character of the symphonic-vocal score, he counted on the presence of two soloists of increasing local fame, the Russian-Argentine soprano Olga Chelavine and the Italian-Argentine baritone Ángel (Angelo) Mattiello, and the choir of the School of Law of the University of Buenos Aires prepared by Manuel Gómez Carrillo.

The concerts repeated on Sunday mornings with free entrance to the Assembly Hall of the School of Law. This venue was an emblematic environment, and it would later be home to the State Radio Symphony: an orchestra that did much for the spread of music in Argentina.[176]

These concerts enjoyed an enormous success and Héctor could include works of consequence, such as those of Richard Strauss, along with Argentine and Italian scores that are today unjustly left to one side: Alberto Williams' *Second Symphony*, Pizzetti's *Canti della stagione alta*, and baroque arrangements by his friend Pick-Mangiagalli. Among the events most remembered from Panizza's cycle at the *porteño* Metropolitan is the first national performance of Carlos Guastavino's *Tres romances argentinos* in May 1950, which had been premiered in London the previous year.[177]

It is interesting to note that Guastavino' s original arrangement was for two pianos, and that the manuscript of the orchestral score by the author contains handwritten indications by Panizza, who —faithful to the Toscaninian line— intervened in the scores when the orchestral effect conceived by the composer, was not, in his judgment, sufficiently well expressed.[178]

During this exhausting year, Héctor reserved energy to dictate to his wife his memoirs in a quite Italianized Spanish, with a large number of slips and imprecisions of fact. Casa Ricordi Americana in Buenos Aires published the memoirs in 1952 under the title *Medio siglo de vida musical.*

Panizza, in his peculiar Spanish, was subject to opinionated statements and a few goads, admittedly affectionate, about his Spanish. Far from being "cocoliche" —the Rioplatense mix of Italian and Spanish dialects spoken by the poorest immigrants, in general illiterate— Panizza's Spanish was acceptable, and very Argentine, but with amusing confusions. One of them manifested when after a performance he offered the musicians his "cumplimientos" instead of "felicitaciones" (congratulations), inappropriately translating the Italian expression "complimenti."[179] Beyond these anecdotes, the maestro conducted during the following seasons of the Colón, always alternating on the podium with other maestros for the rehearsals and performances entrusted to him, and thus remaining in Buenos Aires, surrounded by respect and esteem.

In 1955 Panizza conducted for the last time at the Teatro Colón. Tributes took place to honor his eighty years of age. The Ricordi hall in Buenos Aires prepared a homage for him on August 8, where the critic Ernesto de la Guardia gave a speech; Delia Rigal, accompanied on the piano by Alberto Grigera, sang several of her *Romanzas* with texts by Verlaine;

Roberto Locatelli and Luis la Via performed the version for two pianos of *Theme and Variations*. The hall was packed and applause rang out for a long time.[180]

In a photograph— likely taken on August 12, the day of his eightieth birthday, which took place in the Argentine capital— one can see him at an advanced age, surrounded by his most prominent collaborators from the Teatro Colón: the Argentine conductor Juan Emilio Martini, the Hungarian maestro Roberto Kinsky, the Italian chorus master Tulio (Tullio) Boni and the German stage director of his last *Aurora*, Otto Erhardt.

Panizza bid farewell to the Argentine public that same week with *Aurora*, whose final performance took place at the Teatro Colón the evening of August 14, 1955. In the morning of that same day a concert took place by the Buenos Aires Symphony Orchestra (today the Buenos Aires Philharmonic). He shared it with the Belgian director, instrumentalist and composer Julio (Jules) Perceval, who assumed the conducting role for the works in which he appeared as soloist; the final stretch fell to Panizza, who occupied the podium for *Theme and Variations*.[181]

His deafness was by then already evident, as was the fact that his career was reaching its end. After this long Rioplatense stay, Héctor decided to spend his final days with his wife in Milan, close to his children and grandchildren, who never left Italy. There is no proof that he conducted again after this.

LETTERS OF OLD AGE

The maestro devoted his final years to a tranquil life, in which he took pleasure in existence, but was always attentive to artistic events, especially in Argentina, where he still had several friends— the product of his final years of intense work.

His interest in the institutional aspects of the Teatro Colón and his tight relationship with its artistic bodies drove him to send a letter of support in 1957 to the members of the Resident Orchestra. In the first semester of that year one of the most talked-about conflicts in the entire history of the Colón took place, which determined the dismissal of the entire Resident and Philharmonic orchestras, in addition to fifteen dancers, for their opposition to a "test of efficiency," which implied the risk of dismissal.

In his missive, Panizza stated that despite his lack of competence to intervene in an "artistic-disciplinary matter," the conflict "cannot be resolved with the dissolution of a resident body like the orchestra of our great opera house [...]. To have left unemployed a resident body like the Orchestra of the Colón is a resolution without precedents and extremely serious. One cannot blame the orchestra for the poor artistic result of the last few seasons, especially the last. There are other reasons for this artistic deterioration..." He then went on to contribute some advice about how the matter should be solved through negotiations with the unions, always defending the integrity of the musicians of the ensemble, "who have brought me so many satisfactions during my long time amongst them."[182]

The friendship that united him in those years to the Argentine double bassist and composer Faustino Del Hoyo is registered by the active correspondence between them, which allows one access to some characteristics of Panizza's stretch of life, lived with lucidity practically until his final days.[183]

Panizza's interest in the 1957 conflict at the Colón continues in a letter to Del Hoyo, which contains caustic statements about his colleagues Calusio and Juan José Castro, and which is worth reproducing almost fully, for along the way its original allows one to form an idea of how the very Italian Panizza expressed himself (the originals are in Spanish).

Milan, May 6, 1957.

No doubt the Second World War left on human beings in general, even among peoples who did not feel it closely, a marked remnant of the "invertibility" [sic] of values, so that a contempt for the feelings of sincerity, honesty, ordinary tolerance has emerged; and as a result arts, politics, education, morality and many other things have suffered a great disturbance; values have been inverted and many years must pass before the return to a beginning, a logical and sane thinking... Will it return to this beginning? It must be hoped so, and soon, for the good of all humanity. A person well informed about what happened amongst the Colón's management and the members of the Resident Orchestra came to visit me. It would seem, from what he says, that the group of the seven instrumentalists was asked for an examination, as the Direction doubted their artistic capacities... the fact is that the examining was an "escuse" [sic] to get rid of those seven musicians for "political" reasons! If this were the case, what happened would be even more serious and cannot be named. To verify this version would require two cellists from the group mentioned, who are capable and very worthy of occupying their position.

And so? What do you think of all this? Do you know anything about what I have just referred to? Are these stories of fantasy or reality? I would like to know the truth.

I have also been told that Mr. D'Urbano has presented his resignation, but that it was not accepted. Was it a resignation in any case or a simple "stopping" [sic] to gain even more strength than he already has? Or is he being held responsible for what happened to fix this situation? Everything is chaotic and incomprehensible...!

I cannot even think about the Teatro Colón, at other times so full of life and movement... now closed, sad, mute. And Castro and Calusio, who share quite a bit of guilt in all this, along with their colleagues on the commission who chose the current General Manager, what do they say? Castro carries on with his concerts, and who knows if he isn't satisfied with what has happened, as he can have his concerts in the magnificent hall of the Colón... and now he conducts almost everything... but Calusio?

Meanwhile, from news that the papers bring, it seems the strikes continue without stop... Now Buenos Aires in the dark...! It seems a lie that the people have not calmed down after so many disruptions and struggles without any result for their wellbeing!

I remain infinitely grateful to you and your colleagues for the affectionate memories. For me [it is] of great satisfaction to know that my words have been understood and appreciated! What a pity that nothing has resulted in favor of the Teatro, for the orchestras or for the public that for so many years has honored us with its presence and its approval, and now finds itself deprived of a little poetry, at a moment so dark and full of uncertainties. May God help us!

To you in particular an affectionate hug and estensible [*sic*] greeting to all your colleagues.

—Héctor Panizza

The Colón reopened that following year, and perhaps as a warm acknowledgement of support, the Pessina Quartet —made up of Osvaldo Pessina on violin, Cayetano Molo on viola, José Bragato on cello, and the legendary concertmaster Carlos Pessina— recorded its *Quartet in C minor* in four movements for the Odeón label. To this day it is a recording that has never been reissued.

For his part, Panizza continued to write regularly to Faustino Del Hoyo and his son, Dr. Ricardo Del Hoyo. Of great interest is the letter signed by the conductor in August 1964: in it he speaks of his completely voluntary decision to retire at eighty years old and explicitly recognizes his deafness; he also expresses his opinions about Héctor Berlioz and Alberto Ginastera —curiously in a negative way with respect to the first and a positive way with respect to the second— on the occasion of the respective premieres at the Colón of *Les Troyens* and *Don Rodrigo*.

He first answers Dr. Ricardo del Hoyo (who could not stop to visit him and his wife in Italy), then his father Faustino, whose letter he received in Rome.:

Milan, June 24, 1964.

We have been in this city, enchanting as ever, for a few days as we have the habit of doing every year, for my wife was born in Rome and likes to give a little greeting to her friends from youth every year.

Mo. Ricci came to visit me in Rome. He spent several years at the Colón. We spoke of everything a little, including friends in common... and he told me that Serafin has also completely left orchestral conducting after an "erculean effort" [sic] to get to the end of *Die Meistersinger*.

In life, especially in ours, it is supremely important "to know how to retire in time." I left the baton at eighty... and I've ended, I believe, quite well, leaving my collaborators with a good memory.

It is hard —believe me Del Hoyo— to leave an active life, and from one day to another, find oneself without knowing how to occupy the time...! I, but [sic], and for this I must give thanks to God, have not lost my spirits and have continued to interest myself in everything that concerns music (though not modern) [sic], theater, concerts, etc... my state of "deafness" annoys me a bit... but I have also come to defeat this with a good acoustic device, and so I can deceive time and easily defeat the "inoperosive life" [sic] with continuous distraction...!

I live a great deal with the "memory" of my past life among you, among all my friends who through their letters I "feel" love me with sincere affection!

A sympathetic note came to me from Sr. Maradini (you must remember him, he belonged to the management of the Teatro Colón in my time) which informs me that the Local Council has unanimously decided to celebrate me on Columbus Day (October 12) with a performance of *Aurora* at the Colón.

Skoczdopole announced to me, and you confirm, the formation of a committee to celebrate me!

Prof. Quaratino, director of the M. de Falla Municipal Conservatory, is thinking of dedicating one of the halls of this conservatory to my name! What more can I ask for?

It honors me and honors my past artistic labor in a form so great, so affectionate that I never could have imagined it... At the start I went through fierce struggles that gave me many heartaches... but "justice" (as my friend Maradini says) sometimes "delays" in arriving... and at last it arrives.

I heard *Les Troyens*, which here was called "La presa di Troia," at the Teatro Lírico in Milan many years ago (in 1899) and frankly it is not possible for me to recall the impression I received at that time...

I am no great admirer of Berlioz' s music... I have the impression that it is somewhat "cold"... it does not throb like Wagner' s music. I have not found in Berlioz that "musicality" one feels in Beethoven... maybe I am wrong... this might be an impression of youth... Berlioz has been a great "transformer" of the instrumental palette... it is true!

Mo. Sebastian... by your letter I perfectly understand the reasons for the contrary opinions about his value; not having a clear baton that squeeses [*sic*] all an artist "feels" is a grave defect that at the moment makes me forget the "qualities" in his favor.

I believe that while I write these lines, in artistic Buenos Aires discussions are taking place about Ginastera's new opera *Don Rodrigo*, which must have been premiered at the Colón... I have great faith in this artist for his talent and his "seriousness"! I hope his success has corresponded to his artistic efforts.

Many thanks to Prof. Puglisi, whom I remember perfectly, for his greeting, which I very friendly return.

In the photo of the Colón's orchestra that I have, I cannot find Prof. Porro... at any rate please be so kind as to greet him cordially in my name, along with Locatelli, La Via, Pessina, Martucci (whose letter I will answer shortly) and all those who remember Maestro Panizza...

Well, my dear and esteemed friend, I leave you — begging you to greet in my name your lovely son Dr. Ricardo. To you our hearty greeting and a big hug from me that squeeses [sic] from it all my unalterable friendship.

—Héctor Panizza

The friendly links with Argentine musicians continued to generate affectionate responses in Panizza's country of origin. On his ninetieth birthday, on August 12, 1965, in Buenos Aires a homage took place in the Casacuberta hall of the Teatro General San Martín, then run by an unparalleled former administrator of the Colón —Cirilo Grassi Díaz— who gave a brief speech. Carlos Pessina and Rodolfo Caracciolo played the *Sonata in A minor* for violin and piano, and the same interpreters as well as the cellist Luis Walter Pratesi played the *Trio in G minor*.[184] Panizza sent a telegram of greeting. At the same time, the National Academy of Fine Arts named him an academic.[185]

A handwritten letter —revealing the good pulse that the ninety-year-old still possessed— informs us that the conductor had considered traveling to Argentina to be present at these tributes.

Milan, August 22, 1965.

Dear friend:

I have received your, as always, affectionate letter. My wife continues to improve, but very slowly! Patience! I have news of the progress of the homages in my honor... and it is with deep emotion that I receive this news... though I believe it has been good for my health to have canceled my trip to Argentina!

Would I have been able to bear so many emotions? I don't believe so... I think this way because of the mere fact that all of you, my good friends, live at this moment only thinking of "celebrating" this old musician... [sic] this puts me in a state of nervousness, happy, it is true, but "nervousness" that lived daily amidst all these festivities would have killed me. Thank you for your affectionate wishes! Many memories from our part of you and your traveling son! A big hug from your very affectionable [sic]

—Héctor Panizza

PS. Write to me!

As part of this same series of homages, *Aurora* was performed at the Teatro Colón beginning on November 12, with conducting by Juan Emilio Martini, staging by Enrique Sivieri and set design by Héctor Basaldúa. The protagonists were soprano Haydée de Rosa and tenor Marcos Cubas. The production was staged again the following year, with the Italian-Argentine tenor Carlos (Carlo) Cossutta in the role of Mariano. Panizza was informed by means of letters and telegrams, to which he makes reference in a brief note of satisfaction sent to the effect.[186]

The final missive that is conserved from the correspondence between Panizza and Del Hoyo is from the start of 1966. In it the Italian-Argentine musician returns to his obsession about *Aurora* (the "theatrical work" of the letter), which he no doubt recognizes as the score that will endure from his not-so-large production.

Milan, January 25,1966.

You can imagine, Del Hoyo my friend, as you are also a sincere artist, the great and intimate pleasure of my heart upon reading all the impressions received when listening to my chamber and stage works.

When I premiered Aurora in 1908 the criticism of some "superuomini" was quite severe toward my work and myself as artist... the audience (as always sincere in its demonstrations) did not understand my work right away!... but with this same sincerity it always has (the audience in general) it has accepted my work with great enthusiasm!

Time has proved me right and the greatest satisfaction an artist can ask for upon presenting his work is the conviction of not having made a mistake when he worked on it!

I am also very happy and satisfied that the translation of the "libretto" from Italian to Spanish has favored its understanding. All the better! Your words with such praise for my work make me proud. Thank you, Del Hoyo my friend!

From the criticism of the newspapers I have also learned of the success achieved by *Aurora* — and the magnificent presentations the work has had due to the merit of the principal and secondary performers, with Martini and Sivieri at the head, who have thus demonstrated to me their regard and fondness for me!

And you do not write anything more...? Do not give up composition in your free moments, it will bring you many well earned satisfactions!

Many memories of your son Ricardo... To you a sincere hug that squeeses [sic] from me all my affectionate friendship.

—Héctor Panizza

[in the margin, handwritten, as a P.S.:] To my good friend Valenti Costa, many greetings, and I now hope for a long letter.

By that time— beyond some short trips to Rome or the hot springs of Chianciano— Panizza did not move from Milan, a city as dear to him as

Buenos Aires. There he died, with his family by his side, on November 27, 1967, at ninety-two years of age, and there his remains rest.

AN ELUSIVE POSTERITY

After his death, little has been remembered of Panizza in his native Argentina. On coming to know of his decease, the National Ministry of Culture decreed a period of mourning.[187]

At the Colón, the following day, a double program was performed with Donizetti's *Rita* and Puccini's *Le Villi*, conducted by his faithful collaborator Juan Emilio Martini. The performance was dedicated to Héctor Panizza, after his death was announced to the audience.[188]

In 1968 a homage took place at Salón Dorado of the Teatro Colón. Participating in the act were Enzo Valenti Ferro, Ferruccio Calusio and Roberto Kinsky, as well as Luisa Sofía, Carlos Pessina, Francisco Amicarelli, and Ángel Mattiello, who performed some of his works. For the occasion, the maestro Martini published through Ricordi Americana a very brief work with the title *Semblanza de Héctor Panizza*, which was given to those attending.[189]

In 1972, the school number 26 in District 19 of the city of Buenos Aires (today school number 9 of District 21) —located on the 5920 Berón de Astrada street, in the Almirante Brown neighborhood of Villa Lugano — was given the name Héctor Panizza.

A commission of homage was formed in 1975 made up of Roberto Kinsky, Juan Emilio Martini, Enrique Sivieri and Roberto Locatelli, to which was added Ferruccio Calusio in representation of the executive power and Floro Ugarte as vice president.

On August 12, 1975, on the exact centenary of his birth, a homage took place on National Radio, in which Mauricio Goldstein Citron and Eric Schueler interpreted his *Sonata for violin and piano*, and a copy of the bust sculpted by his daughter Valeria was uncovered in the foyer of the Teatro Colón.[190]

Opening on September 7, 1975, *Bizancio* was revived at the Colón for the last time, with musical conducting by Juan Emilio Martini and stage directing by Eduardo Lanfredi. The cast was headed by soprano Nina Carini as Empress Augusta and, alternating as Emperor Basilio, basses Víctor de Narké and Jorge Algorta, the Uruguayan disciple of Panizza; among others, Adriana Cantelli, Carlos Guichandut, and Renato Cesari also sang.[191]

Starting in the '80s only *Aurora* seemed to represent our artist in the weak Argentine music scene. Limiting ourselves to the Teatro Colón, the emblematic opera was revived in 1983, once again under Martini's baton; the staging was by Fernando Heredia, with a cast led by Mabel Veleris and Liborio Simonella.[192] It was once again performed in 1999, under Bruno D'Astoli's baton, staging by Eduardo Rodríguez Arguibel and the female leading role sung by Martha Colalillo, in circumstances that guaranteed a remarkable success. The debut tenor Darío Volonté breathed a new energy into the "Canción de la bandera," not only through the strength of his singing, but also because he had been one of the survivors of the warship *General Belgrano* sinking by an English submarine in the 1982 Malvinas (Falklands) War. During those performances, the audience demanded an encore of the "Canción," almost uniquely in the short history of the Colón; only Amedeo Bassi, Beniamino Gigli, and Plácido Domingo had been requested to encore during an opera performance.[193]

That representation of *Aurora* was accompanied by an special issue of the magazine *Revista Teatro Colón* dedicated to the work and its composer, transforming that number —in the midst of continuing general disinterest— into required reading for all those who want to know about Panizza and his most fortunate opera.[194]

Shortly afterward a sound recording and film of one of his performances began to circulate, recordings that lack official approval but are highly useful for all interested in the work.[195]

Since then, very little has been done to revindicate the career of Héctor Panizza from the artistic standpoint, whether as composer or performer, beyond the recurrence of that brief celebrated highlight of *Aurora*. On the occasion of Panizza's ninetieth birthday *La Prensa* complained about this lack of recognition, speaking the truth although using popular examples: "This Argentine musician [Panizza], a man of art, is less known and celebrated in his land than Don Luis Ángel Firpo [a famous boxer] and Mr. Tesorieri [Américo Tesorieri, goalkeeper of the Boca Juniors club]. Signs of the times, for in North America a Lindbergh or Pershing are likewise given more national glory than a Thomas Edison."[196]

Image 1. Panizza Portrait, ca. 1930

Héctor Panizza, about 1930. Teatro Colón. Archive of *La Nación*.

Image 2. Panizza Portrait, ca.1904.

Héctor Panizza in about 1904, with a gaze that expresses the illusions of one who has everything ahead of him.

Image 3. Opening Night, Metropolitan Opera, 1938

Image 4. Panizza Caricature

Caras y Caretas dedicates to Panizza one of the famous caricatures by Cao on the occasion of the premiere of *Medio Evo latino*. Teatro de la Ópera, Buenos Aires. 1901 season.

Image 5. Poster for premiere of *Il fidanzato del mare*

Poster for the Argentine premiere of *Il fidanzato del mare*. Teatro de la Ópera, Buenos Aires, 1897 season.

Image 6. Poster for the world premiere of *Medio Evo latino*

Poster for the world premiere of *Medio Evo latino* under the baton of Toscanini. Teatro de la Ópera, Buenos Aires. 1901 season.

Image 7. Cordero Dedication by Panizza

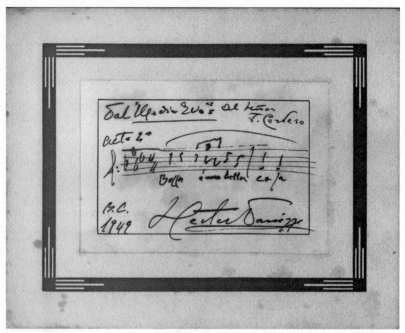

Dedication by Panizza to Sr. I. Cordero, with a musical quotation from Act II of *Medio Evo latino*. 1949. Alberto Bellucci Collection.

Image 8. Panizza Advertisement

Advertisement for a piano of the period published in *Caras y Caretas* with handwritten recommendation and picture of Héctor Panizza. Buenos Aires, August 28, 1908.

Image 9. Panizza Rehearses

Panizza rehearsing *Aurora* with Amedeo Bassi and Titta Ruffo at the Teatro Colón. 1908 season.

Image 10. Puccini Letter to Panizza

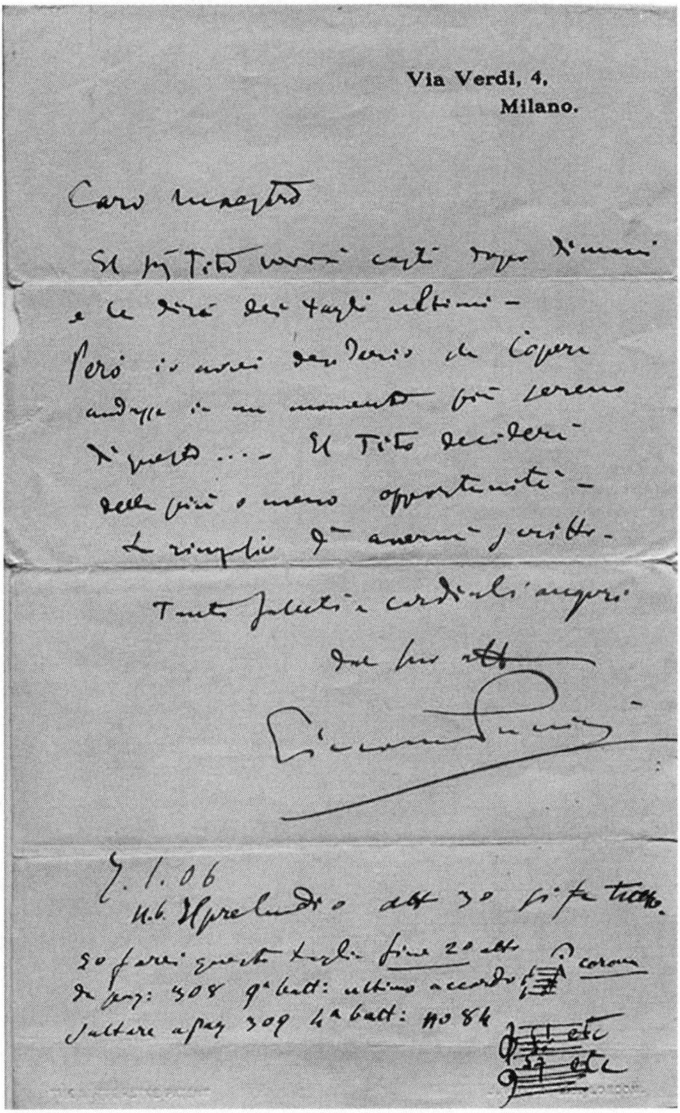

Via Verdi, 4,
Milano.

Caro maestro

Il sig. Tito verrà costì dopo domani
e le dirà dei tagli ultimi –
Però io avrei desiderio di sapere
anche se in un momento più sereno
di questo ... – Il Tito deciderà
della più o meno opportunità –
La ringrazio d'avermi scritto.

Tanti saluti e cordiali auguri
dal suo aff
Giacomo Puccini

2.1.06
N.B. Il preludio atto 3° si fa tutto.
2° farei questo taglio fine 2° atto
da pag: 308 9a batt: ultimo accordo corona
saltare a pag 309 4a batt: no 84 etc

Letter from Giacomo Puccini after the performances in Genoa of *Madama Butterfly* conducted by Panizza. Milan, January 2, 1906.

Image 11. Grieg Letter to Panizza

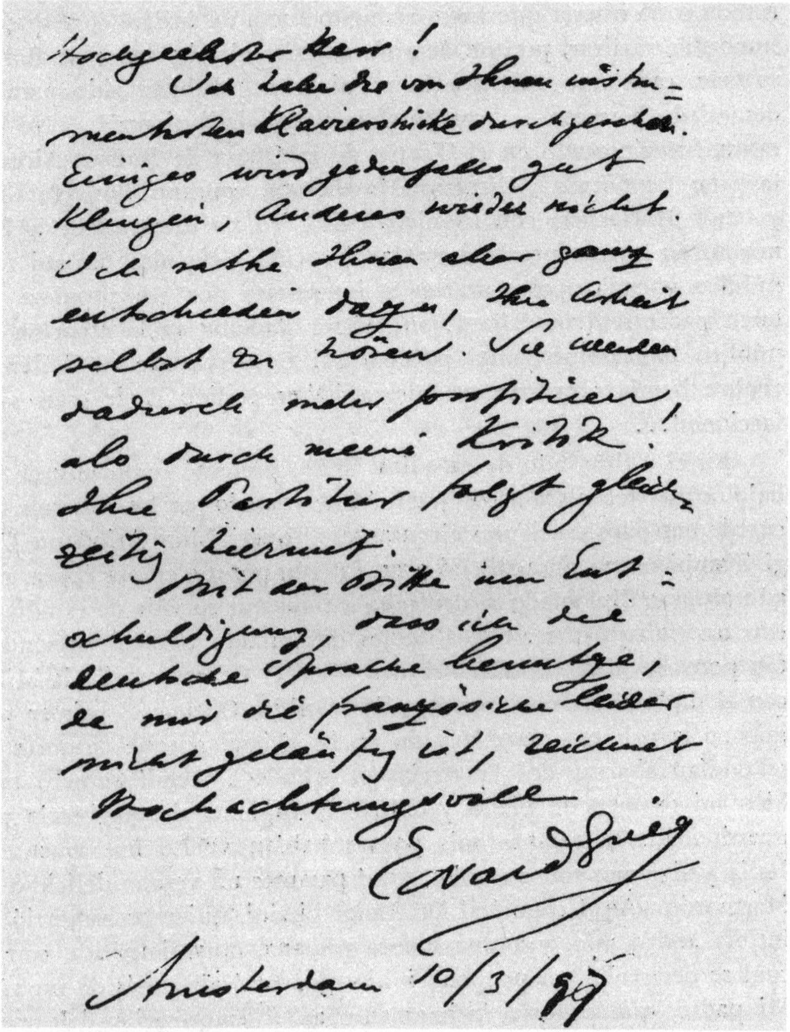

Hochgeehrter Herr!

Ich habe die von Ihnen instrumentirten Klavierstücke durchgesehen. Einiges wird jedenfalls gut klingen, Anderes wieder nicht. Ich rathe Ihnen aber ganz entschieden dazu, Ihre Arbeit selbst zu hören. Sie werden dadurch mehr profitiren, als durch meine Kritik! Ihre Partitur folgt gleichzeitig hiermit.

Mit der Bitte um Entschuldigung, dass ich die deutsche Sprache benutze, da mir die französische leider nicht geläufig ist, zeichnet

Hochachtungsvolle

Edvard Grieg

Amsterdam 10/3/97

Letter from Edvard Grieg to Héctor Panizza praising his arrangements of *Lyric Pieces*. Amsterdam, March 10, 1897.

Image 12. Strauss Letter to Panizza

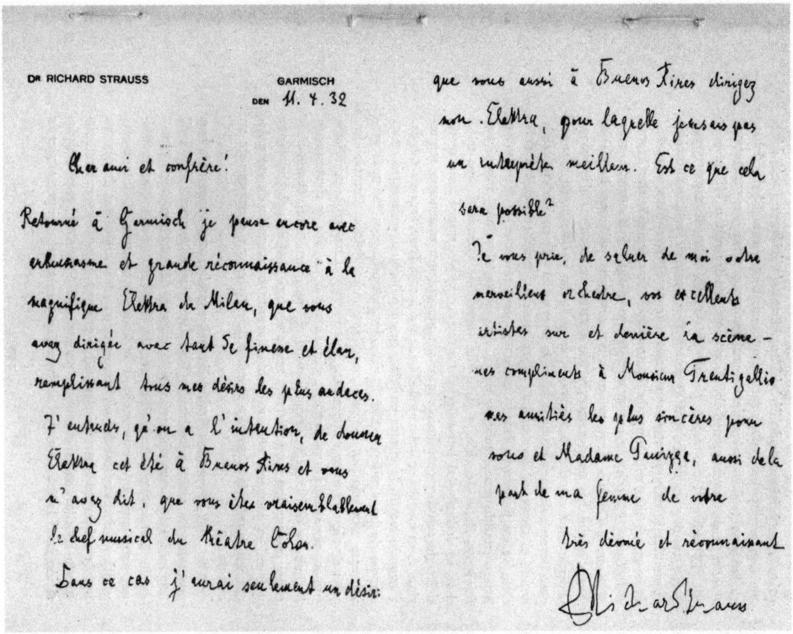

DR RICHARD STRAUSS

GARMISCH
DEN 11. 4. 32

Cher ami et confrère!

Retourné à Garmisch je pense encore avec enthousiasme et grande réconnaissance à la magnifique Elektra de Milan, que vous avez dirigée avec tant de finesse et élan, remplissant tous mes désirs les plus audaces.

J'entends, qu'on a l'intention, de donner Elektra cet été à Buenos Aires et vous m'avez dit, que vous êtes vraisemblablement le chef musical du Théâtre Colon.

Dans ce cas j'aurai seulement un désir: que vous aussi à Buenos Aires dirigez mon Elektra, pour laquelle je ne sais pas un interprète meilleur. Est ce que cela sera possible?

Je vous prie, de saluer de moi votre merveilleux orchestre, vos excellents artistes sur et derrière la scène - mes compliments à Monsieur Trentigallio mes amitiés les plus sincères pour vous et Madame Panizza, aussi de la part de ma femme de votre

très dévoué et réconnaissant

Richard Strauss

Letter from Richard Strauss to Panizza recommending him as the conductor for his *Elektra* at the Teatro Colón. Garmisch, April 11, 1932.

Image 13. Panizza Portrait, 1920

Panizza at his peak, around 1920. From the archive of *La Prensa*.

Image 14. Panizza Portrait (1923)

In 1923 the director dedicated this photo to the tenor Giovanni Martinelli, with whom he would record an impressive *Aida* at the Met in 1941.

Image 15. Panizza Portrait (1929)

Portrait signed in 1929 to the stage director Rodolfo Franco, with whom Panizza worked during that season at the Teatro Colón.

Image 16. Panizza at Piano

Photo dedicated to the soprano Hina Spani. Buenos Aires, 1939. From the archive of the Superior Institute of Art at the Teatro Colón.

Image 17. La Scala Playbill

Playbill from the Teatro alla Scala in Milan during the season that it reopened as an autonomous entity, 1921–22. Ettore Panizza's name appears on exactly the same level as that of Arturo Toscanini, in strict alphabetical order.

Image 18. Panizza Portrait, 1927

The musician in 1927, doing honor to fine dining. From the archive of *La Nación*.

Image 19. Colon Group Photo

Panizza is honored at the Teatro Colón on October 2, 1941. In front of him, with the bowtie, is the composer Alberto Williams. From the archive of *La Prensa*.

Image 20. Panizza on the Podium, 1950

Héctor Panizza on the podium of the State Symphony Orchestra (today the National Symphony Orchestra). Teatro Metropolitan. Buenos Aires, May 9, 1950. From the archive of *La Prensa*.

Image 21. Panizza on the Podium

Panizza on the podium of the Teatro Colón with the brand-new Resident Orchestra, 1927 season.

Image 22. Panizza with Met Cast, 1935

La Traviata cast members Lawrence Tibbett (Germont), Richard Crooks (Alfredo), Lucrezia Bori (Violetta),
and conductor Ettore Panizza, backstage after the opening night perfomrance with Paul Cravath,
Chairman of the Met's Board of Directors, and General Manager, Edward Johnson.

La Traviata. Above, the manager of the Met, Edward Johnson, Lawrence Tibbett,
Richard Crooks, Lucrezia Bori, Panizza, and Paul Cravath, from the board of directors
of the Met. 1935 season.

Image 23. Movie Poster

A poster from the launch of the film *La signora delle camelie* by Carmine Gallone in the United States. Panizza bears the credit as conductor of the soundtrack.

Image 24. Panizza Birthday

Panizza celebrates his 80th birthday at the Teatro Colón, surrounded (from left to right) by Otto Erhardt, Juan Emilio Martini, Roberto Kinsky, and Tullio Boni. 1955 season.

Image 25. Front of Panizza's Letter to Faustino

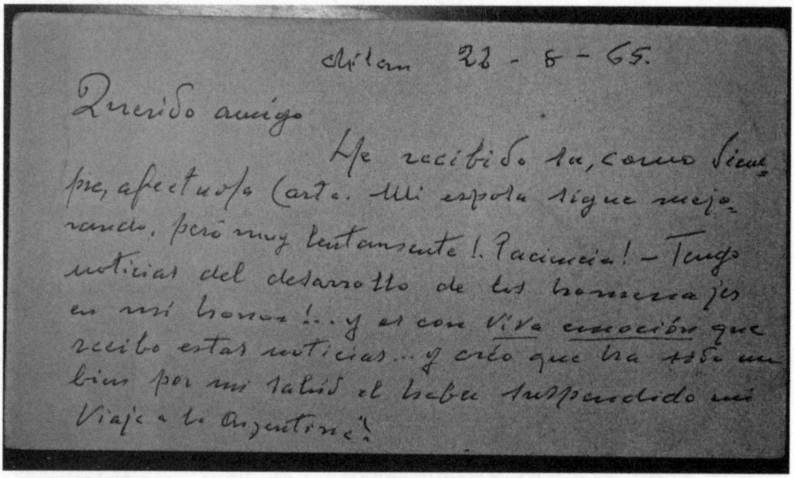

Milán 22 - 8 - 65.

Querido amigo

He recibido tu, como siempre, afectuosa carta. Mi esposa sigue mejorando, pero muy lentamente! Paciencia! — Tengo noticias del desarrollo de los homenajes en mi honor!... y es con viva emoción que recibo estas noticias... y créo que ha sido un bien por mi talvéz el haber suspendido mi viaje a la Argentina!

Image 26. Back of Letter to Faustino

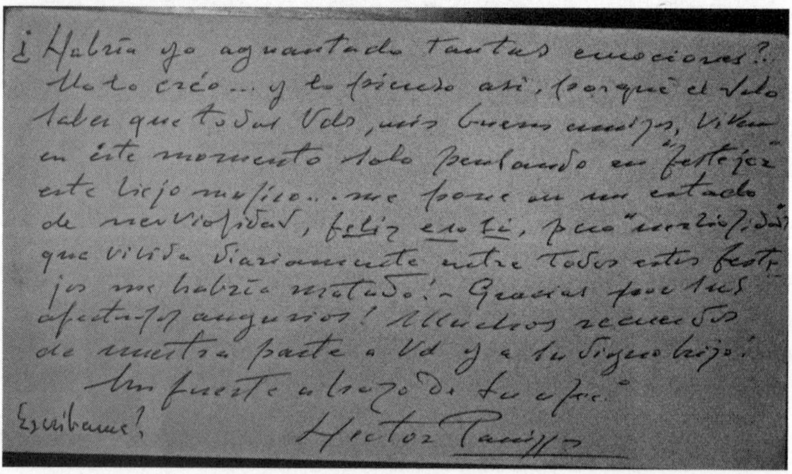

¿Habría yo aguantado tantas emociones?.. No lo créo... y lo pienso así, porqué el solo saber que todos Vds, mis buenos amigos, viven en éste momento solo pensando en "festejar" este hijo músico... me pone en un estado de nerviosidad, feliz eso sí, pero "nerviosidad" que vivida diariamente entre todos estos festejos me habría matado! — Gracias por tus afectuosos augurios! Muchos recuerdos de nuestra parte a Vd y a tu dignísimo hijo!

Un fuerte abrazo de tu afmo.

Escribame!

Héctor Panizza

Letter from Héctor Panizza to Faustino del Hoyo, dated in Milan on August 22, 1965. Panizza was then ninety years old. Institute of Ethnomusicology of the City.

Image 27. Panizza Smoking

Rare photo of Panizza with a cigarette in hand. From the archive of *La Prensa*.

Image 28. Panizza's Ideal Portrait

Panizza the composer: how he would have preferred to be remembered.

Image 29. Panizza After Performance (1938)

The maestro with Lawrence Tibbett, Giovanni Martinelli, Maria Caniglia, and Edward Johnson after a performance of *Otello*. Metropolitan Opera. New York, 1938.

Image 30. Panizza After Performance, 1955

Marcos Cubas, Héctor Panizza, Nicola Rossi-Lemeni, Víctor Damiani in *L'amore dei tre re*. Photo by Juan Pedro Damiani. Teatro Colón. 1955 season.

PART TWO

THE WORK

CHAPTER 7

THE COMPOSER

Héctor Panizza's initial training in Buenos Aires was guided by his father and included piano, violin, and timpani lessons, as well as initial studies in composition. This last discipline quickly captured the attention of the young musician to the pleasure of his father, a composer himself in addition to an instrumentalist, as has been seen.

Panizza's musical studies continued and culminated in what currently is known as the "Giuseppe Verdi" Conservatory of Milan, where he was the classmate of another performer destined for fame who —like him — would have a productive link with Arturo Toscanini: Tullio Serafin, today recognized by all for his brilliant career as opera conductor, in particular in New York, Rome, and Milan itself.[197]

Héctor deliberately chose the Italian teachers with whom he studied. His piano teacher Giuseppe Frugatta was a composer in addition to being a soloist, and also had among his students another Argentine linked with Toscanini: Ferruccio Calusio. Amintore Galli, his harmony teacher, was a prestigious composer, musicologist, and specialized journalist. Michele Saladino, his teacher of counterpoint and fugue, also counted Mascagni among his disciples. Vincenzo Ferroni, his teacher of composition, was a composer as prolific in his day as he is little known in ours. Finally, Antonio Bazzini, who guided Panizza in the orchestral practices, in addition to being a teacher—with Puccini and Catalani as previous students— was a violinist, composer and, at that time, director of the Conservatory.[198]

At the end of his studies, Héctor received a diploma in both piano and composition (the latter with the highest marks). It was a classic example of academic "coupling" during the time—when there still did not exist either a career or a specific course intended to prepare those who had the disposition for conducting, for preparing concerts, and for the work inherent to that environment.

For our artist, it soon became clear that knowledge of the keyboard would only be a means to two ends: conducting and composition. The musician threw himself with equal conviction and enthusiasm into both careers, with the idea of carrying them out in parallel and the hope of achieving a similar success in them both. Several illustrious figures had done just this.

Without a doubt his initial ambitions did not materialize: Panizza passed into history as a professional composer, but without coming to stand out at an international level. This in no way means that some of his works do not deserve to be heard again, however, along with those of other contemporary composers equally forgotten.

Concerning his style, Panizza found himself close to the veristic *Giovane Scuola* and in the same line as the principal Italian composers of his generation, particularly the ones devoted to opera such as Franchetti, Cilea, Giordano, Montemezzi (who was born in the same year as him), Alfano, Wolf-Ferrari, and Zandonai. Wagner (and some Russian composers to a lesser degree) could certainly be added to these names whose use of the orchestral palette fascinated Panizza. He did not seek to generate his own musical revolutions or adhere to the revolutions of others. Rather, he continued to develop as much in the instrumental as in the vocal— the melodic language and tonal harmony he learned from his maestros in Milan and which began to coalesce in an exciting way during his youth and middle age.

It is worth taking a look at his main compositions; unfortunately today almost are all forgotten by the public and ignored by musicologists, with an almost non-existent discography and difficult to consult even for researchers, for neither do the printed scores circulate—as they should—which in their moment were published commercially.

THE MUSICAL THEATER

Leaving aside the two short zarzuelas from his youth mentioned in the biographical section, which were never performed or published, and at the moment are impossible to trace (*El autor del crimen, El ultimo invento*), Panizza's first operatic attempt was an academic work that earned him the composition prize at the Conservatory of Milan.

Il fidanzato del mare, a "lyrical novella" (lyrical tale or story) in one act, whose title can be translated as *The Groom of the Sea*, with a libretto by the poet and journalist Romeo Carugati —an author highly influenced by the realism of Giovanni Verga and especially his most famous novel, *Los Malavoglia*— is about a family of fishermen. Given the element just mentioned it is not difficult to connect this score with the veristic movement then prevailing in the field of Italian opera.[199]

The protagonists of this love story with a tragic end are Vito (tenor), the "fiancé" of the title, and Maria (soprano), accompanied by a mixed choir which represents small-town women and fishermen, since the story develops —as the title and literary preferences of the librettist make it easy to imagine— on the maritime coast. The opera is brief and the plot simple: Maria is betrothed to Vito, who goes out to sea with other boatmen; a storm provokes the unhappy outcome: the only man who does not return to solid ground is, of course, Vito himself.[200]

Il fidanzato del mare was initially performed in the Conservatory of Milan, and later had its official debut at the Teatro de la Ópera in Buenos Aires on August 15, 1897, with the famous conductor Edoardo Mascheroni on the podium; the singers were tenor Michele Mariacher and soprano Carmen Bonaplata-Bau (who would take on, in the same performance, the leading roles of *Tannhäuser*). After those performances, the composer preferred to remove the opera from circulation and the work was never again performed; Héctor even decided not to include it in the official catalogue of his compositions.[201]

Panizza's second opera is perhaps the most curious of his four: *Medioevo latino* (known in Argentina as *Medio Evo latino*) is defined as a "trilogy" and was composed on the basis of a commission by the editor Giulio Ricordi. The original libretto, as we have seen, belongs to Luigi Illica, the prolific literary collaborator of Puccini, Mascagni, Giordano, Catalani, Franchetti, Alfano, Montemezzi, and other notable composers of this generation.

The work innovates as much in the text— one of the most elaborate that emerged from Illica's pen— as in the music. The composer himself, in an introductory note to the libretto, explained his intention: to offer a vision at once dramatic, historical and human of the Middle Ages in three Latin countries, through the different parts of the trilogy: *The Cruzades* or *La crociata* (Italy), *The Courts of Love* or *Per l'amore* (France) and *The Inquisition* or *Per l'umanità* (Spain).

The first part of the triptych, whose action takes place between the years 1000 and 1050, is situated in a feudal castle in Italy, where the Prince there (baritone) hosts a traveling Bard (tenor). After suffering hallucinations, the noble ends up confessing that he has killed many people, among them his own brother, guilty of having looked at his Lady (soprano). To redeem himself, the aristocrat, at the behest of a Hermit (bass), must join the Crusades, thus leaving his comfortable life and also his beloved.

The second story centers on courtly love and takes place in Provence, between the years 1200 and 1250. There is a court of love in which the Castilian Lady (soprano) proposes to decipher an "alphabet of love" presented to her by a Knight (bass). The latter, however, only intends to take possession of a golden flower that the woman wears on her corset, to offer it to the lady Auxehay (mezzosoprano). On opening the court, an Arabian knight who feigns blindness —Il Faidi (baritone)— returns the flower to the Castilian Lady and reveals the deception. The two knights challenge one another to a duel and Il Faidi wins, to the sorrow of the Castilian Lady, who faints.

The third part develops in Cadiz, between 1400 and 1500. The Catholic Kings have just expelled the Moors. A Lord (baritone) betrays his Lady (mezzosoprano) with the Moorish woman Aydée (soprano), who lives in his palace. A Friar (bass) reports him and the husband asks for forgiveness, but after the premonition of a Gypsy (mezzosoprano) surrenders to his hidden lover, whom he kisses. At that moment appear the Lady, the Friar, and the Holy Office with Torquemada himself (baritone) at the head. The husband accuses his wife of sorcery and she is condemned to the bonfire, despite the good efforts of the civil Poet (tenor). The news arrives that a Genoese navigator has won the support of the kings and is about to set sail for the Indies. The Poet shows scorn toward Europe due to its squalor and sings to the ideal represented by the New World yet to be discovered.[202]

The trilogy, long and also complex at the musical level, requires a reliable cast and contains prominent arias for tenor, mezzosoprano, and soprano (such as *In mia segreta camera del core*, which the Lady sings in the first part of the opera).

The world premiere took place at the Politeama Genovese, with the maestro Edoardo Vitale as musical conductor and a cast headed by the tenor Amedeo Bassi, on November 17, 1900.

The success of the first production resulted in the programming of the title at the Teatro de la Ópera in Buenos Aires for the next year, an opportunity that marked the meeting and first artistic collaboration —at the start rather tense, as was seen in the first part of this book— between Panizza and Toscanini. The leading cast, entirely Italian, was excellent: the soprano was Amelia Pinto (Lady, Castilian, Aydée), the tenor Giuseppe Borgatti (Bard, Troubadour, Poet), the baritone Mario Sammarco (Prince, Faidi, Lord), and the bass Remo Ercolani (Astrologer, Hermit, Friar). It would be very interesting to listen to it sometime in our day, among other reasons because the opera met with interest in Buenos Aires even more than in Genoa.[203]

For a great variety of factors, Panizza's third work for the stage is the only one that has achieved a certain durability, although only in Argentina: *Aurora*, an opera in three acts with an interlude (described as "epic," it might be added). The work was commissioned in 1906 and was concluded at the beginning of 1908. As has already been mentioned, the libretto this time was taken on by two authors: the Argentine politician, journalist, and writer Héctor Quesada Casal drafted the plot, while once again Luigi Illica wrote the verses in Italian. The result was a libretto that worked but was historically very imprecise, beginning with the fact that the Jesuits had already been expelled from America before the time in which the tale occurs.[204]

The action takes place in 1810, in the Argentine city of Córdoba, still dominated by the Spanish. The local governor Don Ignacio del Puente (baritone) represents the Iberian forces, who are challenged by Mariano (tenor), a Jesuit novice who soon turns revolutionary. The classic melodramatic contradiction between patriotic duty and amorous sentiment will come to the fore with the meeting between Mariano and the daughter of don Ignacio Aurora (soprano). In contrast with what happens with Calaf and Turandot in Puccini, this meeting is more auditory than visual.

A few episodes are presented as in some way connected to another three operas with verses by Illica: Franchetti's *Germania* (the first scenes of both works, conceived as a *scherzo*, are very similar), Puccini's *Tosca* (its *Te Deum* does not seem very far away) and, in a lesser measure, Giordano's *Andrea Chénier* (compare the respective final scenes). The music, for its part, is undeniably close to the epic veristic style of Giordano himself, with all the positive and negative connotations that can be attributed to it, including among the former a rich orchestration and among the latter certain heaviness in the musical discourse.[205]

Apart from the "Canción de la bandera," the most efficient moments in the score are doubtlessly the animated exchanges with the spy Lavín (bass), the brief interlude of the first act that describes the agitation in Mariano's soul, the end of the second act, the heroic exhortation of Lucas (baritone), the last duet and the finale, with the death of the protagonist over a brief quote from the Argentine National Anthem.

Aurora had its first performance during the inaugural season of the new Teatro Colón in Buenos Aires, on September 5, 1908, with the composer conducting and an absolutely stellar cast headed by the Italian singers Maria Farneti, Amedeo Bassi, and Titta Ruffo. The audience received it warmly but, as often happens, certain critics did not find it to their taste: some *porteño* journalists found it distasteful that a work with a patriotic plot made no direct reference to Argentine popular music and was sung in Italian by Italians. As has been said, the opera rose again to the stage of the Colón the following year, under Giuseppe Barone's baton, also Italian, and with Hariclea Darclée as the protagonist. *Aurora*'s revival, with a notably more Ibero-American profile, had to wait until the 1945 season, on the occasion of the evening of the national gala on July 9. Panizza presided from the pit and the Argentine Delia Rigal, the Spanish Antonio Vela, and the Uruguayan Víctor Damiani performed the main roles. It was on this occasion that he entrusted the Spanish version of the text to Ángel Petitta and Josué Quesada, son of the original author, Héctor Quesada.

Panizza took advantage of the moment to examine several details of the music, particularly where the orchestration was concerned. An almost Wagnerian density at certain moments of the score was an authentic challenge for the voices onstage. The singers had to sing mostly at the center of their tessituras and were for this reason less likely to rise above the sound of the orchestra.

From then on, *Aurora* was performed only in this jumbled Spanish translation, which contains some of the least happy verses in memory, many neologisms, and a good number of frankly incomprehensible expressions. The famous intervention of the tenor during the epic interlude, "Alta pel cielo, un'aquila guerriera / ardita s'erge in volo trionfale" thus became "Alta en el cielo, un águila guerrera / audaz se eleva a vuelo triunfal" [High in the sky, a warrior eagle / bravely rises in triumphal flight].

In Argentina, rather than eagles there are condors, the Argentine flag is sky-blue not blue, the word "irradial" does not exist in Spanish supposedly translating the Italian adjective "irradiale," and the verse "il rostro d'or punta di freccia appare" was poorly inverted into *castellano* ignoring that "rostro" in Italian in this context means "beak," certainly not "face." We quote these matters merely as examples, limiting ourselves to the points that concern the "Canción de la bandera" on which with very sound judgment the writer Juan Sasturain has taken note.[206] The translation of "porpora il teso collo e forma stelo" for "y forma estela al purpurado cuello" is also erroneous, as it translates "stelo" as "estela" [trail] rather than "tallo" [stem]. It is also very doubtful to link the color purple with the Argentine flag, which never had any element of that color, which was identified on the contrary —ironically— with the Spanish realists during the wars of independence, to which *Aurora* intends to render homage from a patriotic perspective.

In short, the translation is deficient, even anti-musical at times. That the composer did not step in to halt such absurdities can only be explained by the fact that Panizza himself always spoke and wrote a Spanish full of italianisms, and therefore perhaps did not believe himself to have the authority necessary to intervene in poetic matters. Such is the resulting nonsense that, in more recent times, Horacio Sanguinetti —in his role as President of the National Academy of Education and a music-loving expert of the tenor repertoire— came to develop and suggest an alternative poetic translation for the Spanish version of the aria.[207]

The truth is that the Spanish text very likely facilitated the circulation of the opera in Argentina, but decreased the chances it was known beyond the limits of the country where it was written.

Despite the problems of the text, it did not take long before this version of the aria for tenor —based on the form of the *triste* creole— became a "national prayer" dedicated to the national flag, through a decree signed by President Perón. A version especially simplified for its performance in school and military contexts was then spread and to this day goes by several names, such as "Canción de la bandera," erroneously as "Canción a la bandera" or "Saludo a la bandera," or even simply and unfortunately as *Aurora*, without any reference to the original context.

This forced popularization did little favor to the work and its composer: today it is not unusual to hear references to the "Canción de la bandera" as a "patriotic march" and it has even come to be symbolically connected with tragedies from Argentine history that took place long after Panizza's lifetime.[208]

The excerpt—in the original operatic version, that is—was recorded in the studio by several tenors, beginning with Amedeo Bassi himself (who curiously committed an error, repeating the word "trionfale" in place of "irradiale").[209] In Argentina it is relatively common to hear it as a concert piece. In recent years it has also been recorded by Argentine tenors Eduardo Ayas and José Cura; the latter interpreted it several times as well during his European concerts with an orchestra, for example in Prague.[210]

Panizza's most successful creation returned to the Colón in 1953, with conducting by Roberto Kinsky and Pili Martorell as Aurora, and in 1955 with the same soprano as an homage to Héctor on his eightieth birthday, conducted by himself as his farewell from the porteño orchestral pit. *Aurora* later returned in 1965, to celebrate the ninetieth birthday of the composer, and in 1966 and 1983, all three times conducted by Juan Emilio Martini, one of the closest collaborators of the Italian-Argentine maestro during his many seasons at the first opera house of Buenos Aires; the sopranos were Haydée De Rosa on the first two occasions and Mabel Veleris on the third.[211]

The Colón programmed it for the last time in 1999, in homage to Martini; it was on this occasion that the Argentine singer and veteran of war Darío Volonté —who was making his first appearance in the venue — passed into the history of the Teatro upon repeating, at the request of the ecstatic public, the famous tenor piece. The other protagonists were the soprano Martha Colalillo —an Argentine singer who had Ferruccio Calusio and Roberto Kinsky as teachers for the repertoire— and the baritone Ricardo Yost, a resident artist who also had the opportunity to work with Kinsky.

Aurora is Panizza's only dramatic work to have been performed in other Argentine cities. In 1966 it rose to the stage of the Teatro Argentino in La Plata, the country's second largest opera house, with two performances and a cast led by the singers Haydée De Rosa, Marcos Cubas, and Ángel Mattiello, accompanied by the Resident Orchestra of the house under the baton of Juan Emilio Martini.

In 1995 the well-known conductor Juan Carlos Zorzi offered a wide selection from *Aurora* in a concert version at the Teatro El Círculo in Rosario, conducting the Provincial Symphonic Orchestra of that city, with Adelaida Negri, Ricardo Ochoa, and Ricardo Yost among the soloists.[212]

In 2001 it was scheduled at the Teatro del Libertador in Córdoba—that is, in the very city where the events narrated by the opera occur, just a few meters from one of the plot's main locations— with a cast headed by Cecilia Lapponi, Darío Volonté, and Ricardo Ortale, accompanied by the Provincial Symphony Orchestra conducted by the maestro Fernando Álvarez.

Finally, in 2012 *Aurora* arrived in Mendoza, with three performances at the Teatro Independencia of the provincial capital led by an energetic group of young local singers, accompanied by the Philharmonic Orchestra of the province conducted by the Brazilian Ligia Amadio.

It would be of the greatest interest to make a studio recording with international commercial distribution of this opera, the most widely performed by the composer and one of the most emblematic of the Argentine repertoire, creating it with standards of philological interpretation, that is, essentially, in the original Italian, respecting all the *tempi* indicated and above all without the cuts that were usually made at the moment of performing it live. It would perhaps be the best way for the fortune that has smiled in Argentina upon Panizza's opera to have an opportunity to spread to the rest of the world. In relation to his other dramatic creations, *Aurora* also exhibits a fundamental advantage: its score and parts are still easily attainable.

Panizza's fourth and final opera was *Bizancio*, a "musical poem" in three acts. The libretto in Italian, with the original title of *Bisanzio*, was entrusted to Gustavo Macchi, who by explicit request of the composer based it on the historical novel of almost the same name by the French writer Auguste Bailly. Strictly speaking, the beginning of its composition precedes that of *Aurora*, but a series of delays by the first librettist and indecision by the composer about the final act extended the creative process for several years.

The plot —probably the weakest of those with which Panizza worked — takes place during the decadence of the Roman Empire. It is about a soldier named Suatari (tenor) who arrives at the court with his brother Aldano (baritone). An insurrection is taking place at that moment, led by Papías (tenor). Aldano has fallen into disgrace with the empress Augusta (soprano) for being the lover of the princess Eudoxia (mezzosoprano), who aspires to the throne. In the context of a public homage to the emperor Basilio (bass), Suatari wants to kill the empress, but his brother prevents it.

In the second act, which takes place in a secret villa belonging to the empress, Aldano begs pardon from Suatari. Augusta, for her part, recognizes that Suatari is a son of hers, whom she bore in secret. In the final act, Eudoxia complains about the relationship of Augusta with Aldano. Suatari, meanwhile, has been blinded. An insurrection suddenly occurs. The troops complain to Aldano for their defense and the emperor Basilio consents. Suatari dies, while Aldano returns hurt and also dies while singing the anthem of his country.[213]

Bizancio made its world debut at the Teatro Colón in Buenos Aires, on July 25, 1939, under the composer's own baton, and the performance was a success. As a result, in 1940 the score and parts were published by the firm Suvini & Zerboni in Milan, due to the impossibility for Ricordi —the editor of the majority of Panizza's works— to print them; Roberto Kinsky took on the responsibility of preparing the studio score for voice and piano. The opera returned to the stage of the Colón in the 1944 season, once again conducted by the composer, and for the last time in 1975, led by Martini.[214]

From then Panizza slept, as is often said, the sleep of the just, though paradoxically without much justice: a performance of his work allows one to appreciate the piece's undeniable musical values, prominent among which are majestic and dramatic vocal lines for the soloist, effective writing for the chorus with a predominantly heroic character and a control over the orchestration that at times seems to refer to the best of Mussorgsky.

To conclude with Panizza's creative activity for the stage, in addition to remembering the concrete but abandoned project of an opera about Napoleon Bonaparte (from which no draft has survived), in this section we will also take note of the excellent arrangements for reduced orchestra he made for *Madama Butterfly, La fanciulla del West,* and *Il trittico —Il tabarro, Suor Angelica,* and *Gianni Schicchi*— by Giacomo Puccini. Save for the reduction of *La fanciulla...,* the remaining versions have been performed on recent dates at the Teatro Avenida in Buenos Aires (with *Gianni Schicchi* performed on three different occasions).[215]

HIS ORCHESTRAL WORKS

Panizza's first two orchestral works one might have knowledge of are those that the composer disowned later in life. He withdrew them from the official list of his compositions: *Gavota para cuerdas* and the symphonic suite *Bodas campestres*, which earned him an award and was premiered at the Teatro Nacional in Buenos Aires in 1892. They do not seem to have been published, given that the scores have not been located to this day. In 1893 a *Minuetto* for string instruments was published in *El Mundo del Arte*, but as a reduction for piano.

The official catalogue, then, was inaugurated with *Tema y variaciones* (*Theme and Variations*, sometimes mentioned as *Tema con variaciones*, in Spanish as well as Italian), a work composed in 1916, later receiving an award in the Certani Competition in Bologna, and published by Suvini & Zerboni in 1920. Ironically, this first "official" composition was the composer's favorite until his final days: Héctor felt particularly proud of this piece which he conducted with the Chicago Symphony Orchestra and included in several concert programs he prepared, just like his *Nocturno* in G flat major (of a second orchestral Nocturne, mentioned by him in an interview, nothing further is known). *Theme and Variations* had its premiere on June 1, 1919, in Milan and was performed in Turin a few days later. Its first performance in Buenos Aires was on November 30, 1920, at the Prince George hall, in the context of the concert series of the Associazione Italiana di Concerti, conducted by Ferruccio Cattelani.[216]

It is known that the work was performed again on September 30, 1923, at the Teatro Politeama, with the orchestra of the Asociación del Profesorado Orquestal, also under maestro Cattelani's baton.[217]

At the Teatro Colón in Buenos Aires it was offered in the years 1934, 1943, 1946, and in the concert of the 1955 season in which Héctor bid farewell definitively to the podium.[218]

Panizza's first symphonic work has a musical structure that is easy to describe. The main theme, presented in *Andante sostenuto* with a 4/4 tempo and key of G minor, seems to reflect the melancholic tone of certain kind of Russian music, and is essentially performed by violas and cellos. Ten variations —two of which can be omitted, by the indication of the author himself— lead to a final section, in duple time, in which elements from the principal variations are mixed.

The work requires powerful orchestral force: three woodwinds, four horns, four trumpets, four trombones, four timpani, glockenspiel, xylophone, triangle, tambourine, bass drum, cymbals, two harps, celesta, and strings.[219]

Panizza wrote a single symphonic-choral piece and the public of Buenos Aires had the opportunity of coming to know it under his own baton: this was the cantata *El rey y la floresta* (*The King and the Forest*, a translation accepted by the author from the Italian title *Il re e la foresta*, originally *Dal re e la foresta*), a "symphonic poem" for soprano, baritone, choir, and orchestra. The libretto belongs to the Italian poet Fausto Salvadori (or Salvatori) who in his time achieved some notoriety as the author of the verses from the *Inno a Roma* to which Puccini set music in 1919 and which was later used by Mussolini's regime.[220]

In the biographical part of this book we have already noted that the work had its premiere in the United States on December 30, 1923, played by an ensemble listed with the name of Chicago Theater Orchestra conducted by Nathaniel Finston, with the soprano Hazel Eden and baritone Benjamin Landsmann as soloists. The piece received an excellent response from the audience, but there is no information about its publication.

This overview of the Italian-Argentine maestro's symphonic work is completed by his orchestrations of Grieg's *Lyric Pieces* for piano, which were praised by the Norwegian composer himself in a letter to the author, as well as the "Himno Nacional Argentino" (Argentine National Anthem) by Blas Parera, whose signed manuscript Panizza dedicated and donated to the Teatro Colón.[221]

INSTRUMENTAL CHAMBER MUSIC

Panizza's production in this genre includes five works from his youth not listed in his official catalogue and apparently never published: a *Suite* in four acts, *Canto de octubre* (*October Song*) for two pianos, a *Scherzo para dos pianos* (*Scherzo for two pianos*), a *Cinco piezas para piano* (*Five piano pieces*), and a *Sonata for cello and piano*. Of greater relevance are the *Cuarteto en Do menor para dos violines, viola y violonchelo* (*Quartet in C minor for two violins, viola and cello*) an important work but somewhat irregular in quality, of academic origin), the *Trío en Sol menor para violín, violonchelo y piano* (*Trio in G minor for violin, cello and piano*), published in Milan by Suvini & Zerboni and Ricordi respectively, the *Sonata en La menor para violín y piano* (*Sonata in A minor for violin and piano*), and the *Réverie* for violin and piano. To these works must be added his own transcription for two pianos of his *Theme and Variations*.

Finally, as has already been said, as a very young man Panizza reduced for piano two pieces that in his day enjoyed a certain popular approval: Gottschalk's *Pasquinade* and Ketten's *La Castagnette*.

Since Panizza's death, his *Sonata for Violín and Piano* has been performed at the Auditorium of the Argentine National Radio, on the centenary of the composer's birth, and his *Trio* was scheduled in Milan a few years ago by the initiative of the Argentine pianist José Luis Juri, thanks to the support of the composer's grandson, also named Ettore Panizza, who lent him the printed copies in his possession. As far as is known, the rest of his instrumental works of chamber music have not been heard again.

VOCAL CHAMBER MUSIC

As was the case with his other genres of composition, Panizza's production in this category began with a youthful work "outside the catalogue," *Flores primaverales* (*Fiori primaverili, Spring Flowers*) for voice and piano.

A second youthful work merited publication in Buenos Aires: the *Ave Maria* for voice, violin or cello, and piano, dedicated to Mrs. Isac de Boneo and premiered by a young Argentine soprano named Amanda Campodónico.[222] Among the works published —in this case, by Ricordi in Milan and Ricordi Americana in Buenos Aires— the composer felt particular pride in his series of nine *Romanzas* for high-pitched voice and piano based on poetry by Paul Verlaine (with their title in the original language but text in Italian): *Chanson d'automne, Green, Colloque sentimental, En sourdine, Sérénade, Mon réve familier, Ariettes oubliées, Clymène,* and *Sagesse*. Other pieces for voice and piano with his signature are *Chanson galante, Je porte sur moi ton image,* and *Quand tu passes,* all using poetry by Armand Silvestre (published in Paris in 1915), *Escape* with verses by Lorraine Noel Finley, *Guitare* using the poem by Victor Hugo (from 1926) and *D'une prison* using poetry by Verlaine (the composer's only work edited by Casa Schirmer in New York).

Such a profusion of French poetry in the vocal chamber creation of the musician is not by chance: in addition to being a great lover of Verlaine, he spoke and wrote French almost as fluidly as Spanish and Italian. This material, a good part of which was published, is available for study and generally requires only two performers (a singer and a pianist). Playing these pieces based on verses by Verlaine would be perhaps the easiest way for today's public to receive an idea of how Panizza composed outside the orchestral medium.

Texts

On only two occasions did the Italian-American maestro take up his pen to write words suitable for publication in the format of a book instead of notes on a score: one in good Italian, written in his own hand, the other in a precarious Spanish, dictated to another person. The first was in 1912, when at the request of Ricordi he revised, brought up to date, and admirably expanded Héctor Berlioz's *Grand traité d'instrumentation et d'orchestration modernes* for its publication by the Milanese publishing label, which can still be profitably consulted today.[223]

The second was in 1952, when he dictated to his second wife *Medio siglo de vida musical* (*Half a Century of Musical Life*), the brief and incomplete autobiographical essay that Ricordi Americana published in Buenos Aires that same year.

From an Opera Aria to a School Song

The process by which the "Canción de la bandera" from *Aurora* passed from being an aria of Italian opera to a school song obligatory in Argentina is certainly complex and deserves further research. Perhaps it must be explained, especially for one who has not lived in Panizza's native country or has not passed through its educational milieus, that a special interest by the state has existed to impose specific songs during school ceremonies, along with the Argentine National Anthem.

The organisation in charge of this type of decision was called the National Council of Education. It was created by decree in 1881, during the first presidency of Julio Argentino Roca, with the aim of standardizing the schools of the federal capital; these had belonged to the Province of Buenos Aires before the City of Buenos Aires became the capital, then passed to under the direct control of the federal authorities. Its first "general superintendent" was Domingo Faustino Sarmiento, who was assisted by nine advisers.

Sarmiento defended at all costs the resources destined for education and founded the magazine *El Monitor de la Educación Común*, which for decades gave an account of the state of public instruction in the country. With the approval in 1884 of the incomparable Act No. 1.420 —which established public, secular, free, and obligatory education— the Council now possessed a legal base to win the battle against illiteracy in Argentina, a policy that put the country in a position of world leadership in educational matters, and that was not consistently followed since then.

Act No. 1.420 was polemical insofar as it abolished religious education in public schools by the Catholic Church, which until then had been obligatory. The liberals of the "Generation of the '80" wanted a country free of ecclesiastic ties and achieved this, perhaps at the cost of putting national leaders in the place of patron saints.

What concerns us here is that the National Council of Education played an active part in the instrumentation of these policies that tended to shape an idea of nationality, strengthened on the basis of a certain paranoia emerging in the dominant classes before the deluge of immigrants.

Education now became strongly regulated and music, an ideal context during school ceremonies, went through the same process. Even in a period still distanced from nationalism like that of the start of the 20th century, the Regulations for Primary Schools published by the *Monitor* established in its Article 22 that "moral and patriotic songs are obligatory for all schools" and in its Article 27 that "during the three days that precede civic holidays, one hour daily will be set aside for readings, recitations and patriotic songs."

It was in 1900, by decree of the Executive Power, that the obligatory teaching of the *Himno Nacional* was established, along with the pieces "La bandera," "Mi bandera," "San Lorenzo," "Tuyutí," "Canción patriótica de 1810," and "Viva la patria."

The method of selection of these songs was rather simple: each year the General Inspection of Music, a body made up of the inspectors who controlled the state of musical teaching in public schools, presented for the consideration of the Council the nominations for songs which were suitable for the official repertoire, the only one authorized to be taught in schools.[224]

By majority vote, the Council approved the inclusion of marches or songs proposed though, in reality, the list did not undergo important changes from year to year, as a more or less canonical list had crystallized around the 1920s. The music teachers had the obligation to "accompany and personally guide students, trying to instill in them greater animation."

By that time, the Argentine state had managed to impose an official liberal history, based on Bartolomé Mitre's account, while *El Monitor de la Educación Común* gave a detailed account of the "school songs" that had to be taught and performed in accordance with each year of primary education. The list included the "Argentine National Anthem," in the lower first grade, and the following year additionally required the "Saludo a la bandera" by Leopoldo Corretjer, "Viva la patria," and the "Himno a Sarmiento." Beginning from third grade and until the final (then sixth) grade, their obligatory nature in school ceremonies was complete and incorporated the "Marcha de San Lorenzo," "Canción nacional," "Himno a la bandera," "Mi bandera," "A los muertos por la patria," "Himno a Rivadavia," and "El tambor de Tacuarí."[225]

The "patriotic song book" has been defined as "the set of patriotic songs established by the public authorities as school repertoire, which must be sung at the different patriotic ceremonies when the dates are celebrated and/or commemorated." It is worth observing that this repertoire, tending to the exaltation of patriotic love, was established as compulsory from third to sixth grade (equivalent to the current seventh) at the primary level for all schools dependent on the National Council of Education.

The song book was made up of the works registered as follows: the "Himno Nacional Argentino" (by Blas Parera and Vicente López y Planes); the songs "Canción patriótica de 1810" (attributed to Esteban de Luca), "La azulada bandera del Plata" (anonymous, attributed to

Blas Parera and harmonized by Josué Teófilo Wilkes); the marches "Mi bandera" (by Juan Imbroisi and Juan Chassaing), "La bandera" (by Pascual Romano and G. J. García), "San Lorenzo" (by Cayetano Silva and Carlos Benielli), "Viva la patria" (by Leopoldo Corretjer and Rafael Obligado), "Marcha del reservista" (by Alberto Cifolelli and Carlos Smith), "Canto al trabajo" (by Cátulo Castillo and Oscar Ivanissevich), "Saludo a la bandera argentina" (by Leopoldo Corretjer) and "Himno a Sarmiento" (by Leopoldo Corretjer).[226]

A thesis on the subject comments, "the analysis of the 'Argentine National Anthem' has been included despite it being a song that surpasses the limits of the school, as it was sung in every type of ceremony, beyond the educational context... *Aurora* (by Héctor Panizza, Héctor Quesada, and Luis Illica) has been considered, even if it was not registered as obligatory, as it was included during the raising of the flag. The 'Himno al libertador general San Martín' (by Arturo Luzzatti y Segundo Argañaraz) has also been considered, for though it was not registered as part of the obligatory song book, it was sung beginning in 1950, which was established as a year of homage to his figure. The analysis of 'Los muchachos peronistas' (anonymous) has been added, because there are indications that this song formed part of the repertoire on the occasion of the patriotic ceremonies during the period studied." In order to form this selection, the National Council of Education ordered polls to research the effects of the music on the emotions of children.

The conclusion of these pioneering survey takers was that the anthem and military marches were an "extremely poewrful generator of love for the country," since according to the children's answers, the reactions produced a certain "pride to be patriotic... something ordered by God; great respect, ... heroism and enthusiasm," and the "desire to laugh and cry at the same time."[227]

The initiatives in this sense soon became controversial. On the one hand, the inspector Miguel Mastroggiani declared: "The honorable National Council of Education, when inagurating the well considered series of measures tending to strengthen in the soul of Argentine children the august feeling of Nation, and to transform the school into the firmest and most indisputable support for the national ideal of our tradition and splendid past, assigned to music, in this great task, the extremely important, it could even be said decisive, role that by its character of poetic vagueness and intense emotism [sic] it is thoroughly able to perform."[228]

Criticism of this position was most clearly expressed by one of the greatest Argentine poets (who was also a journalist for La Prensa), Enrique Banchs. In a text that surprises not only due to its prose but also because it was published in the Monitor itself, he writes: "In our songs the overblown and false patriotism of the parochial newspapers predominates. It has crossed the border that separates the sublime from the ridiculous. [...] The treacherous patriotic-literary aim that engenders those songs is generally decided by San Martín and Belgrano. These are names that should not leave the history texts [...]. Children absolutely lack the notion of proportions in history. A pretty lesson of falsity is imposed upon them, then, when presenting to them these agents of Independence with uncharacteristically colossal profiles, great to the point of stupidity. The reality is that they were human and did no more than fulfill their duty. Maybe instilling a child with the notion that these men fulfilled their duty and did things inspired by reason and not delirium, he will feel able to do what they did in similar circumstances. As long as they represent for the child's mind swellings of genius, divinity, the infinite, they are immoral models, because their life does not offer itself to imitation. They cannot even be loved [...] Historical literature, when it is created with criteria that foment the wondrous and heroic, has for a child the danger that obsessed by the brilliance of the past, he does not leave his circle, and scorns the present time for being vulgar and low, not fit to be dedicated any effort [...] It would be worth more for children to know that all times are overwhelmingly similar; that vulgarity is the heritage of all the human ages." Banchs continued: "The current school song which assumes the main part of teaching tends, like an arrow toward the target, to fix in the mood of children the idea that being an Argentine is an exceptional privilege, a letter affirming nobility. The honor of being born in Argentine territory is a fortune shared with numerous families of insects. Our ancestors did some remarkable things, for example win battles. The child venerates the past glories but does not take credit for them. He played no part in those roles."[229]

And what about *Aurora*? It is worth noting that, despite the success the "Canción de la bandera" had in its debut at the Colón in 1908, and the two recordings that began to circulate of it, no educational authority considered the aria of an Italian opera suitable music for shaping the desired national identity, especially as its text was not in Spanish, which was and remains the official language of Argentina.

Equally adverse had been the fate, three years before, of the school hymn the newspaper *La Prensa* had entrusted to its guest Giacomo Puccini: "Dios y patria" (God and Homeland), the only work with text in Spanish that was set to music by the composer from Lucca, who wrote it in Buenos Aires. Sent to the Council by the powerful newspaper, in spite of its illustrious author and catchy and simple music, it did not receive even the consideration of the official agency, falling into oblivion until its rediscovery in 2006.[230]

But in itself the title of Puccini's work already predicted that the efforts by the liberals to replace religious saints with military heroes would end up generating a symbolic structure and social mentality more than favorable for the establishment of the Argentine Catholic nationalism that would begin in the 1930s.

According to Carlos Escudé, the seed of nationalism goes back precisely to the year 1908, with the assumption of José María Ramos Mejía to the head of the National Council of Education. With his project, he "buried the spirit of Act No. 1.420, which had guided education with views to progress, in this way getting rid of its liberal and progressive character in which a direct relationship had been established between education and economy. Distancing himself from Sarmiento's liberalism, Mejía imposed a model that subordinated the individual to the State, inculcating undisputed norms and leaving only the forms without the content of European civilization. This project came close to authoritarian and dogmatic nationalism, imbued with jingoism and militarism. Its actions to manipulate consciences preached unquestionable moral values, achieving the brainwashing that would conclude in what Mejía called the construction of the *homo patrioticus.*"[231]

It is in this context that the great paradox of Panizza's *Aurora* is produced: harshly criticized by the rising nationalism, years later —when it was fully established— the "Canción de la bandera" started to be taken as an emblem of this same tendency, through the "opportune" operation of translating it into Spanish, as Rodolfo Arizaga put it.[232]

Proof of this paradox is that the most severe of Panizza's detractors in 1908 —Miguel Mastroggiani, the Inspector of Music working on the Council, and Julio V. Ochoa, his unfortunate batterer during the decade of the '40s from his managerial post at the Colón— were an active part of the nationalist tendencies that ended up imposing Panizza's hymn and forging the circle of relations within which the composer-conductor moved ideologically to the end of his days, without coming to evaluate the political consequences that this event might assume.

In 1948, during Perón's first presidency, the National Council of Education, an autonomous body within the Ministry of Justice and Public Instruction, began to function under the brand-new Secretary's Office of Education. (It could not be given the rank of Ministry because the National Constitution of 1853 limited the number of departments to eight, which was modified with the Constitution of 1949.)

First as Secretary's Office of State and later as Ministry, education came to have an exclusive government department overseen by a figure who would be key in the passage of *Aurora* from an aria of Italian opera to an obligatory school song: Oscar Ivanissevich. He was an Argentine doctor, of Croatian ancestry, who promoted a nationalist educational policy with Catholic roots. He was given a copy of the translation of *Aurora* that had been sung during the evening of July 9, 1945, while under the presidency of Farrell (with Colonel Perón as vice president *de facto*). When Ivanissevich held the role of minister he established the obligatory nature of the "Canción de la bandera" at the moment of raising and lowering the national flag, notwithstanding the various marches and songs mentioned that refer to the national insignia. His decree was endorsed by the then-President Perón.

The reason for adding one more song to so many existing ones about the national flag may seem curious. The symbol had taken on greater prominence since the "Pledge to the flag" was established in 1909 and the form of the oath was approved for all schools in the country. In 1945 several pieces had already been in force for some time: the song *La azulada bandera del Plata*, attributed to Blas Parera, today unknown; the already mentioned march *La bandera*, dedicated to Mastrogianni (which begins with the famous verses: "Glorious ensign of my country, / the Paraná in its breezes wrapped round you"); the even more used "Mi bandera," subtitled "Patriotic song of the Argentine army" ("Here is the idolized flag, / the ensign Belgrano bequeathed to us"); and the "Greeting to the Argentine Flag" by Corretjer (which begins with the verses "All hail Argentina, blue and white flag, / shred of the sky where the sun reigns"), also sung to this day.

Faced with such competition, the "Canción de la Bandera" posed significant *a priori* obstacles: the text does not contain "expressions about equality, the people, family, work, echoes in other peoples, freedom, heroism, or fidelity to the flag, just as no resonant images are noted," while the music, as has been said, "does not present any element that can be assimilated to the national forms of composition, whether folkloric or native."[233]

In the column of assets, it was said that "some content coincides with the principles that would see the construction of national identity for the Peronist project be made visible in different textual units [...] The principle 'love for country' is materialized in the content about 'country' which in the text says: 'It is the flag of my country (...)' whose

continuation '(...) of the risen sun that God has given me' is displayed
in the content about 'God' that refers to the stated 'Christian values.'
Even if there is not an explicit materialization of the stated 'memory
of the heroic action of the leaders,' which is expressed in the content
about 'glory,' the text which says: 'High in the sky, a warrior eagle /
bravely rises in triumphal flight' can be considered to be referring to
this expression, as it can be inferred that the glory is a consequence of
the triumph of which the verse speaks. As far as literary resources, the
expression repeated three times in the text: 'it is the flag of my country, /
of the risen sun God has given me' provides an account of the alliance
between the Argentine nation and divinity, which is the projection of
the rapprochement of State and Church that has characterized school
life during the greater part of the 20th century."[234]

To this analysis a peculiar trait can be added: far from being a military
march, the "Canción de la bandera," with its slow tempo and melodic
lyricism, in every case resembles the most widespread songs that Catholic
parishioners sang in the churches. The tendency to slow down and
generate undue *rubatos* that its musical discourse permits, along with the
ostinato of its accompaniment, goes perfectly with the plaintive rhetoric
which had come to almost exclusively characterize the musical side
of the Catholic liturgy in Argentina, whose greatest exponent was the
nationalist song whose refrain prays: "All hail divine focus of love, / all
hail the Argentine people, Sacred Heart." In fact, not a few times "Alta
en el cielo" has been alluded to as a secular prayer, whose final dramatic
effect is the statement in first person: "It is the flag of my country," which
gives prominence to the subject who sings.

As the merits or strengths of the lyrics were therefore quite relative,
no doubt Ivanissevich's own enthusiasm must be taken into account to
explain the decision that *Aurora* would be added to the well-stocked
mandatory book of school songs about the flag.

History gave one more proof of the functionary's persistent enthusiasm.
With the return of General Perón to the government in 1973, Ivanissevich

returned to overseeing the Ministry of Education, putting into place policies that tended to silence the movements of the left then highly active in Argentina, which he pompously came to call the "Ivanissevich Mission." On September 10, 1974, Teacher's Day, with Perón now deceased and his widow María Estela Martínez in the presidential chair, Ivanissevich delivered a speech at the Teatro Colón about the state of education. In it he said: "We create with Perón the first Ministry of Education in the Republic. Every morning at the schools the Argentine flag was raised to the chords of the march *Aurora*, which instills in teachers and students an emotional state of self-improvement."[235]

One week later, through Resolution 158, the Ministry established the following:

Buenos Aires, September 18, 1974.

Art. 1 — Mandate that in the teaching establishments dependent on this Ministry the proceeding will be to sing the verses of the song "Aurora" by maestro Héctor Panizza at the moment of performing the raising of the national flag.

Art. 2 — The National Council of Education and National Council of Technical Education are invited to adopt the same behavior in the establishments of their respective jurisdictions.

Art. 3 — [De forma].[236]

The National Council of Education finally disappeared in 1978, when the military dicatorship began the transference of the primary schools to the provinces and what was then the Muncipality of the City of Buenos Aires, a process that concluded in the 1990s with the transfer of the secondary schools. The Argentine national state practically ceased to administer the primary and secondary schools, but reserved the right to implement educational policies at the federal level.

With the coming of democracy, which emerged during the delegation from the national state to the provincial autonomies, the obligatory nature of the school songs passed to being one more alternative before a line-up of popular songs, even commercial music, fated to substitute for the military marches and nationalist songs that had fallen into discredit.

In spite of this, the "Canción de la bandera," its obligatory nature now relaxed, continued to be sung in many of the country's schools and remains the solitary prop by which the name of Héctor Panizza is still known in Argentina.

THE COMPOSER AT THE PRESENT

This essential digression now complete, one fact is beyond doubt: today Panizza's music has been forgotten, partially left to one side in Argentina, and completely ignored throughout the rest of the world. If it is often complex to join an international canon from a peripheral place like Argentina, the national duality of Panizza and development of his career in places absolutely central in the west could compensate for that disadvantage of origin; even so, they were not enough to grant him a lasting fame.

It is difficult to say if this oblivion is deserved or not, or if Panizza's legacy will gain more attention in the near future. The exact cause of his obscurity is unknown, and it is necessary to formulate some considerations, to reflect on certain variables that may have provoked this result.

The first consideration is of a practical order and strongly supported by evidence: Panizza did not at any time privilege his compositional activity; he even came to express himself openly in that sense. From his youth, frenetic activity as music director prevented him from composing with regularity, which is necessary in order to produce a more substantive number of works and achieve stylistic development and qualitative improvement.

The second consideration is of a historical and contextual nature: Héctor grew up studying, reading, and listening to the music of the Italian *Giovane Scuola* of Puccini, Mascagni, Leoncavallo, Giordano, Catalani, Cilea, Franchetti, and Perosi. This school presented a program that broke with the past and advocated for the elimination of fixed acts in the opera and for a richer orchestration. These were innovations that had been deployed by the mature Verdi, and naturally by Wagner in Germany, but at the same time they guaranteed certain continuity as far as the importance of vocal and instrumental melody in a tonal, harmonic scheme. Panizza did not desire to move from this position and, in fact, never did.

The third consideration is a direct consequence of the previous one and comes from Héctor himself, who —as we previously saw— justified his preference for conducting over composition by affirming that his style was what we have just summarized and not the one gradually taking its place thanks to Respighi, Pizzetti, Pick-Mangiagalli, Malipiero, Casella, de Sabata, Menotti, and the atonal composers. Héctor himself felt, then, that his music was "set back" significantly in relation to the more modern taste, and so it seemed to him prudent to desist from musical creation or to foster it the least amount possible.[237]

The fourth consideration is ours: we believe that of all the composers of the period whom Panizza respected and admired, the one who most closely shared his form of writing was his personal friend Umberto Giordano. Giordano was the author of fifteen operas (if one includes the first one, *Marina*, which was unfinished; the second version of *Siberia*; and *Giove e Pompei*, composed with Franchetti). These were solidly written from the musical point of view, reasonably functional in their drama, and without pretentions to contributing extraordinary novelties to the contemporary opera scene.

Of all of his compositions, *Andrea Chénier* is the only one that has been established in the international repertoire and discreetly maintains itself to this day. It is thus worth wondering why only his *Chénier* survived the test of time. Perhaps because, unlike the rest of his creations, it is full of the melodically inspired romanzas the public easily retains and remembers with pleasure: three for tenor ("Un dì all'azzurro spazio;" "Sì, fui soldato;" "Come un bel dì di maggio"), two for baritone ("Son sessant'anni, oh vecchio, che tu servi;" "Nemico della patria") and one, particularly heart-rending, for soprano ("La mamma morta"). Six inspired romanzas— in addition to an equally effective couple of duets and finale— can no doubt determine the success and inclusion in the current repertoire of an opera, which otherwise might have been judged as minor.

What can be concluded from what we have just mentioned? Panizza's operas closely follow Giordano's model: they are written with comparable musical skill, a similar dramatic functionality, and a seeming lack of revolutionary pretensions; but none of them contain a comparable number of moments that are authentically memorable for the average listener. And something similar can be said of the rest of his works.

Whoever listens to *Andrea Chénier* for the first time —then as now— very possibly leaves the theater at the end of the performance singing four or five of the six fragments noted above. Whoever attends a performance of *Aurora* upon returning home will in all probability not retain more than the "Canción de la bandera," a song of quality comparable to those of Giordano... but only one.

Finally, the symphonic and above all operatic production of Panizza is not exactly characterized by its technical simplicity or low cost of production. Only a major opera house can dispose of the economic and artistic means to properly produce one of the three great operas by our biographical subject, each one of which requires a cast with powerful voices, a large choir, and an excellent orchestra, as well as a new staging production, considered especially for the specific occasion and therefore expensive in the case of possible revivals or subsequent tours.

The recent crisis and current restructuring of the international opera market calls for prudence and encourages seasons that tend to be conservative, made up of popular titles with an assured success; to aim to revive a difficult, expensive, and unknown work by a rarely performed composer is an aspiration that is challenging to realize.

Perhaps in this chain of intertwined factors there exists the subtle but definite difference between the relative endurance of a part of Giordano's creation and the almost non-existence of that of Panizza, in particular within a genre like that of the opera, in which the constant favor of a numerous public is fundamental: where Umberto knew how to save himself partially and *in extremis*, Héctor remained hardly below the minimum of required melody.

As if all the previous were not enough, we have seen that in his own country Panizza was universally accepted as a conductor but often attacked as a composer for his lack of "national commitment" at the melodic level and even for the "Wagnerianism" of his orchestral writing. Such can be the cruel and sometimes unfair mechanism of selection by the public and by history (in this case, the history of music).

CHAPTER 8

THE CONDUCTOR

As occurred with some of his more or less contemporary important Italian colleagues — Luigi Mancinelli, Gino Marinuzzi, and above all Victor de Sabata, not to mention Pietro Mascagni— Héctor Panizza was at the same time a composer and a conductor, and this is the way he liked to introduce himself.

As we have seen, he considered being a pianist a simple —and in those years, almost inevitable— part of his musical education: a useful working tool at the hour of studying, composing, and rehearsing, but nothing else. He never sought to introduce himself in public as an instrumentalist, contrary to what happened with famous conductors like Leonard Bernstein or, to mention the example of one of Panizza's contemporaries, Antonino Votto.[238]

A simple walk through his professional path, however, shows that what made Panizza known, and permitted him to develop an international career as successful as it was lucrative, was his ability on the podium, from which he dominated a repertoire as vast as it was heterogenous with absolute reliability.

Once he graduated from the Conservatory in Milan where he was "discovered" by the head of the institution, Antonio Bazzini, Héctor quickly took control of the profession of "maestro concertatore," at first working as a "substitute" —today we would say "assistant conductor" or "coach"— in the opera under the orders of Edoardo Mascheroni, the prestigious conductor of *La Wally's* and *Falstaff's* world premieres, much appreciated by Verdi. Thus the young man soon found himself in conditions to climb onstage, passing from the piano to the podium.

A fervent admirer of Felix Weingartner, a good friend of Hans Richter, and finally a close collaborator of Arturo Toscanini, by diverse circumstances Héctor Panizza is today a conductor who is less known internationally than the others mentioned, even in the land where he was born and in Italy where his parents and children were born. But it is fair to say that the quantity, variety, and quality of his presentation as a conductor make him by all rights equivalent to those authentic idols of the baton. Not in vain were his talents admired and explicitly endorsed by composers as unlike as Boito, Charpentier, Giordano, Puccini, Richard Strauss, and Zandonai.

At the performing level, Panizza's art is clearly located in the wake of Toscanini, even before he worked with the great conductor of Parma. If the latter chose him as his main collaborator during the golden age of La Scala in Milan, it is because he had evidently already identified in the Argentine maestro a style of work and aesthetic ideals similar to his own.

The years of working elbow to elbow with Arturo would do the rest, and would end up shaping Héctor as a "Toscaninian" conductor: absolutely committed to his work, energetic, precise, perfectionist, demanding with his musicians, faithful to the letter, and even more loyal to the spirit of the works he had to perform.

REPERTOIRE WITHOUT BOUNDARIES

Héctor Panizza studied and conducted an impressive number of compositions in all genres, spanning the opera, ballet, symphonic-choral repertoire, concerts for soloist and orchestra, and symphonic works.

The heart of Panizza's repertoire was of course the musical theater; it included more than 120 operas from some sixty composers, which range from the baroque to world premieres, beginning with Jean-Philippe Rameau and arriving at Gian Carlo Menotti; between the birth of the first and death of the second there stretch a trifling 324 years.

This repertoire included many indisputable masterpieces and several minor pieces, along with titles unusual for their time and better known in ours, and vice versa. The maestro's scope of interest showed hardly any limitations on style or nationality, and without prejudice he often conducted French, German, and Russian operas in Italian translation, which furthermore was common practice then; the "almost" prevails for, as far as one knows, Panizza never conducted atonal works. In a time in which it was extremely unusual to listen to older music, Héctor took charge of a remarkable baroque opera: Rameau's *Castor et Pollux*. Equally unusual and absolutely significant was the interest he showed in Gluck, with repeated interpretations of *Orfeo ed Euridice*, *Alceste*, *Armide*, *Iphigénie en Tauride*, and *Iphigénie en Aulide*. (This interest was partly shared with Toscanini and later inherited by the most Toscaninian maestro of our days, Riccardo Muti, who conducted and recorded several operas by Gluck.)

For reasons difficult to imagine, Mozart's operas were scarcely represented in Panizza's repertoire, which only included somewhat late performances of *Le Nozze di Figaro* and *Don Giovanni*, though with great success. Other rarely frequented composers whom he offered, besides the genius from Salzburg, were as dissimilar as Cimarosa's *Il matrimonio segreto*, Spontini's *Fernando Cortez*, Halévy's *La juive*, and Meyerbeer's *Les Huguenots* and *Dinorah*.

The *bel canto* is present in his repertoire with several traditional titles and a couple that in his years were not so, with a certain predilection for the serious genre over the comic, perhaps dictated by his own personality: Rossini's *Il barbiere di Siviglia, Mosè,* and *Guglielmo Tell;* Donizetti's *Don Pasquale, Lucia di Lammermoor, L'elisir d'amore, Lucrezia Borgia,* and *Linda di Chamounix;* and Bellini's *Norma, I puritani,* and *La sonnambula.* Proceeding in tentative chronological order by composer, we will also mention his performances of Von Flotow' s *Martha,* Thomas' *Mignon* and two operas by Gounod: *Faust* and *Roméo et Juliette.*

As in the case of Toscanini, the central place in Panizza's dramatic repertoire was occupied by Wagnerian dramas and Verdian operas. Héctor was one of the greatest promoters of Wagner's music in Italy, one more reason to regret that in his native country he was not permitted to diligently conduct the operas of that composer whom he admired so much and knew so well. He was the interpreter of almost the entire traditional Wagnerian canon: *Der fliegende Holländer, Lohengrin, Tannhäuser, Tristan und Isolde, Parsifal,* and the complete *Ring: Das Rheingold, Die Walküre, Siegfried,* and *Götterdämerung.*

Panizza bore Verdi's style in the blood, just like his famous colleague from Parma. And Verdi was perhaps the composer who brought the most unanimous success to Panizza, who was constantly praised on both the European and North American continents for his extraordinary renderings of *La traviata, Aïda, Simon Boccanegra, Falstaff, Otello, Il trovatore, Un ballo in maschera, Macbeth, Don Carlo, Rigoletto, Ernani, La forza del destino,* and even a much less known work like *I lombardi alla prima crociata.*

To confirm the high reputation Héctor enjoyed as an interpreter of Verdi, it is sufficient to note two brief excerpts of criticism published by the press of Buenos Aires, which are representative of dozens of other similar reviews. About his *Boccanegra* at the Teatro Colón it was written: "Maestro Héctor Panizza reedited his dramatic and nuanced version of 1935, achieving a perfect adjustment of the difficult choral sections, in which he translated the feelings of the masses and protagonists with singular vigor. The audience awarded the performances of all with warm applause."[239]

A few years later, the critics' admiration for his Verdian approach continued unfazed: "At the Teatro Colón the opera *Aïda* resumed its tradition last night with rare success. It must be said that on this occasion everything matched to put in evidence the unfading beauties of Verdi's universal creation. Héctor Panizza served him with prestige and enthusiasm, before a scene with first-class singers and counting on an orchestra of the first rank, who responded to all his demands."[240]

Aïda always brought him tremendous success, no matter the place it fell to him to conduct it. About his performances at the Met it was said: "He was always happy to go somewhat beyond in his expressive inflection, adjusting the phrasing to favor spontaneity and —I am thinking above all of the several broadcasts of *Aida*— slowing down significantly during emotionally charged passages. The richly ironic lack of the initial reference of Amneris to Aïda *alla Panizza* is a good example. And the entrance of Aida indicated by his baton can be so sad and fragile in its unhurried speed that one seems to see the eyes of Radamès always following this endangered creature with great love over the big stage."[241] Other works frequented with success were Offenbach's *Les contes d' Hoffmann* and Filippo Marchetti's *Ruy Blas*; Ponchielli's *La Gioconda* and *Il figliuol prodigo*; Saint-Saëns' *Samson et Dalila*, Delibe's *Lakmé*, *Maria Tudor* by the talented Brazilian Carlos Gomes and Bizet's *Carmen*, in addition to Mussorgsky's *Boris Godunov* and *Khovanchina*. Panizza was also a respected interpreter of Boito's *Mefistofele*, a composer with whom he cultivated a very friendly relationship based on mutual admiration.

Panizza also conducted Massenet's *Manon*, *Thaïs*, *Le roi de Lahore*, *Grisélidis*, and *Cléopatre*; Rimsky-Korsakov' s *The Tale of Tsar Saltan* and *Sadkó*; *Loreley*, *La falce*, *Dejanice*, *La Wally* by Catalani (the composer so admired by Toscanini), and Humperdinck' s *Hänsel und Gretel*.

Another very substantial chapter in his work as *maestro concertatore* was due to Puccini, with *Turandot* (with conducting starting from the fourth performance of its first production, as we have seen), *Tosca*, *La bohème*, *Madama Butterfly*, *Manon Lescaut*, *La fanciulla del West* (his reduction for orchestra was commissioned and praised by Puccini himself), *Il trittico* made up by *Il tabarro*, *Suor Angelica*, and *Gianni Schicchi*, *La rondine*, and even the youthful *Le Villi*; in short, all of the dramatic work by the maestro from Lucca, with the single exception of *Edgar*, undoubtedly the composer's weakest opera.

As has already been mentioned, Panizza enjoyed Puccini's explicit admiration. Friendly short letters written after Puccini heard Panizza conduct *Madama Butterfly* and *Manon Lescaut* (one of them in verse, mentioned above) bear witness to this, and include a letter Puccini wrote in 1910 to the musicologist and cellist Maurice Kufferath, co-director of the Théâtre Royal of the Monnaie in Brussels: "I know that in Brussels in May, for the exhibition at the Monnaie, there will also be Italian opera. And I also know they are looking for an orchestra conductor. I recommend to you maestro Ettore Panizza, who conducts at Covent Garden. He is an artist of uncommon merit and experience." The recommendation fell on deaf ears, but this was not too important.[242]

Authors contemporary to the great Tuscan composer mentioned in Panizza's contracts were Franchetti (*Germania, La figlia di Iorio,* and *Cristoforo Colombo*), Mascagni (not only the popular *Cavalleria rusticana,* but also *Iris, Zanetto, Lodoletta,* and *Isabeau,* the opera premiered by its own composer in Buenos Aires), Dukas (*Ariane et Barbebleue*), Cilea (*Adriana Lecouvreur*) and his much-admired Giordano (*Andrea Chénier, Fedora, Siberia, Madame Sans-Gêne,* and *Mese mariano*). Panizza also conducted *Louise* by Charpentier, an author who had a special esteem for him.

Another creator from the same time who especially trusted Panizza as performer of his works —even coming to record his praises in writing — was Richard Strauss. Our maestro conducted his *Der Rosenkavalier,*

Elektra, and *Salomé* and in 1932, Strauss praised the Ambrosian *Elektra* via letter and requested that the Teatro Colón assign the concert to Panizza when it chose its music directors. The original, translated from French, says:

> Dear friend and companion: back from Garmisch, I still remember with enthusiasm and great appreciation the magnificent *Elettra* [in Italian, in the original] from Milan, which you have conducted with all of your delicacy and impetus, satisfying all my boldest desires. I understand that the intention exists of offering *Elettra* in Buenos Aires this summer and I have been told you will probably be the music director at the Teatro Colón. In this case, I have only one wish: that you also conduct my *Elettra* in Buenos Aires, as I do not know a better interpreter. Will this be possible? I ask you to give my greetings to your marvelous orchestra and excellent artists who work onstage and behind the scenes, my greetings to señor Trentigallio [Trentinaglia?], and my most sincere friendship to you and Mrs. Panizza, also on the part of my wife. From your very sincerely devoted and grateful
>
> [signature] Richard Strauss.[243]

The artistic managers of the Colón —to the great frustration of the Italian-Argentine— preferred to count on German conductors for the German repertoire so that, once again, a famous recommendation was of no use.

In addition to this, Panizza personally conducted two of his own four operas —*Aurora* and *Bizancio*— as well as those of many authors who were his contemporaries, today almost completely forgotten.

Some composers born between 1868 and 1884 —from the same generation as Panizza, who was born in 1875— formed part of the repertoire of our biographical subject, such as Frédéric D'Erlanger (*Tess*), Elmerico Fracassi (*Finlandia*), Attilio Parelli (world debut of *Fanfulla*), Ubaldo Pacchierotti (*Il santo* and debut of *Eidelberga mia!*), Vittorio Gnecchi (*Cassandra*), Ezio Camussi (*La Dubarry*), Arrigo Pedrollo (*Delitto e castigo*),

Vincenzo Michetti (*Maria di Magdala* and *La Maddalena*), Francesco Santoliquido (*La favola di Helda*), Luigi Ferrari Trecate (*La bella e il mostro*), and Lamberto Pavanelli (*Vanna*). In other words, operas that very possibly no reader has had the chance to hear a single note.

Some titles and names from the same generation that in certain cases are a bit more familiar to the opera-going public of today are Henri Rabaud's *Marouf*, Franco Alfano's *Il principe Zilah*, Italo Montemezzi's *L'amore dei tre re*, Ottorino Respighi's *La campana sommersa*, Ildebrando Pizzetti's *Lo straniero*, Riccardo Pick-Mangiagalli's *Basi e bote* and Gian Francesco Malipiero's *Giulio Cesare*.

Héctor's collaboration with Ermanno Wolf-Ferrari was important, with the latter presenting the Milan premiere of *Sly* —taken up again in our time as a vehicle for the brilliance of José Carreras and Plácido Domingo— and additionally conducting *I quatro rusteghi*, *Il segreto di Susanna*, *La vita nova*, *I gioielli della Madonna* and *La vedova scaltra*. No less relevant was Panizza's relationship with Riccardo Zandonai, who had a blind confidence in Panizza's talent, to the point of trusting to him the absolute premieres of *Francesca da Rimini* (in Turin) as well as *Conchita* and *Melenis* (both in Milan). From Guido Bianchini, an Italian composer born only two years after Zandonai, Panizza directed *Thien-Hoa*.

In addition to presenting for the first time in America *Svanda the Bagpiper* by the Czech Jaromír Weinberger, Panizza showed a great aesthetic range and inexhaustible enthusiasm for study, taking upon himself the world premieres of operas as dissimilar as Pietro Canonica's *La sposa di Corinto*, Edoardo Berlendis' *Il pastore*, Felipe Boero's *El matrero*, Giuseppe Pietri's *Maristella*, Raúl Espoile's *La ciudad roja*, Victor de Sabata's *Il macigno* and John Seymour's *In the Pasha's Garden*, in addition to Gian Carlo Menotti's *The Island God* (in the Italian version *Ilo e Zeus*).

Some sources mention that Panizza conducted the first performance of Alfredo Casella's ballet *Il convento veneziano* (also known by the French title of *Le couvent sous l'eau*), performed in Milan, apparently in 1925. The information is plausible, all the more so since a studio recording of two excerpts from this ballet exists, conducted by Panizza. To this can be added the "mimo-symphonic comedy" *Il carillon magico* by Riccardo Pick-Mangiagalli, a choreographic work conceptually similar to Bartók's *The Miraculous Mandarin.*[244]

As far as the symphonic, choral, and symphonic-choral repertoire that Héctor Panizza embraced —along with numerous orchestral highlights belonging to operas by authors familiar to him whom we have already mentioned— there is also an enormous variety of large and small scores, as immortal then as they are today relegated to oblivion.

The heterogeneous list of composers he took on in concert —or in the recording studio— includes the names Alfano, Amfitheatrof, Bach, Bartók, Beethoven, Boccherini, Boëllmann, Brahms, Casella, Tchaikovsky, Cimarosa, Corelli, Coronaro, Debussy, de Falla, de Sabata, D'Indy, Dohnányi, Dvořák, Elgar, Ferrari Trecate, Gianneo, Glazunov, Guastavino, Haydn, Holst, Imbroisi, Lalo, Liadov, López Buchardo, Mancinelli, Martucci, Mendelssohn, Mozart, Nápravník, Pedrollo, Perosi, Pick-Mangiagalli, Piaggio, Pizzetti, Prokofiev, Rabaud, Rachmaninoff, Ravel, Respighi, Rossini, Scarlatti, Schumann, Scriabin, Sebastiani, Sibelius, Sinigaglia, Sonzogno, Strauss, Stravinsky, Vivaldi, Wagner, Vaughan Williams, Weber, Williams, Zamacois, and Zandonai.[245]

To this list (which is not complete, but is at least highly indicative) it can be added that Panizza also conducted his own orchestral works, such as the *Nocturno, Theme and Variations,* and the symphonic-choral poem *The King and the Forest.*

Collaboration with Soloists

More than six decades of uninterrupted work on the podium and visiting the principal musical centers of Europe and America, put Héctor Panizza in direct contact with the best soloists of various generations, as much in the instrumental category as —above all— in the vocal. Practically all the best singers from the Italian, French, and German schools who were active between the final years of the 19th century and the first half of the 20th century featured in his performances.

Of course it is impossible and unnecessary to mention them exhaustively. Because of this the following will include only a panoramic vision of names still familiar today. On occasion, brief references to a singer mentioned in the world premieres of important operas are added, so the reader can have a clearer idea of the historical relevance of some of them. (The artists are mentioned from upper to lower register and, within each voice, ordered by chronological order of birth.)

Panizza had the opportunity to work with authentic divas of the soprano voice. Let us recall the names of Hariclea Darclée (the protagonist of *Tosca*'s world premiere), Nellie Melba, Luisa Tetrazzini, Selma Kurz, Rosina Storchio (who created the role of *Madama Butterfly*), Maria Farneti (the creator of the leading role of *Aurora*), Emmy Destinn (the first protagonist of Strauss' *Salomé*), and Geneviève Vix (who participated in the premiere of Ravel's *L' heure espagnole*).

The somewhat younger sopranos with whom he worked include Lucrezia Bori, the "divine" Claudia Muzio (the first Giorgietta in *Il tabarro* and first protagonist of Zandonai's *Melenis*, whose premiere was conducted by Panizza himself, as has been mentioned) and Gilda Dalla Rizza (the creator of the role of Magda in Puccini's *La rondine*). The career of the British Eva Turner received strong backing on the part of Héctor, who also worked with Giannina Arangi-Lombardi, Rosa Raisa (the first protagonist of *Turandot*), Rosa Ponselle, Lily Pons, and Grace Moore.

Some notable interpreters with the same vocal range who sang under the Italian-Argentine maestro's baton were Gina Cigna, Bidu Sayão, Maria Caniglia (creator, among others, of the role of Rossana in Alfano's *Cyrano di Bergerac*), Zinka Milanov, Rose Bampton, Jarmila Novotná, Licia Albanese, and the unforgettable Victoria de los Ángeles.

From the Teatro Colón in Buenos Aires our director also spread the names of two young Argentine sopranos who would give much to speak about, the first as a relevant figure from the porteño opera house itself and the second as a star at the Metropolitan Opera in New York: Helena Arizmendi, the disciple of María Barrientos who made her first lead debut at the Colón as Mimì in Puccini's *La bohème*, and Delia Rigal, introduced as Amelia in Verdi's *Simon Boccanegra*.

Among the mezzosopranos and contraltos who sang at Panizza's orders at least seven artists deserve to be remembered, five of them Italian: the exuberant Gabriella Besanzoni; Conchita Supervía from Spain; Gianna Pederzini, a member of the cast in the world premiere of Poulenc's *Dialogues des Carmélites*; Bruna Castagna, who after a shining but brief career chose Argentina as his country of residence; Ebe Stignani, with a torrential voice; Risë Stevens from the United States; and the great Fedora Barbieri, who died in 2003.

The list of tenors who shared operatic productions with our conductor is simply overwhelming and allows us to mention a colossus of this vocal range whom Panizza did not come to conduct but did accompany on the piano during rehearsals. While in a Buenos Aires radio interview in the '60s, Héctor commented that the first Verdian Othello Francesco Tamagno's voice was so powerful that it "had left him deaf."[246]

We must name, in chronological order, at least the following tenors who performed under our artist's baton: Alessandro Bonci, Giuseppe Borgatti (the first protagonist of Giordano's *Andrea Chénier*), Amedeo Bassi (a great favorite of Panizza, who chose him to debut *Medio Evo latino* as well as *Aurora*), the legendary Enrico Caruso (the first Dick Johnson in *La fanciulla del West*, who sang the only two performances of *Chénier* during his career in London in 1907, with Panizza on the podium), Leo Slezak, Giovanni Zenatello (the creator of Pinkerton in *Madama Butterfly*), and John McCormack.

Somewhat younger than the preceding list, the following singers also performed with Héctor: the great Aureliano Pertile (who was featured in the first casts of operas as dissimilar as Boito's *Nerone*, Wolf-Ferrari's *Sly*, Felipe Boero's *Tucumán* and Constantino Gaito's *Ollantay*), Giovanni

Martinelli (who debuted Zandonai's *Melenis* with Panizza) and Francesco Merli; an authentically Olympian Italian trio made up of Tito Schipa, Beniamino Gigli —who referred to Héctor as a "god"— and Giacomo Lauri-Volpi; and also René Maison, Galliano Masini, Georges Thill, Jan Kiepura, Raoul Jobin, and Jussi Björling.

The list of baritones and basses who also had the opportunity to work with the maestro was significant as well. The legendary Mattia Battistini, Mario Ancona (the first Silvio in *Pagliacci*), Antonio Scotti, Mario Sammarco (creator of the role of Gérard in *Andrea Chénier*), Marcel Journet, Eugenio Giraldoni (Scarpia in the debut of *Tosca*) and the deep bass Mansueto Gaudio.

To this list can be added Riccardo Stracciari, Titta Ruffo (who participated in the first performance of *Aurora*), Vanni Marcoux, Nazzareno De Angelis, Giuseppe Danise (the initial interpreter of Victor de Sabata's *Il macigno*, whose premiere was not directed by Panizza, as will be remembered), Carlo Galeffi (the first Manfredo in Montemezzi's *L'amore dei tre re*), Tancredi Pasero, Ezio Pinza, Lawrence Tibbett, and Salvatore Baccaloni, the principal performer of the comic repertoire for bass in his time.

Regarding the bass voices born in the 20th century, we can mention the Hungarian Alexander De Svéd and the Italian Gino Bechi. In this context, the case of the baritone Leonard Warren is interesting, as he was discovered and launched to stardom by Panizza with the role of Paolo in *Simon Boccanegra* at the New York Met, and he was an artist whom Panizza also later occupied himself personally to hire in Buenos Aires.

Panizza's interaction with the Argentine Carlos Guichandut is also notable, as he had him debut as a baritone as the lead in *Rigoletto* at the Teatro Colón. Among the historical singers of the porteño opera house it is not too much to remember the special regard of our director for the Italian-Argentine baritone Ángel Mattiello, already mentioned.

The profession of opera stage director was just starting to become independent in the years Panizza found himself active as *maestro concertatore*, but this did not prevent him from presiding over performances whose *régie* was in the care of artists as emblematic as the poet Gabriele D'Annunzio. The list of stage directors with whom Panizza worked includes the names of Giovacchino Forzano (Puccini's librettist), Margarita Wallmann, Otto Erhardt, Carlo Piccinato, Josef Gielen, Marcello Govoni, Lothar Wallerstein, and Mario Frigerio.

Faithful to the Toscaninian concept that the opera's music director was also generally responsible for everything shown to the audience, Panizza never stopped personally overseeing the quality and coherence of the staging. Delia Rigal remembered that, on the occasion of his first *Armide* at the Colón (1945), "despite being the conductor, nothing that happened onstage was external to him. In that time, the conductor's influence was also very great on the stage and was respected. Panizza was very meticulous."[247]

Even if Panizza's activity as symphonic conductor was undoutedly inferior in quantity to his work at the opera house, it would be hasty to say the same about its quality. Even if the detail of the artist's activity at concerts is somewhat more difficult to reconstruct for the contemporary researcher, there are indications of its variety and excellence, even reflected in his interesting discography. We know, for example, that in addition to conducting concert versions of operas with the singers already mentioned, he accompanied the pianists Rudolf Firkusny (Czech), Mieczyslaw Horszowski (Polish), Alexander Borowsky (Russian) and Mario Zanfi (Italian), the violinist Franz von Vecsey (Hungarian), and the cellists Arturo Bonucci and Onorina Semino (Italian).

Within the Argentine milieu, he also directed pianists like Lía Cimaglia Espinosa, Roberto Locatelli and Marisa Regules, the violinist Rodolfo Zubrisky, and the Pessina Quartet, led by the maestro Carlos Pessina.

MUSICAL GEOGRAPHY

Contrary to what tends to happen today, a few decades ago the great artistic careers in the field of cultured music were not limited to the major cities of the world; they included them in a prominent way, of course, but this presence in the most significant cultural centers did not dissuade the great performer, even after his consecration, from visiting small cities and theaters, often taking on tour an opera that had already been premiered on a larger stage. Panizza was no exception.

Thus in his adopted Italy, Héctor conducted at the Teatro alla Scala in Milan, at the Teatro Costanzi (later Teatro dell'Opera) in Rome, and at the majority of the main opera houses of the peninsula: the Teatro di San Carlo in Naples, the Massimo in Palermo, the Carlo Felice in Genoa, the Regio in Turin, the Comunale in Bologna, the Verdi in Trieste, and at the festivals of the Arena in Verona and the Maggio Musicale Fiorentino (at the Teatro Comunale in Florence).

But this activity did not prevent him from also appearing on alternative stages in those same cities, such as the Politeama Genovese, the Politeama Garibaldi in Palermo, the theaters of the Popolo, della Esposizione, and Dal Verme in Milan, and the Teatro Filarmonico in Verona.

In the same way, the Chiabrera in Savona, the Sociale in Treviso, the Grande in Brescia, the Donizetti in Bérgamo, the Sala Grande of the Conservatorio "Giuseppe Verdi" in Milan, the Auditorio de la Radio in Rome, the concert hall of the Conservatorio di San Pietro a Majella in Naples, the Casino in San Remo, the Anfiteatro Cidneo in Brescia, and the Villa Reale in Monza counted on his presence.

From the rest of Europe, his performances at the Royal Opera House Covent Garden in London and the Staatsoper in Vienna are particularly important. In France, his work extended in Paris from the Opéra Comique, to the Théâtre des Champs-Élysées, to the Casino in Nice.

In Berlin he presented at the Städtische Oper (today Deustche Oper) in the district of Charlottenburg, and his stays in Zurich included both the Opernhaus and the Tonhalle. In Spain, in addition to conducting at the Real de Madrid and the Liceo in Barcelona, he also worked at the Teatro Olimpia in Valencia, and in venues in Bilbao and San Sebastián, not to mention other smaller cities.

Moving from Europe to America, the most important is the long tenure at the Metropolitan Opera in New York, with countless performances at its site, with no prejudice against his also leading perfomances with the same company at the Auditorium in Brooklyn, as well as with the troupes of Chicago on the main stage of that city, the Auditorium.

What is interesting in this case is that Panizza participated in various national tours for the Met and could thus travel through the United States, also leading performances in New Orleans (Municipal Auditorium), Boston (Opera House), Philadelphia (Academy of Music), Cleveland (Public Hall), Newark (Mosque Theater), Baltimore (Lyric Theater), Hartford (Bushnell Memorial Hall), Dallas (Auditorium), Rochester (Eastman Theater), Richmond (Mosque Auditorium), Birmingham (Auditorium), and Salt Lake City.

In South America, Panizza's baton led operas at the municipal theaters of Rio de Janeiro and São Paulo, at the Municipal in Santiago de Chile and at the Solís in Montevideo, for the Uruguayan S.O.D.R.E. In his native Argentina, in addition to his prominent performances at the Teatro Colón, he held concerts at the Teatro Metropolitan and Assembly Hall at the School of Law of the University of Buenos Aires, both in the Argentine capital, as well as at the Auditorium of the Casino in Mar del Plata.

Panizza also received a proposal to conduct in Oceania: he was invited by soprano Nellie Melba to tour in Australia, but preferred to decline the invitation as he did not have the will to embark on such a long journey. It is more than clear that he was not lacking in offers of work and could permit himself to choose the ones that seemed most interesting.

In any case, if something confirms the extraordinary and absolutely "ecumenical" character of Héctor Panizza's career as a conductor, it is his status for several years as principal musical referent of the three most important opera houses in the world.

Indeed, Panizza was principal director at the Royal Opera House Covent Garden in London between 1907 and 1914; he worked together with Toscanini conducting at the Teatro alla Scala in Milan between 1921 and 1932; and he was director of the Italian repertoire at the Metropolitan Opera in New York between 1934 and 1942, a responsibility inherited by Tullio Serafin.

Additionally, in a time in which the Teatro Colón was no doubt located among the five principal opera houses in the world, Panizza was a constant presence in the porteño opera house between 1942 and 1955, in addition to his numerous activities in previous seasons. And as if all the previous were not enough, it is worth remembering that in 1932 the position of Resident Director at the Staatsoper in Vienna was offered to him, a responsability he rejected simply because the conditions the contract proposed did not seem to him sufficiently attractive.

One does not know of any other maestro —before, contemporary with, or after Panizza— who, in addition to developing a tireless activity as guest conductor invited to so many cities in the western world, was the Principal Conductor or Music Director at the Scala, Covent Garden, the Met and the Colón, and was also offered this position at the Viennese Staatsoper.

Undoubtedly, Héctor Panizza's international career was one of the most impressive in the history of music performance.

THE CONDUCTOR NOWADAYS

One of the most authoritative voices in the Argentine musical environment was known to be Enzo Valenti Ferro, the fondly remembered music critic and manager of the Teatro Colón; this is how he summarized his opinion of Panizza as a conductor: "By now, it seems unnecessary to highlight that Héctor Panizza has been one of the most relevant orchestra conductors of his time. Deeply knowledgeable of his profession and a repertoire that, as was often the case with contemporary maestros, did not recognize limitations as it covered essentially everything more or less enduring that had been written in the field of musical drama, Panizza additionally belonged to that lineage of maestros for whom musically conducting an opera did not mean neglecting the rest of the elements of the performance but, on the contrary, including them wisely and with an authority in the matter of his responsibilities no one dared to dispute. His versions had a musical quality above all, that is, respect for the words, a precise capture of the musical thought, and an expressive eloquence. Skill, professional seriousness, lucid interpretive talent, style and tradition were blended harmoniously in this great maestro whose presentation at the Met in New York merited this judgment: *An admirable musician, with a keen understanding of what must be expressed in the theater.*[248]

To listen to some of Panizza's main studio and live recordings is to embrace Valenti Ferro's judgment, as well as understand the reasons why the career we have come to summarize existed and developed to such extremes. In this respect, it has been written: "A dynamo with pince-nez who worked with Toscanini, Panizza was a conductor with fire and taste, force and poetry. His performances were precise and *decise* but, with the exception of a Puccini that was slightly dry yet admirable all the same, in no way superficially muscular. His scene of the Chamber of the Council in Verdi's *Simon Boccanegra* was heart-wrenching, and the charm he cast on the final pages of Bellini's *Norma*, with the soprano and tenor rising to the funeral pyre, was no less powerful."[249]

Objectively, Panizza was an extraordinary conductor, no doubt one of the best of his time and comparable in quality and style to Toscanini, of whom in life he was considered the main descendant, above all in terms of the interpretation of opera.

When an outraged Argentine instrumentalist told him of the excesses of certain young batons in their *tempi*, Héctor replied using a reference to his mentor from Parma: "When Toscanini heard one of these performances he became furious... He said to me 'The race of the *tempi* —as you write to me— is *in fashion*. All of them take off sprinting. They are thoughtless! Remember that the word always has to be understood; that is the guide that gives the precise *tempo*... but now *modern* conductors don't give a *fig* what the artist meant to be understood or not understood... What is important is to sprint, for they believe (the ignorant and uncultured) that sprinting is how one enlivens the music that is performed'..."[250]

Within the repertoire recorded in the studio by the Italian-Argentine the historical recording of Mendelssohn's *Sinfonia "Italiana"* deserves to be mentioned, as Panizza's rendering has a beautiful sound and solid architechtonic proportions. It is significant the way the melodic line of the second movement, the *Andante con moto*, is expressed, as Panizza — like Toscanini and few others, even among our contemporaries— tends to respect the *legato* of phrasing and the multiple indications referring to nuance and articulation; that is, he does not unify the discourse, as is often the case, into a single *cantabile* line without letting the precise signs of musical markings which the composer meant to be heard in the score, with the detail that characterized him.[251]

Among those same official recordings it is particularly interesting to listen to "Nun sei bedankt, mein lieber Schwan" (in Italian, "Mercè, mercè, cigno gentil") from *Lohengrin*, in which one can appreciate Panizza's Wagnerian expertise. The dreaminess of the tenor voice, the precision of the choral interventions and the delicate transparence of the orchestral accompaniment speak to a superior sensibility for this repertoire, expressed in a version in which the use of the Italian language was in no way detrimental to the final result, even accentuating its profoundly lyrical character.[252]

From his multiple New York broadcasts an excellent demonstration of his command of the *belcantista* repertoire is the performance of Bellini's *Norma* presented on February 20, 1937, at the Metropolitan Opera, with an outstanding cast.

The energetic version of the overture, with a rapid tempo full of contrasts in articulation and dynamics, is a wonderful example of what Héctor achieved with an orchestra that was not then the first rank ensemble it is today. The end of the first act achieves a level of incandescence worthy of historical Toscaninian evenings, but presents an unwritten *fermata* in which Gina Cigna launches a terrific high note, which the Parmesan maestro would certainly not have allowed her at La Scala. The opera's last scene, in which Bellini's *crescendi* are deployed to their final consequences and the ensemble speaks to an absolute precision, deservedly unleashed a unanimous and thunderous standing ovation by the Met's audience.[253]

Of the many top-notch Verdian performances Héctor offered at the Met, the *Otello* from January 18, 1941 (a year before his departure from New York), has features that make it authentically equal, and even rival, the legendary recording Toscanini made with the NBC orchestra six years later, for which it seems to be an almost involuntary preparation.

This was perhaps the high point of the work by the maestro from Busseto, and along with *Falstaff* is perhaps the most difficult to perform. The opera was subject to an interpretation in which clarity, emphasis, and melodiousness are married to scrupulous work by the cast, choir, and orchestra, with a constant double vigilance over the architectonic structure of the work and the legion of details studding the writing of the mature Verdi. The initial storm has an overwhelming intensity, and Jago's *Credo* is as macabre as can be imagined, with an absolutely moving finale.

One must also consider that this extreme of technical and artistic perfection was achieved by Panizza in a live performance, while Toscanini worked with soloists, choral singers, and instrumentalists who were not acting, who were very close to the podium and entirely dependant on his baton at every moment. The Toscaninian miracle (his *Otello* for radio is considered by many, from a critical perspective, the best opera recording ever made) loses none of its impact when confronted by this comparison, but at least finds a certain context, which is not unimportant. In short, this was an extraordinary work by Panizza and perhaps one of the most powerful examples of both his interpretative mastery and his capacity to conduct a live performance of a highly complex work.[254]

In the United States, as the years went by, the echoes of Héctor's tenure at the Metropolitan Opera and his *Otello* in particular did not fade. On March 9, 2003, the primary newspaper in New York published an article about *Otello* reporting that Valery Gergiev was preparing to conduct at the Met. The author dedicated a good part of the article to Panizza's approach and to him in general: "With Toscanini's departure, in 1915, the Met's Italian wing was entrusted to superior leaders: first Tullio Serafin, then Panizza. Born in Buenos Aires and trained in Milan, Panizza (today barely a name) conducted from 1921 to 1932 at La Scala, where Toscanini esteemed him. (So did Richard Strauss, who arranged for him to conduct 'Elektra' in Vienna.) His Met years were 1934 to 1942. For all his extensive European career, which also included Covent Garden, Panizza called the Met orchestra 'as fine a theater orchestra as I have seen in the world.' He was greeted by [the tenor Giovanni] Martinelli in New York as an old friend and colleague."

The article went on: "In the 1938 *Otello*, it is Panizza who stylistically binds his Italian Otello, German Desdemona and American Iago. Compared with Toscanini, he favors a broader play of tempo. But the velocity and precision, the taut filaments of tone, the keen timbres, the clipped, attenuated phrasings are all Italianate Toscanini trademarks. Like Toscanini, Panizza will bolt suddenly to the end of a scorching musical sentence; like Toscanini's, his musicians respond like lightning. And Panizza is a master at controlling the show while showcasing his cast; calibrating Martinelli's titanic climaxes and magisterial breadth of phrase, he achieves a unity."[255]

There is no doubt that, as was the case with the performances of his mentor from Parma, most of Panizza's recordings have not aged. In their time, they were almost revolutionary for their use of electric emphasis.

Today they sound contemporary, though their forceful immediacy brings a greater quality than many interpretations heard today, live or digital.

As we have seen, the Argentine added one quality to those of his distinguished mentor: the will and capacity to negotiate musical variables with the vocal soloists so that they could feel comfortable, occasionally conceding them a high note or a dilation of the pulse, not explicitly foreseen by the composer but conducive to the excellent use of their melodic resources. This, no doubt, is one of the reasons why singers respected and feared Toscanini and why Panizza was admired and loved by them.

An additional piece of information for those who wish to understand more about this comparison between Panizza and Toscanini, particularly in terms of their respective discographic productions (which today are the only source to artistically evaluate them): At eighty years of age, Panizza was troubled by a deafness he could no longer hide and was forced to leave the podium forever. This, after many years without recording in the studio and having left New York, the city that was by then already one of the greatest musical centers in the world. At eighty-two years old, Toscanini, who spent a good part of the year in New York, began the long series of recordings with the NBC orchestra, which today constitute his principal material legacy.

Toscanini only retired at eighty-seven years of age, and not due to problems of hearing: his prodigious memory had failed him for the first and last time.

CHAPTER 9

PANIZZA AND THE COLÓN

Héctor Panizza's professional and personal link to the Teatro Colón of Buenos Aires spans almost half a century. This bond became more noticeable toward the 1930s and strengthened definitively from the beginning of the Second World War.

It is clear that as an artist, Panizza's connection with his native country transcended the Teatro Colón, for it had its start before the new building of this opera house opened, with the premieres of his student opera *Il fidanzato del mare* in 1897 and *Medio Evo latino* in 1901, both at the Teatro de la Ópera. In the mature stage of his life, as has been seen in the preceding pages, Héctor also intervened in the formative process of the Argentine National Symphony Orchestra, in the beginning of the musical activity at the Mar del Plata Auditorium and, at the end of his life, in a concert inaugurating the first years of the current Buenos Aires Philharmonic Orchestra.

Yet what these golden-years activities mean for Panizza (in terms of the construction of his public image in Argentina) pales in comparison to the prodigious number of seasons he spent spearheading the music direction of opera performances at the Colón. During the first season of the new Teatro Colón, in 1908, Héctor premiered *Aurora*, his most significant opera, practically on the eve of the centenary of the first national government, celebrated in 1910; and during his final season at the Teatro, in 1955, his title of farewell was also *Aurora*.

In the meantime, Héctor Panizza conducted almost 600 performances at the Teatro Colón, with more than sixty different titles —several of them world or local debuts— over twenty-one seasons. These are both convincing numbers, and very difficult to match by other maestros who worked at that venue in Buenos Aires, whether Argentines or foreigners.[256]

Even for those familiar with Panizza's work, it is a surprise to analyze the artistic level of these seasons, due to the identity of the repertoires he took on in an opera house like the Colón (which is now a theater of *stagione*, but that in its years of glory debuted and revived a large number of performances each season, just as at Toscanini's La Scala) and the quality of the singers he conducted, in many cases the best ones at the moment for their respective roles.

The critical reception of his activity at the Colón and Argentina seems rather schematic. As a composer, he exposed himself to the predictable doubts of the nationalists since he anchored himself in the European tradition in general and the Italian one in particular, generating severe criticisms such as those of Miguel Mastroggiani in *La Razón*.[257]

One of the founding fathers of Argentine music, Alberto Williams, oriented him the following way in an article published in the magazine at his conservatory in the 1930s: "The composers Hermann Bermberg, Justino Clerice, Héctor Panizza, Eduardo García Mansilla and Rameti (Hilarión Moreno), who have lived abroad, as well as Clementino Del Ponte and Alfonso Thibaud, who fixed their residence here, have not felt the influence of Argentinianism."[258]

As an interpreter, in contrast, he was invariably showered in praises, to such an extent that even when the performances were not satisfactory from the point of view —for instance— of the vocal casts, the excellence of his work always remained safe from criticism.[259]

He found his greatest defender as a manager in Gastón Talamón, from *La Prensa*, a man of pure nationalist inspiration whose ideas matched Panizza's. A defense that seems paradoxical if one takes into account that Talamón could have emphatically opposed the Italianism of *Aurora* and Panizza's consecration in the United States, a country he detested, along with many nationalists at the time like the writer Manuel Gálvez.[260]

More interesting are the testimonies that foreign singers, after their stop at the Colón, offered about his musicality from the podium. After the *Aida* of 1949, for example, Beniamino Gigli cried out: "Come si canta con quest'uomo! È un dio."[261]

Local singers were also not sparing with their praise. Soprano Helena Arizmendi often repeated: "Panizza's hands are sacred" in relation to the confidence inspired by his tempi and his ability to accompany the vocal line with flexibility.[262]

Héctor's activity crossed over from the first phase of the Teatro Colón, which was practically a building conceded to impresarios and companies —in general Italian— which took charge of seasons, to its second phase as a municipal organism, with the creation of resident artistic bodies —orchestra, choir and ballet— in 1925 and its effective implementation in the '30s, which speaks to his enormous capacity to adapt himself to different forms of work and institutional structures.

It is clear that for Panizza, the Teatro Colón had transformed into the leading opera house in Argentina, and starting in 1930, all of Latin America. His tenure there represents something more than a milestone in his extensive career. Tugged at by his double citizenship, as has been said, Panizza constantly complained about feeling himself Argentine in Italy and Italian in Argentina, as well as about the absurd pseudo-nationalist criteria that in his country attempted to confine him to Italian opera and the reduced Argentine repertoire.

The matter was clear to at least some of the musical critics of the period. It is enough to mention the following reflection published by the newspaper *El Mundo* in 1936: "We think that the Colón has done poorly in not offering the opportunities to conduct symphonic concerts to Mr. Panizza since, in addition to offering the public artistic works of value, he would have given the lie to that kind of conspiracy which exists that claims Latin directors are incapable of making symphonic music." [263]

Five years later, Mariano Antonio Barrenechea, critic of *La Nación*, gave a partial vision of the subject in his most widely read book: "Héctor Panizza, although born in Buenos Aires, can be considered an Italian artist, having spent his whole artistic career in Italy, to which he has given all his activity."[264]

To some extent Barrenechea continued the line represented by his newspaper, which had defined Panizza in the following way: "Mr. Panizza was born in Buenos Aires and followed his musical studies with official Argentine scholarships; in Italy, however, he is considered an Italian maestro, due not only to his paternal citizenship, which is legal there, but also to the Italian school which has educated and inspired him."[265]

If Panizza's career at the Colón proves anything, it is that this close association with Italy was not exclusive, at least in the field of opera, since several artistic managers at this house trusted him with not only ample programming during their seasons but also works of very diverse origins, including Wagner. It is true, however, that for specifically German works he often had to yield many operas to Central-European conductors who guaranteed a high standard for that repertoire, especially beginning in the '30s: this was the case with Erich Kleiber and Fritz Busch, trained at the highest level, who happened to work with the Teatro Colón Resident Orchestra.

ARTISTIC JOURNEY

Panizza's artistic course at the Colón began on September 5, 1908, with the debut of his opera *Aurora* in the original Italian. The honor fell to Héctor to inaugurate the tradition of programming an Argentine opera for every season, a tradition that has not always been observed.

Aurora's premiere was announced, as has been mentioned, as a "great artistic event." From the start it was planned to circulate it widely, to such a degree that the handbill included the score for song and piano from the Romanza of the first act and reproduced sketches of the set design by Pio Collivadino.

After twenty days of intense rehearsals, Panizza conducted his creation before the Gran Compañía Lírica Italiana and, as has been seen, he assigned several famous peninsular singers to the main roles, beginning with the excellent soprano Maria Farneti for the protagonist.

The composer also managed for the opera to be repeated the following year, with conducting by another Italian, Giuseppe Barone, and a different international diva playing Aurora, Hariclea Darclée.

The "Canción de la bandera" was quickly characterized as an independent piece, so much so that in 1908 Amedeo Bassi was asked to sing it during a benefit performance of *Pagliacci*, and in 1909 Florencio Constantino sang it before the *Cavalleria rusticana*.

After his inaugural *Aurora* —the redundancy is merited here— Panizza did not work at the Colón again until 1921. That year Héctor's baton led *Manon* (with Vallin and Borgioli), *Il barbiere di Siviglia* (with Barrientos), *Götterdämmerung*, *Don Pasquale*, *Les Huguenots*, *Faust* (with Martinelli, Vallin, and Didur), *Marouf*, *Un ballo in maschera*, *I puritani*, *Il trovatore*, *Grisélidis* by Massenet (translated as *Griselda*), and *La sonnambula*, works invariably sung in Italian, as was the custom during those years. The conductor was also invited to the gala to celebrate the national holiday of July 9, where he took charge of the fourth act of *Les Huguenots*, while his colleague Giorgio Polacco took on segments from the Italian repertoire.

The eclecticism of the repertoire, about which a local musical authority like Roberto Caamaño expressed his reservations, earned him the disapproval of a state official (an inspector of music, as well as critic), the previously mentioned Miguel Mastroggiani, who beginning from this time became one of his detractors. The critics in general continued to accompany Panizza in a positive way, however, without including particularly original or specific considerations that deserve to be reproduced.

It is worth it, in contrast, to quote a couple of journalistic interviews that Panizza gave before and during this isolated visit which found him at an inflection point in his international career, given that he was on the point of sharing the *cartellone* with Toscanini during the reopening of La Scala.

In a preview published in Argentina in 1921, the journalist introduced him without failing to allude, once again, to the famous theme of his nationality: "We thought we would find ourselves before a true Italian, who hardly knows our language, and have had the pleasant surprise of confirming that despite his long residence in Europe, in Italy above all, he is a *creole*, more so than some sons of foreigners who have not left Argentina."

For his part, Panizza blended observations of an economic sort with other more artistic ones, returning of course to his ubiquitous nationalist complex: "During the journey I have rehearsed *Götterdämmerung*. You already know how many difficulties the organization of a company offers. The war has destroyed four generations, and Yankee gold monopolizes the good singers. It has been a triumph to get so many artists to come here from North America. I know the orchestra is good, as my eminent friend Richard Strauss said when he found out I was coming to the Colón."

He still wished to emphasize that he was a composer: "I am bringing two nocturnes for orchestra, ready to be played, and a symphonic poem for orchestra, solos and choir, *El rey en la selva* [sic], which I need to arrange," to which the journalist added: "He has *Bizancio* completely arranged." And as a form of farewell he argued, with a tone of warning and even resentment: "I arrive at the Colón by personal merit and not by origin. [...] Each time at Covent Garden, La Scala, etcetera I obtained some triumph, I mentally shared it with Argentina, the country of my birth and my heart."[266]

Now in Argentina, in 1921 Panizza gave an interview to *Caras y Caretas*, after having directed his first Wagner at the Colón (*Götterdämmerung*), where he was given a lively standing ovation. It is worth reproducing the circumlocutions of the journalist to describe this success, as far as he refers, euphemistically and elaborately, to the attacks of the press during the previous performance of *Aurora*: "The audience of the great Argentine opera house, heterogeneous and jumbled in the nuances of culture, and also spectators whose presence has to adjust itself to irreducible social demands, forgot about conventionalisms, at times very deep-rooted, and dispensing with many minor animosities and pintoresque rivalries, added its enthusiasm and warmly showed it in prolonged applause. Accentuating its significance before the maestro, this spontaneous and unanimous admiration was added to the high merit of showing his work in a hall of his native city, at an auditorium whose constituents had perhaps only known about Héctor Panizza's talent what the journalistic accounts had repeated on so many occasions. The reality is that it was not, then, a matter of 'old friends....'"

In the following line Panizza affirmed: "Few times in my artistic career have I been applauded in this way [...]. In Trieste I was recently subject to affectionate displays when I conducted some of Beethoven's symphonies, a short time after Trieste returned to being Italian."

He then made a show of his love for Argentina, which was perhaps necessary to mitigate the critics of his Europeanism: "How I long to see the Plaza de Mayo! It is a feverish desire, like that of a schoolboy, and I still have not been able to fulfill it. But I have already stopped for some time on Suipacha street in front the house where I was born, that is, not in front of the house itself, for other buildings have now been raised on that site." And the journalist clarified: "Panizza's childhood home was torn down —in an extraordinary coincidence— to facilitate the construction of the stage of the Teatro de la Ópera, where the musician, years later, premiered his first work."[267]

Héctor returned in 1927 to conduct eight works, with several artists of the first rank: Lauri-Volpi and Muzio in *Il trovatore*; Muzio, Fleta and Galeffi in *Tosca*; Galeffi, Dal Monte, Schipa and Pinza in *Il barbiere di Siviglia*. Two of the works —*Manon* and *Thaïs*— included choreographies by Bronislava Nijinska (later seasons would be arranged by Boris Romanov).

In the 1929 season the marathon was even longer: Panizza was in charge of fourteen titles between May 25 —a patriotic date that opened the *stagione*— and August 15. The revival of *Turandot* stood out, with Raisa and Thill singing, set design by Galileo Chini, and costumes by Umberto Brunelleschi, just as during its debut in Buenos Aires in 1926, when Gino Marinuzzi had conducted it. Raisa as well as Chini and Brunelleschi corresponded in their turn to the original team from the opera's world premiere, when —as we have seen— Panizza participated beginning with its fourth performance.

In addition to *Madama Butterfly* with Dalla Rizza and Mirassou, and *Lucia di Lammermoor* with Sayão and Pertile, Héctor intervened in a world premiere of an Argentina opera not of his authorship: this was Felipe Boero's *El matrero* by Felipe Boero, a very effective work whose indigenous folkloric cut, as much in theme as in the verses and music, transformed it at the end of the 20th century into the most performed Argentine opera, surpassing *Aurora* itself, which "weighs in" at second place.[268]

The Argentine critics appreciated the Italian Panizza as a demiurge of local premieres, which indicated an Argentine folkloric inspiration he had not demonstrated at the moment of composing. This occurred with *El matrero*, about whose approach it was written: "The performance of *El matrero* contributed greatly to its success. Héctor Panizza, first of all, was the best ally of the composer. We are not going to sing his praises once more. With his usual great authority and an evident fondness for his compatriot he presented the work of Mr. Boero with perfect spiritual understanding, making for an attentive execution."[269]

The following year Panizza returned for a season that showed his versatility: once again he conducted *Götterdämmerung* and *Don Carlo*, *L'elisir d'amore* (with Schipa, Romelli and Baccaloni) and the local premiere of Pizzetti's *Lo straniero*, Gluck's *Orfeo ed Euridice* and Rimski-Korsakov's *Sadkó* (sung in French), in addition to a revival of *El matrero*, among other titles. His arrival at the "Conte Rosso" along with Alfredo Casella, Lina Romelli and Boris Romanov was widely covered by the local press.[270]

In 1934, with the composer Athos Palma now at the head of the Colón, Panizza contributed to local knowledge of the French repertoire with Dukas' *Ariane et Barbe-bleue*; he also conducted a notable *Falstaff* with Baccaloni, Damiani, Marengo, Fleischer, von Pataky, and De Paolis in a healthy practice of joining Rioplatense artists with foreigners. He also continued with his Gluck project, conducting *Alceste*.

This visit was preceded by an interview carried out in Naples by the general consul Arturo Lagorio and published in *Caras y Caretas*, in which the topic of nationality permeates the whole text, leading to the formulation of somewhat unusual claims. Panizza notes: "there are within me several conflicting feelings [...] I am going to my country with some precaution, for I cannot forget the harsh attacks that were made on me [...] But in modern times one must overcome the old proverbs: I also wish to triumph in my nation, and I want to give the best of myself to my country, to which I feel linked by the flower of my youth [...] I always travel with my Argentine passport. And Mussolini also knows this."[271]

He then continues: "If at times I insist on my nationality it is because some would like me to forget it. [...] I, along with Athos Palma and the Neapolitan maestro, director of the conservatory orchestra [from Naples], will attempt for our symphonic music to be heard. At the same time we will introduce some values that have come from the San Pietro a Majella Conservatory, worthy of Argentine critical judgement."

The journalist —who was a diplomat in the government of President Agustín Pedro Justo— concludes with an affirmation of his own, which expresses, among other things, his personal vision of politics: "If on this last trip there were those who did not wish to recognize his musical science, which flourished in his revision of Berlioz' s *Traité*; if at that time it was not believed that Toscanini glimpsed in Panizza a magnificent future... now is the moment to accept the verdicts of Austria, Germany and Italy, which publicly consider him the heir to the artistic scepter left by Toscanini."[272]

In each one of the following seasons, alongside operas usually performed in European seasons, the maestro contributed something new to the Teatro Colón: in 1935 it was the forgotten *Svanda the Bagpiper* (*Svanda dudák*) by Jaromír Weinberger (sung in Italian); in 1936 it was Gian Francesco Malipiero's *Giulio Cesare* and the debut of another Argentine opera, *La ciudad roja* by Raúl Espoile; in 1939 it was the world premiere of his own *Bizancio*, with Cigna and De Paolis, in a full season in which he also took charge of Zandonai's *Conchita* and a *Boris Godunov* sung, once again, in Italian.

After his absence during the two seasons in which Toscanini returned to Buenos Aires to offer symphonic concerts (in 1940 with the NBC orchestra and in 1941 with the Teatro Colón Resident Orchestra), Panizza established himself at the opera house on Libertad Street. Beginning in 1942 and from then on, with the only exceptions in 1950 and 1953, he worked there until his retirement in 1955.[273]

During this period, begun in the midst of war, with many European artists prepared to work at the Colón, Ferruccio Calusio appointed General Director of the Teatro in 1944, and a Panizza already approaching seventy years old, it was logical that the number of works he conducted would decrease to an average of five or six per season. What did not decrease, on the other hand, was the importance and variety of the operas chosen, or his eagerness for personal development. He thus led *Carmen* in French, alternating with performances in Italian, in 1942; he insisted on Gluck, this time with *Armida* (featuring Rose Bampton) in 1943; he restaged *Bizancio* with Rigal in 1944, and presented titles like *Otello* and Montemezzi' s *L'amore dei tre re*.

Two important events once again put his skills as symphonic interpreter on display: in 1943 he conducted Rudolf Firkusny —the pianist who had awoken such fervor in Buenos Aires— in the *"Emperor"* Concerto by Beethoven; three years later, he led the Argentine debut of Rachmaninoff's *Piano Concerto No. 3*, with Marisa Regules as soloist.

By 1945, Panizza had additionally managed to closely identify himself with a distinguished group of important Argentine singers, whom he featured in different operas. A paradigmatic case was his revival of Gluck's *Armida* with one of his favorite students, Delia Rigal, along with Clara Oyuela, Felipe Romito, Tota de Igarzábal, Ángel Mattiello, Helena Arizmendi, and Nilda Hoffmann, who had shared the marquee with an artist of the stature of Canadian tenor Raoul Jobin. The same practice continued into 1946, in a *Simon Boccanegra* in which Rigal sang with Leonard Warren. In 1947 Panizza conducted *Fedora* by his friend Umberto Giordano for the first time at the Colón, and *Norma* with Caniglia, Vela, Barbieri and Vaghi, among other titles with no less brilliant casts. He also successfully restaged Boero's *El matrero*. At a date as late as 1949, and already bordering on seventy-five years of age, Panizza arranged another novelty: Gluck's *Iphigénie en Áulide*. In 1951, *Adriana Lecouvreur* was a heartfelt homage to its author Francesco Cilea, who had died in November of the previous year.

Beginning with the following season, with the rapid progression of his deafness, Panizza had to share the podium during the performances of several operas: in *Armida* with Juan Emilio Martini, and in *Madama Butterfly* with Bruno Mari. In 1953 his beloved *Aurora* was in charge of Roberto Kinsky. In 1954, in Verdi's *Otello* Martini once again assisted him. Only in 1955, as a concession to the celebration of his eighty years, did he exclusively occupy the podium in *L'amore dei tre re* and his final *Aurora*, with Pili Martorell, whose final performance was on August 14.

INSTITUTIONAL PROJECTS

Panizza's interest in the Teatro Colón always transcended his musical profession. He turned his gaze toward the Teatro as not only a place of high artistic realization, but also a cultural and social institution. It is clear that during a great part of his life he wagered on the idea of being artistic director of the house or at least influencing its production system and legal framework. Very possibly he imagined a Colón organized in a form similar to that of Toscanini's La Scala, in which maestros like Calusio, Kinsky, and Martini were to him what he, Calusio, and Votto had been for the great Parmesan conductor.

In 1929, after the close of a season of enormous activity, the musically influential group Camuatí began preparations before the mayor of Buenos Aires for "Panizza to be general director of the opera season of the Teatro Colón in 1930, due to his performance at international venues for thirty years, and his Argentine nationality."[274]

The highest moment of this aspiration occurred in 1933, when from Milan, Héctor offered his services as artistic director to the City Council of Buenos Aires. The municipalization of the Colón was in its beginning phase and in February 1933 Mayor Mariano de Vedia y Mitre invited a board of prominent figures to choose an artistic director for the opera house. The body was made up of Victoria Ocampo, Alberto Prebisch, and Constantino Gaito. The latter, an important Argentine composer, promoted Panizza to the board that was unfortunately averse to him and which, to Panizza's displeasure, ended up nominating Juan José Castro, about whose experience as an opera conductor he had his doubts.

This fact determined, in March of that same year, the first crisis of the new directorate: Gaito's resignation. Several influential newspapers of the period —*Crítica, La Vanguardia*— deplored the refusal to designate

Panizza and used his figure against Castro. Gastón Talamón, the critic from *La Prensa* who for years was Héctor's battering ram in Argentina (and who when Gaito resigned formed part of the previously mentioned Camuatí group) even wrote that Panizza was the "natural director" for the Colón, while the Catholic magazine *Criterio* indicated that Panizza should also be hired in order to limit the influence of Castro and the one who along with him had been named staging director of the Colón, Héctor Basaldúa.[275]

He was never a member of the general or artistic management of the Colón, though president de facto Ramírez later offered such a position to him. However, Panizza filed two great projects for the Teatro's institutional restructuring which, even if they could not be carried out, merited a spirited defense from their promoter.

The first was the "unification" of the Teatro alla Scala in Milan with the Teatro Colón in Buenos Aires. This cause was a fruit from his experience forming La Scala with Arturo Toscanini. With the efficacy of this new structure already proven, toward 1925 Panizza and the general director Angelo Scandiani considered the possibility of moving the artistic bodies of La Scala to Buenos Aires, taking advantage of the fact that part of the respective seasons were given in different periods of the year.

As one knows, while in the northern hemisphere it is summer, in the south it is winter, and this would permit the visit of artists and even complete casts to Argentina. In that period the Colón was developing the kernel of its operatic season (including most of the debuts and new productions) between May and September, while La Scala carried out its own between December and April. The assembly was thus perfectly possible.

Panizza, who knew as well as Toscanini of these alternatives that permitted them, like many colleagues, to count on an uninterrupted year of work, convinced the Argentine ambassador in Rome of the project and, with his endorsement, communicated it to the local administration of Buenos Aires. The response he received, in tersely bureaucratic language, was for the enthusiastic Panizza a bucket of cold water: "La Scala must be up for tender like any other participatee."[276]

It is worth remembering that until 1925 the Colón had been functioning as a rented opera house, without an activity of its own, conceded to impresarios who had to "win" the season by "participating" through public bidding.

The dry response invited La Scala to submit like any other enterprise, taking into account neither its status as a nonprofit autonomous organization, nor much less its enormous historical prestige and incomparable artistic quality.

The story ended the following way: the season was finally entrusted to the impresario Ottavio Scotto and neither Panizza nor Toscanini insisted further on the proposal. The flow of artists from La Scala to Argentina continued to be intense all the same, with singers (both in leading and secondary roles), maestros like Ferruccio Calusio, stage directors like Margarita (Margarete) Wallmann and even prompters like Otello Ceroni arriving.

Toward the beginning of the '40s, Panizza was frequently consulted by officials and media outlets on different points relating to Argentine musical life. In 1943, the magazine *El Mercurio Musical*, the bulletin of the defunct Argentine Musical Chamber of Commerce, consulted a number of composers about the value of the decision by the national government — still in the hands of President Ramón Castillo— to "make official" a Day of Music on November 22. Panizza was consulted second, immediately after the patriarch Alberto Williams, and did not deprive himself of giving his affirmative and enthusiastic point of view: "Aside from concerts, open-air festivals and performances in closed spaces, more student contests for the youth could be held...," he opined.[277]

This public exposition led Panizza to present a second institutional project to the Colón: its "nationalization," the correct term if one takes into account that this opera house depends, to this day, on the City

Council of Buenos Aires. Panizza handed the papers to the president de facto General Ramírez, after he assumed the position following the coup d'état on June 1943, but it had been drawn up between 1940 and 1941.[278]

From that time until the constitutional reform of 1994, the inhabitants of the city of Buenos Aires could not choose their own mayor, who was designated directly by the president of the nation —that is, by the head of Argentine executive national power— as a consequence of the metropolis being ceded to the federal government as capital of the republic. Although one thing did not necesarily imply another, in Argentina it operated in this way for more than a century.

This fact was not unimportant: if the president designated the mayor, and the latter the Secretary of Culture and general director of the Teatro Colón, this meant that the federal state had complete power over the theater. Panizza's project aimed, then, at an economic reasoning. The maestro considered that in the context of the city's local budget, the Colón would never be able to access a level of financing on its own sufficiently important to develop a far-reaching artistic project.

Behind this argument rested the idea that the Colón should be maintained directly by the national state so that it sent its performances to the provinces. He did not think that this idea only contributed to strengthening the supremacy of Buenos Aires as against the "interior" of the country —the way the entire rest of the national territory is often curiously defined from the Argentine capital— which, with the unique exception of the Teatro Argentino in La Plata, never came to develop completely professional and self-sufficient opera houses. In many aspects Argentina —today just as before— continues to be a country with a single great city and this is perhaps one of the keys of its political, social, and cultural regression.

Of the shelved and never seriously considered "Panizza Project," the idea of transforming the Colón into an autonomous institution remains of interest —something that finally happened in 2009, at least formally, through a law riddled with contradictions and uncertain phrasing— as does the idea of creating a special tax to sustain it, which in its draft could consist of a tax for radio broadcasts or other activities (like football), copying European initiatives implemented during those times. With this self-sufficiency and greater financing, Panizza proposed a working outline that forms the most substantial and partially current part of his project.

In accordance with this outline of activities, the Teatro Colón had to create an area for experimental opera —an objective in part satisfied with the foundation of the Center of Experimentation by Sergio Renán and Gerardo Gandini in 1990— which worked in a space alternative to the main hall (which is also the case currently).

With this complementary activity, the Colón had to organize in the first place a concert season (copied from the Italian scheme of that time, where symphonic series, with the same orchestra dedicated to the opera, preceded or followed the opera season). Immediately afterward, when winter arrived, the official operatic season opened. When this was completed, in spring, the Teatro had to carry out tours with opera or ballet performances in the provinces, while in Buenos Aires, with the people not involved in the *tournées* (taking into account that the Argentine provincial opera houses have much less capacity than that of the Colón), an experimental cycle had to be developed. Finally, in summer performances had to be produced in the open air, in spaces especially adapted for operas, ballets, and concerts.

The project was complemented with two other aspects of interest. The first was the creation of a retirement fund exclusively for the Colón's personnel, a pressing matter to this day, in which the dancers cannot retire until the general legal age of retirement, thus blocking the place for younger generations in the time they take to continue performing (even if the current debate is not about a fund but a differential regime).

The second was the creation of a National Symphony Orchestra, given that during this time the Argentine capital did not have an official orchestra for exclusive use in concerts. Panizza considered it necessary — despite the fact that the Resident Orchestra of the Teatro Colón was also taking on the symphonic repertoire— to form an ensemble that during the winter, when the Resident Orchestra was occupied with the official opera season, could offer concerts in the provinces.

Panizza's project was partly taken up in this aspect by the first government of Perón (ex-vice president *de facto* of Ramírez, as has been said), through his appointed mayor, with the creation in 1946 of the Municipal Theater Symphony Orchestra, later called City of Buenos Aires Symphony Orchestra, finally rebaptized as Buenos Aires Philharmonic Orchestra, which to this day has its home at the Teatro Colón.[279]

In an even more specific fashion, in 1948 one of the ideas of the Italian-Argentine became reality with the creation of the National Symphony Orchestra, in whose arrangements, as we have seen, Héctor Panizza was personally involved.

CHAPTER 10

THE TOSCANINIAN LEGACY

If something defined Héctor Panizza's brilliant activity as music director, it was his long relationship with Arturo Toscanini and the artistic work developed by his side, over several years, at the Teatro alla Scala de Milan. The consequences of this double link — with what were, at the time, the greatest conductor and the finest opera house in the world— accompanied Héctor for his entire subsequent career.

This influence continued even after his death, given that there existed and still exist maestros who, directly or indirectly, follow the Toscanini and Panizza line: artists who strongly identify with the type of work they both displayed while working together at La Scala and who attempt to follow the route they inaugurated.

It is undeniable: the point of maximum glory of Toscanini's talent coincided with the most glorious moment of the opera in Milan, and with the establishment of an exemplary form to perform the musical repertoire in general and the operatic in particular; and there, in the first rank, an active participant in all this, was our Italian-Argentine.

Panizza knew perfectly well who Toscanini was before having any dealings with him, as he had already seen him conduct and deeply admired him. Let us remember that beginning in 1896 the maestro from Parma increasingly developed his career in Italy, and two years later was already the principal conductor at La Scala (that is, he was invited to conduct a substantial number of the titles programmed, but had no direct input in the outline of the seasons).

Panizza recalls in almost mystical tones that as a student at the Conservatory of Milan, "I was a regular spectator at his performances in La Scala, indeed one could say I did not miss the chance to see practically any of them. From my location, in the upper circle naturally, I could follow his work with devotion, trying not to miss a movement of his baton or the slightest of his gestures [...]. There I had the sensation that little by little, Toscanini's soul was penetrating into mine."[280]

The two maestros finally struck up a personal relationship in 1901. As we have already seen, Panizza's *Medio Evo latino* had enjoyed a successful world premiere in 1900 and the Teatro de la Ópera in Buenos Aires scheduled it for its season the following year, entrusting the podium to that rising star of the baton, Arturo Toscanini. The young Héctor was delighted by the choice, knowing that his opera would be in the best hands and that the audience in his city would appreciate it in a superb performance.

After the incidents narrated in the first part of this work, the two artists achieved an agreement and the premiere could take place. The performance was a success and sealed the beginning of a relationship of collaboration and friendship that, even if it was not for life, would extend over many years. A significant and certainly not minor detail: such collaboration was limited to the work of Héctor as conductor, for as composer, after the experience of *Medio Evo...*, Toscanini never again conducted or programmed his music.

THE GOLDEN YEARS OF LA SCALA

Fifteen years after these events, Héctor was now a prestigious maestro, and during the 1916-1917 season he had the opportunity to make his opera debut at the Teatro alla Scala, where until then he had only conducted two concert programs. On this occasion he took on nine operas by eight different composers. The results were very positive, and from on it was clear throughout all of Italy that the surname Panizza was a synonym for quality on the operatic podium.

Panizza's artistic growth did not pass unnoticed by Toscanini. A key moment thus arrived in the relationship between the two great musicians when, in 1921, Toscanini returned to La Scala as artistic director, that is, not only as the principal conductor but with full powers of programming over all aspects of music and staging.

The incorruptible maestro from Parma was now going to have within reach everything necessary so that his professional creed of meticulousness, precision, and fidelity to the composer was no longer an interminable crusade of singlehanded combat — production by production— orchestras, choirs, casts, and collaborating maestros of the second rank or insufficiently disciplined. Now his aesthetic and ethical values could be the base for a musical institution that, with him at its head, would become a model of artistic seriousness, and ultimately the most important opera house in the world.

He thus carried out what might be referred to as "Toscaninian operatic reform." In that context, Toscanini — who had respect for very few colleagues and admiration for almost none— chose one person to be his closest collaborator (and at the start, the only one) in the conducting of all the performances he organized: the maestro Panizza. Héctor thus transformed into Arturo's associate during the great Toscaninian management of La Scala between 1921 and 1929.

For Harvey Sachs, no doubt the principal world expert on Arturo Toscanini, "...what made Toscanini so important in the history of musical performance was his work as a reformer in the opera house and in his approach to musical interpretation; in this, neither Panizza nor anyone else of that period equaled him. Mahler might have achieved something similar in the opera house had he lived twenty years longer, but he died too soon (...). Panizza followed Toscanini in his mission, and was certainly one of his most faithful followers."[281]

As is known, Toscanini never gave lessons — with the partial exception, perhaps, of his advice to the young Guido Cantelli, with whom he identified to such an extent that he referred to him as "a son"— and in fact he thought that orchestral direction could not be the subject of specific study: so much was this the case that in 1950 he commented sarcastically on the publication of the first manual for conducting technique worthy of that name. [282]

But he did have faithful collaborators and assistants who learned from his interpretative mastery over years of labor together; Panizza, already a respected colleague, became one of the first and most principal ones during the *scaligeri* years. Arturo's confidence toward Héctor was evidently not limited to his capacity as a conductor and choral trainer: it also extended to the selection of artistic personnel. Let us not forget that Toscanini, on assuming his position, created an orchestra from scratch, a choir and a fledgling body of maestros, or as were then called in Italy, "substitutes." The excellent ensemble Panizza had just put together for the concerts at the Casino of San Remo was the basis for the brand-new orchestra of the Teatro alla Scala: Héctor's recommendation was enough to allocate certain positions or at least guarantee the audition of the instrumentalist recommended.

The *cartellone* that announced La Scala's first season under the aegis of the maestro from Parma featured thirteen operatic performances, with only two conductors mentioned — let us not forget— in alphabetical order: Ettore Panizza and Arturo Toscanini; a full declaration of intentions, and an explicit guarantee of the musical capacity of the Argentine.

When programming only thirteen operas (one of them Puccini's *Trittico*) Toscanini and Panizza wanted to be sure they had enough time to establish the quality canons they desired for the Teatro. Once that was achieved, the productivity of La Scala as far as titles and performances grew year after year, to reach up to forty-five productions and over 200 performances per season. This is undoubtedly a record no opera house in the world could have competed against. Once a title had been duly prepared, it could be maintained on the bill for several years, requiring increasingly fewer rehearsals. La Scala thus suddenly became a theater "*de repertorio*," but each of its performances bore the label of quality belonging to a theater "*de stagione.*"

The Milanese opera house's seasons included, in addition, a strong commitment to contemporary music, which was embodied with the world premieres of Puccini's *Turandot*, Boito's *Nerone*, Giordano's *Le cena delle beffe* and *Il re*, Pizzetti's *Debora e Jaele* and *Fra Gherardo*, Zandonai's *I cavalieri de Ekebù*, Respighi's *Belfagor*, Wolf-Ferrari's *Sly*, Lualdi's *Il diavolo nel campanile*, Ferrari Trecate's *La bella e il mostro*, Pedrollo's *Delitto e castigo*, Bianchini's *Tien-Hoa*, and Guarino's *Madame di Challant*.

As one can see on this interesting list, not one case considers Panizza, or his status as composer. For some reason, very possibly of an ethical order, it did not seem correct to program operas that belonged to one of the resident directors of the institution, to the detriment of other composers.

This legendary chapter in the history of La Scala and in musical interpretation was officially inaugurated on December 26, 1921. That day the Teatro opened its doors again after three years of inactivity, and reorganized as an autonomous entity. The first performance was dedicated to Verdi's final opera, *Falstaff*, under Toscanini's baton and with the baritone Mariano Stabile in the title role. This was followed by Wagner's final opera, *Parsifal*, in Panizza's hands, with the tenor Amedeo Bassi as protagonist. Verdi and Wagner, Toscanini and Panizza: from the start, it was a clear declaration of what would come.

At the margin of the numerous anecdotes in this intense relationship between two great maestros, there is no doubt that from their collaboration emerged an Italian and *scaligera* (and therefore, to an extent, also Toscaninian and Panizzian) line of conductors, particularly among those who have dedicated a good part of their energies to opera, which to a certain extent continues to our day.

This authentic cultural heritage consists of a method of assembling the different stages of an opera production that demands long and thorough work on the part of the music director and his assistant conductors. The work is carried out initially in airtight compartments: at the piano, with a vocal cast on one side and the chorus on the other (the so-called "camerino" and "stage" rehearsals), and also in a separated form with the orchestra (the "reading" rehearsals). Only on a second occasion are these three elements united, in what are referred to —not casually— as rehearsals "a l'italiana."

In a parallel form, the singers also carry out "scene" rehearsals under the guidance of a stage director (in Panizza's time, often a *maestro sostituto* with extra-musical concerns), working with the accompaniment of piano, also under the supervision of the music director. Only in the final instance, generally a week before the premiere, are all the factors mentioned brought together in what are referred to as "ensemble" rehearsals (often one for each act of the opera), followed by pre-general and general ("dress") rehearsals.

One cannot say that Toscanini and Panizza invented this system of preparation of an opera performance, but it was established at La Scala in an exclusive manner, and there it was perfected and brought to its maximum expression, as much in the demands of quality as in the working times. As a corollary, under the baton of these maestros an opera production was never staged for the first time without a precise scheme of daily rehearsals for more than a month. The final results were, in all cases and with no detriment to any artists who could make a greater impression than that of their colleagues, brilliant collective works.

For this reason, at La Scala at the time and even in several Italian theaters today, the playbills list the name of the "maestro concertatore" and orchestra conductor. To name the person with the greatest musical — and in that period, generally artistic— responsibility for an opera production as a simple conductor would clearly be reductive, all the more when working in the way we have just described.

Everything was aimed at understanding the message of the composer and performing it in his own style, down to the smallest detail, without the interferences or personal caprices, in a constant work of deepening into the letter and spirit of the work. Naturally, this scheme of production alone did not work miracles: it had to be brought to life through the artistic principles that Panizza shared with Toscanini, which can be summarized in a phrase the latter spoke before Carlo Maria Giulini: "Bisogna essere artisti... non dei mestieranti" (It is necessary to be artists... not merely craftsmen).[283]

They sought no more and no less than the perfect performance, with the application of criteria that attempted to be objective, or as objective as possible. Whim, improvisation, approximation and mediocrity were discarded completely, in any of their multiple aspects, including many of the liberties traditionally conceded to soloist singers beyond what was explicitly indicated by the composer.

One of the criteria that Toscanini imposed for the first time and that today is followed in all of the world's opera houses is that a singer is not authorized to repeat an aria, no matter how many rounds of applause and bravos his performance received, for to do so would be to break the indispensable dramatic and musical continuity imagined by the librettist and the composer. Other measures in this sense were the positioning of the orchestral pit in such a way that the instrumentalists and conductor were less visible to the public, and the total or almost total dimming of the lights during the performance.

At present there are still maestros devoted to the operatic repertoire —generally trained in Latin countries— who rehearse in accordance with the working plan and ethical-aesthetic criteria we have just mentioned, all the more so in opera houses that work season by season, as do La Scala, Covent Garden, and the Colón today.

It is a different case with conductors from Anglo-Saxon countries who come to the opera from the symphonic field, above all if they work in repertory theaters — like the Metropolitan in New York, the Staatsoper in Vienna, or the Deutsche Oper in Berlin— where the method of production generally implies rehearsal times which are shorter and almost non-existent in the case of restagings.

Panizza's presence on the Milanese podium during this period spanned fifty-nine productions (including restagings) and six different concert programs, for a total of approximately 300 performances, marked by great successes and authentic milestones.

Héctor's performance at La Scala included events it is not too much to say were historical. During the 1925-1926 season Ettore directed the four-day Wagnerian *Tetralogía*, which had never been performed at La Scala. During the 1927-1928 season he did so again, offering for the first time, in rapid succession and the correct order, the four operas from this cycle, not once but twice. Toscanini, as is known, was extremely sparing in his praise toward other musicians, above all in public. One of the few people whom he praised before third parties was Panizza, whom he often called "il bravo Ettore" (the adjective, difficult to translate into English, suggests a combination of the terms "good" and "capable").

COLLABORATORS WITH THEIR OWN TALENT

The other musician — who immediately became a close collaborator— to whom Toscanini referred as "bravo," upon hearing him play the piano for the first time, was Antonino Votto, a Neapolitan who at twenty-five years old was brought by Panizza to La Scala to audition as assistant conductor, later working for several seasons under his supervision. Votto passed the audition brilliantly, provoking Arturo's unexpected praise, which in turn triggered the following commentary on Héctor's part: "You should really buy yourself a bottle of wine and get drunk, because Toscanini never says 'bravo' to anybody!"[284]

During his management, Toscanini and Panizza assigned Votto the conducting of fifty-nine opera performances. Later the Neapolitan developed a career of the first rank as a conductor beyond La Scala, including many performances and recordings with Maria Callas. Votto remained in constant touch with Toscanini until 1956, and worked at the Milanese opera house for over half a century. Herbert von Karajan, who invited him several times to conduct at the Staatsoper in Vienna, particularly respected him.

As we will see in what follows, in his maturity Antonino was also one of the main heirs of Toscanini, from his chair of orchestral conducting at the "Giuseppe Verdi" Conservatory in Milan, created especially for him. During the first season at La Scala shared between Toscanini and Panizza, along with Votto, there worked with Votto as collaborating maestro — in fact, as *primus inter pares*— another Argentine of Italian origin: Ferruccio Calusio, who would later conduct at the Teatro Colón, the Metropolitan Opera and La Scala itself. At their side was also Sergio Failoni from Verona, a maestro who later came to develop a good career as a conductor and would have had an even greater one, were it not for an explosive temperament which soon made him fall out with Arturo himself.

The fourth and final assistant who was present at the start of Toscanini's new management was Mario Frigerio, the music stage manager. With the years Frigerio turned increasingly toward opera stage direction, becoming an artist in demand by many theaters. Completing the musical staff was the maestro Vittore Veneziani, in charge of the preparation of the brand-new chorus.

In 1923 Toscanini invited Vittorio Gui to make his first presentation at the Milanese opera house with Strauss' *Salomé*. Gui, who exactly ten years later founded the Maggio Musicale Fiorentino festival, would remember the generosity of the great maestro and did not spare him praise regarding his artistic commitment and the way things worked at La Scala during his management. (Further conductors at the Florence festival, Mario Rossi, Bruno Bartoletti, Riccardo Muti and Zubin Mehta, would also be Toscaninians.)

In 1924 the Parmesan conductor added to the staff at La Scala a musician who had already been *maestro sostituto* under him between 1907 and 1909: Gabriele Santini. Beginning that same year, Santini conducted numerous Verdian and veristic operas, and even the first Milan performance of Ravel's *L'heure espagnole*. Santini later had an important career, centered in Italy, which included two periods at the head of the Teatro dell'Opera in Rome.

Other guest maestros were Antonio Guarnieri, Arturo Lucon and Antonio Sabino, and other composers included Strauss, Mascagni and Stravinsky, who interpreted their own works.

In subsequent seasons, assistants included Eduardo Fornarini, Leopoldo Gennai, Guido Ragni, Emilio Rossi, Vittorio Ruffo, Pietro Cimara, Pietro Clausetti and Norberto Mola, the pianist and conductor who in 1955 became the highly regarded principal Chorus Director at the Teatro alla Scala. All of them zealously retained and transmitted to their disciples what they had learned working with Toscanini and Panizza.

A RIVAL AND A RUPTURE

During these years Toscanini's great competitor was Victor de Sabata, unanimously considered his only rival, with whom he no longer had dealings. By then Toscanini was a fervent anti-fascist, and de Sabata was a friend of Benito Mussolini. De Sabata is currently better known than Panizza, but less known than Toscanini (perhaps for similar reasons, as we will see further on).[285]

Finding himself with an orchestra and public fanatical about Toscanini, Panizza, Calusio, and Votto, it was not easy for the evident musical authority of this maestro to gain recognition, as de Sabata had not been part of the foundational achievement of La Scala as a self-governing institution. Despite this, he did achieve outstanding interpretations, and his approach to Wagner's *Tristan und Isolde* was so sublime that for him it meant becoming the second foreign conductor to be hired at the Wagnerian temple of Bayreuth (the first, ironically, had been Toscanini himself).

Regrettable and unfair episodes were in no short supply for de Sabata or others, which give an idea of how obsessed Milanese musicians and music lovers were with Toscanini and his group. In 1931, de Sabata found himself rehearsing Massenet's *Manon*; faced with the repeated resistence by some instrumentalists to perform specific passages as he insisted, after the final rehearsal the maestro refused to conduct the opera.

The Teatro's management requested that Panizza take over the production without any preparation, which Héctor did with his usual professionalism, in addition to an admirable quota of cold blood and a good result. At one moment of the premiere, however, a spectator evidently less Toscaninian and more "de Sabatian" than the majority shouted at Panizza: "Shame on you, it's not your work!" referring to the fact that the performance had been entirely prepared by de Sabata.

Victor de Sabata was, in addition to a great maestro, an authentic gentleman. Despite his rivalry with Toscanini, the hostile climate with which he was received at La Scala, and his adherence to fascism, during his *scaligero* tenure he did not cease to invite the conductors who had been close collaborators of the previous management: thus Panizza, along with Votto, Failoni and Santini, continued to tread the Milanese podium.

The turning point for the relationship between Toscanini and Panizza was, as we have seen, 1938. By then Arturo had taken a clear position in relation to Hitler's Germany and refused to perform again in that country. That year, when our musician — who did not have the slightest interest in ideological or political subjects and apparently did not profess particular libertarian ideals— accepted to work in Berlin, Toscanini grew furious and cut all communication with him. The maestro from Parma included him among the "artists who do not deserve to be counted among men but among slaves."[286]

It is curious that this phrase, even with Panizza referred to as a "slave," leaves open the possibility that one can continue to consider him an "artist," a word which for Toscanini was without a doubt a form of praise and not a minor qualification if one considers that Arturo's furious outbursts knew no limit. Wilhelm Furtwängler, for whose style he also felt no affinity, as it seemed to him absolutely subjective and arbitrary, also merited this opinion.

As we have seen, Héctor returned to La Scala for the last time after the war, between 1947 and 1948, to conduct — among other works— unforgettable versions of Strauss' *Der Rosenkavalier* and Wagner's *Parsifal,* the beloved German repertoire he always regretted not frequenting more intensely in London, New York, and above all his native Buenos Aires.

FROM EUROPE TO AMERICA

It is worth telling the story of two young and talented Jewish musicians, one Austrian and the other Hungarian. In the second half of the '30s they worked as accompanying pianists and musical assistants at the Salzburg Festival. There they closely followed Toscanini's work in operas by Mozart, Beethoven, Wagner and Verdi. One of them even went down to the pit during the performances to play the *glockenspiel* in *Die Zauberflöte,* which was then recorded in radio broadcasts, today accessible through compact discs.

Both musicians were stupefied by their admiration for the work displayed by the Italian maestro, who came to Austria to show the system of work he had implemented with Panizza in Italy. They had the opportunity to talk with Toscanini, listen to his anecdotes and receive some advice. These experiences were certainly defining, so that later on Erich Leinsdorf and Georg Solti — such were the names of these young men— became extraordinary symphonic and opera conductors whom everybody remembers today and whose discographic legacy we continue to enjoy.[287]

Tullio Serafin, for his part, needs no further introduction, for he was one of the great opera conductors of his generation. During the first period of Toscanini at La Scala, the twenty-something Serafin played second viola between 1899 and 1900, and worked as his assistant between 1901 and 1902, along with the veteran Pietro Sormani. In 1903 Toscanini left La Scala and Serafin set out on his brilliant operatic and recording career, which would lead him to become a music reference in Verona, Rome, Milan, and Buenos Aires, and to be appointed principal director of the Italian repertoire at the Metropolitan Opera in New York.

In an interesting work of his authorship, Serafin partly gives the lie to the legend of the Toscaninian school as passively submissive to the printed notes, and informs his readers of the changes that seem to him allowed and even necessary in some scores.[288]

As we have seen, upon arriving at the Met in 1934, Panizza was assigned almost the entire Italian repertoire (or to be more specific, the repertoire in Italian, which is quite a bit more ample), taking upon himself precisely the responsability that Serafin had exercised until then. The artistic bodies of the New York opera house (where Toscanini had also worked), critics and spectators in that big city felt they were thus guaranteed continuity of intentions and style. The praise for Panizza's work was unanimous.

At the Metropolitan Opera, Panizza worked hand in hand with two Italian musicians younger than him who lived in New York, with the first serving as assistant conductor and the second as chorus trainer: Gennaro Papi and Fausto Cleva. Both became regular conductors in the pit of the Met for the Italian repertoire when, in 1942, Héctor decided to leave New York. Thus they continued the Panizza line, which was essentially that of Toscanini. An extremely young pianist studying directing from the United States (Cincinnati, to be exact), encountered Cleva's work and became his attentive disciple. This was James Levine, who would later successfully run the Met for many years.

It is very interesting to see maestro Levine — a complete musician and omnivore with an enormous symphonic repertoire, until recently still active as a chamber pianist— rehearse an Italian opera. He played the piano himself with the performers, as well as read the score in front of the orchestra. The form in which he worked — practical and dynamic yet also detail-oriented and punctilious, with a great emphasis on the intentionality of the musical phrase and handling of the poetic text— as well as his interest in vocal quality come directly from the Toscanini and Panizza line, through Fausto Cleva. Levine stated in numerous interviews that he felt an immense admiration for the great Arturo, which comes as no surprise.

Another Italian maestro living in the United States, Dick Marzollo, was responsible for spreading in North America the working method of Toscanini and Serafin, to whom he was assistant. A remarkable director who received his teachings was the North American James Conlon, who visited him over the course of seventeen years and learned from him the secrets of the Italian opera repertoire. Marzollo, an excellent pianist, was the trainer whom several of the best singers from the United States trusted, among them the legendary baritone Cornell MacNeil.

Somewhat further to the south, an artist who developed under the wing of Héctor Panizza at the Teatro Colón in Buenos Aires was Roberto Kinsky, a maestro with great merits of his own who was for years a pillar at the Colón. The Hungarian Kinsky undoubtedly complemented his musical formation of a German cut with the more Italian way of working transmitted to him by Panizza.

The Argentine director Juan Emilio Martini, who worked permanently at the Colón for more than fifty years, also had the opportunity to collaborate closely with Panizza, Calusio and Votto; without having studied formally with any of these maestros, he considered himself a disciple of them all and inherited several scores from Héctor's pocket. In

1988 he published a brief work about the interpretation of Italian opera, evidently inspired by Serafin's book.[289]

Martini had met Panizza in 1934, the year the Italian-Argentine had just taken over the Italian wing of the Met. "He was the living, real, burning exponent of the high achiever," he recalls in a text in which he clearly expresses his vision of the school Panizza represented: "Héctor Panizza and Tullio Serafin, who left this world with a difference of a few months, and for fifty years of intense activity were the owners of diametrically opposed techniques and working regimes, were in my understanding the last representatives of the simultaneous orchestra conductor and *maestro concertatore*, the single person responsible for a performance in both its musical and stage aspects. Their words and decisions were indisputable law. Both left their profession at the precise moment that a new authority emerged at the forefront in the opera houses: the stage director."

Martini understood that "Panizza possessed the true gesture that governs each musical fragment and here the comparison with the masterful technique of Toscanini clearly emerges."[290]

Naturally, not only Martini but several other resident maestros of the Teatro Colón knew Panizza, Calusio, Votto and Kinsky, and had worked repeatedly with them; today many have died and the rest are retired or in the process of doing so.

In the first group, we would like to mention Jorge Fontenla, who recently passed away. A versatile musician (pianist, director, composer, teacher and manager), he was an untiring worker and authentic creator of artistic and cultural events in Argentina. Close to ninety years of age, maestro Fontenla still recalled with pleasure and gratitude seeing Panizza direct and working with Kinsky.[291]

In the second group, it is necessary to at least mention Vicente La Ferla, a musician with international experience as an orchestra and opera conductor, choral trainer, accompanying pianist, music stage director and teacher of the operatic repertoire — in addition to appreciated collaborator of Fernando Previtali— who studied with Franco Ferrara in Siena and even came to occupy the position of artistic secretary at the Teatro alla Scala during Claudio Abbado's management.

Maestro La Ferla still remembers his first meeting with Panizza, in the '40s: "When I was an adolescent studying at the Municipal Conservatory it was obligatory to form part of the Student Choir; its director was the maestro Luis Ochoa, who also belonged to the institution. We were invited to sing the Argentine National Anthem at a gala performance for a national holiday at the Teatro Colón. The singers, with their white uniforms, were located in tiered stands which spanned the whole width of the stage."

La Ferla went on: "When the curtain rose that majestic hall appeared before our astonished eyes, and the audience in formal dress broke into applause to greet us. There before the Colón's Resident Orchestra, we saw the conductor, maestro Héctor Panizza, who smiled at us in a friendly way. Raising the baton he attacked the introduction to the Argentine National Anthem. I will never forget his gesture, solemn and at the same time worthy of a general. This conductor's gesture has been imprinted on my retina for my entire life."[292]

With Panizza and Votto in Milan, but above all with Calusio and Kinsky in Buenos Aires, Miguel Ángel Veltri (known abroad as Michelangelo, exactly as occurred with Panizza's first name) had a productive relationship. This Argentine of Italian ancestry was the assistant conductor at the Teatro Colón and later had a prominent international career, including performances on the main stages of Milan, London, Vienna, Paris, Barcelona and above all the Met in New York. It does not seem chance that the first opera he heard in his life was a *Faust* conducted at the Colón by Serafin. Over the course of his life, in more than one interview, he defended the conducting school from which he had emerged, and of which he felt himself a proud link in the chain.[293]

THE VOTTO SCHOOL

Antonino Votto, Panizza's protegé at La Scala, began to teach orchestral conducting at the Conservatory of Milan in 1941. From his pedagogical activity at that prestigious house emerged Claudio Abbado, as well as Riccardo Muti, maestros who came to be — among other roles— music directors at La Scala, the second succeeding the first.

Antonino did not elaborate a systematized program —by then teaching in the specialty was just starting to appear in the world's conservatories— and instead taught through practice, through anecdotal stories about his work at the Ambrosian opera house and recommendations as lapidary as "Direttore si nasce, poi si diventa" (A director is born, and later comes to be one), "La maggior parte della musica è in due" (The majority of music may be conducted in 2/2 time) and "Non rompete le scatole all'orchestra," a colorful expression that out of modesty we will not dare to translate. [294]

He also taught, of course, by example of his own musical work, which included playing the piano and conducting 127 operas from memory, a bit like Toscanini himself. Even today Muti remembers with astonishment when he saw his maestro rehearsing an extremely complex opera like Verdi's *Falstaff* without the score, without even having it on the music stand; when the astonished student asked about this, the teacher replied that it was the logical consequence of having worked for so many years alongside his mentor from Parma.

In 1942, after a year of teaching, Votto prepared a series of notes for his students, which circulated from that time at the Conservatory and was recently published in 1999. They make up the synthesis of his advice for the profession of conductor.[295]

Claudio Abbado, who came from a distinguished family of Milanese musicians, after graduating from his studies with Votto continued in Vienna with Hans Swarowsky, a learned conductor and profoundly Germanophile pedagogue who all the same considered Toscanini an authentic reference forsymphonic and opera interpretation.[296] Although the extremely young Claudio had been able to admire Toscanini's rehearsals and performances, he ended up forming himself as a much less Mediterranean and more *mittel-european* conductor than Toscanini, Votto, or Muti, in both matters of repertoire and body language on the podium. In addition, Abbado's somewhat withdrawn personality and deeply courteous behavior when working with other musicians were light years away from the profile of his classmate Muti, as well as that of Toscanini himself.

Abbado always took on the opera repertoire following the conducting guidelines defined by Toscanini and Panizza in Milan, however, preparing the soloist singers above all through extensive rehearsals in the dressing room, on the piano. Even today one can appreciate this detail in the film that shows him rehearsing and conducting Verdi's *Messa da requiem*, with the artistic bodies of La Scala; the type of musical interaction one sees between Abbado and the bass Samuel Ramey from the United States is a good example of this.[297]

In this context Riccardo Muti, a Neapolitan like Votto, is undoubtedly the most notable case among the great conductors still active. Launching to fame in 1967 as the winner of the "Guido Cantelli" conducting contest, Muti fully embraced the teachings of his maestro and La Scala's heritage received from the latter. This includes certain attempts to imitate Toscanini in his gestures, his repertoire, his interpretative decisions, his surly demeanor when conducting, even his cutting attitudes, as well of course in his strongly top-down way of managing La Scala during the period he was music director of the Milanese opera house.

This is a case in which the identification with the model is absolute, clearly sought and even brought to fever pitch, with some attitudes of extreme musical rigidity and excesses of pontification before the mass media that neither Toscanini nor Votto nor Panizza would ever have imagined, for they were rather more pragmatic, flexible, and low-profile musicians. Even today Muti does not let an opportunity pass to mention

Votto as his mentor, who furthermore came even to be his best man during his wedding with Cristina Mazzavillani.

Other important musicians who studied directing with Antonino Votto in Milan were Maurizio Pollini, Claudio Scimone, Pinchas Steinberg, Luciano Berio, Enza Ferrari and the already mentioned Guido Cantelli.

Evidently the rest of Votto's students did not achieve universal fame like those mentioned here, but many had satisfactory careers. One of his students, Ronaldo Rosa (as far as one knows, the only Argentine to graduate under his guidance at the "Giuseppe Verdi" Conservatory), continues the heritage received from Antonino, above all by means of his teaching activity, having instilled many aspects of this form of work to Argentine artists today making their careers.[298]

ADMIRERS AND IMITATORS

Another great follower of Toscanini, in whom admiration at times became emulation, was no doubt Lorin Maazel. A violinist and composer, in addition to conductor, the French-American was a child prodigy who came to know Toscanini personally: the old maestro saw him direct at eleven years of age in New York and afterward, caressing his head, said to him with a mixture of astonishment and tenderness: "May God bless you."

There were also other well-known conductors who positioned themselves, to some degree, within the Toscanini-Panizza line. In most of the cases they did not have any personal contact with these maestros, though some saw them conduct when they were still young.

Herbert von Karajan once declared that he felt fascination as much for Toscanini' s energy and strict precision as for, at the other extreme, Furtwängler' s flexibility and capacity of improvisation. By his own admission, from his first years in his job he sought a style of conducting that would permit him to combine the best of both worlds; it is not easy to say if he achieved this goal or not, but undoubtedly he has achieved many things during his long and meteoric career as a conductor of operas, concerts and in recordings.

It is little wonder that the passage of Karajan through La Scala was for him as for as for the Teatro a very special moment, particularly the unforgettable Verdian *Messa da requiem* performed in honor of Toscanini in 1967, with a quartet of incomparable soloists including Leontyne Price, Fiorenza Cossotto, Luciano Pavarotti, and Nicolai Ghiaurov.[299]

In this context at least ten Italian conductors must be mentioned, specialized in the peninsular opera repertoire of the 19th century, which with a greater or lesser grade of intensity and awareness followed the course laid out by Toscanini and Panizza in the golden years of La Scala, on occasions bringing it to theaters where neither of those two titans ever worked. All of these maestros were born between 1902 and 1932.

We think for example of Oliviero De Fabritiis, a close collaborator of Serafin in Rome, who also had the opportunity to conduct at La Scala. Another case is that of Fernando Previtali, assistant to Gui in Florence and Genoa, who in 1951 wrote a *Guida allo studio della direzione d'orchestra* in which he explains the way to conduct an orchestra and arrange an opera that we have been discussing.[300]

Gianandrea Gavazzeni was conductor at La Scala for many years, and a musicologist and refined author of many books of of the greatest interest. Between 1924 and 1929 he could attend almost all the performances directed by Toscanini and Panizza at the Milanese opera house.

It is also fundamental to mention Franco Ferrara, who played bass under Toscanini's baton at the Teatro Comunale of Bolonia and witnessed along with Ottorino Respighi the famous 1931 episode in which a group of Mussolini's supporters slapped the maestro of Parma for having refused to perform the fascist party hymn, *Giovinezza*. Afflicted by a health problem, Ferrara left conducting and dedicated himself from an early age to teaching, giving courses on specific topics in which almost all the main conductors in the contemporary scene participated.

Even without having direct dealings with either Toscanini or Panizza, Francesco Molinari-Pradelli situated himself in their wake, giving proof of this in his performances at La Scala and many recordings of Italian opera. Renato Cellini, for his part, saw Toscanini and Panizza conduct very often, for he was the son of Enzio Cellini, stage director of the Milanese opera house in the '20s; Renato later conducted a great number of performances at the Met, after Panizza left New York.

Closer to our days we can point to Lamberto Gardelli, assistant to Serafin for eight years and today widely remembered for his excellent recordings of Verdi's less-known operas, and Anton Guadagno, who was a collaborator of Karajan and enjoyed an distinguished career, above all in the United States and Austria.

Bruno Bartoletti, for his part, was a direct disciple of Serafin and knew how to hold high the flag of the Italian conducting school, especially in Rome, Florence, Copenhagen, and Chicago, cities where he was principal director. Finally we come to Giuseppe Patanè, a habitual presence on the podium of La Scala for many years with a considerable discography; maestro Patanè was another of those batons with the ability to take on any title from the usual opera repertoire without even looking at the score.

What can be said about that unique case, the legendary Carlos Kleiber? He was a great enthusiast of Toscanini's records and when it fell to him to conduct at La Scala, he took advantage of the opportunity to ask the most experienced instrumentalists what it was like to play under Arturo's baton, and how the director from Parma achieved specific musical results.[301] Carlos' artistic sensitivity at times seemed to distance him from the Italian model, however. His incomparable lightness, extreme subtlety, and almost inventive flexibility at the moment of making music are not virtues that can be easily linked with Toscanini (who had, needless to say, others that were different and of no less value).

Furthermore, the quota of strict Toscanianian rigor and perfectionism in Carlos' conducting was surely a paternal inheritance. Let us remember that Toscanini invited Erich Kleiber twice to conduct in New York and that on hearing his first concert, wrote to him in a letter that "non ci fu male" (it wasn't bad), almost exaggerated praise for someone characterized by his relentless judgments.[302]

This transmission of Toscaninian concepts from father to son should not be surprising: it is enough to listen to Erich's albums and see the few surviving pieces of footage to realize that Kleiber the father, in his style of conducting and musical criteria, was something like a German Toscanini. [303]

But Carlos had another great influence from the school of Italian opera conducting: Alberto Erede, a Genovese director with a long international career and significant discographic work, specializing in the peninsular repertoire and well versed in the work of Toscanini. Carlos was his assistant — along with the pianist Richard Trimborn— at the Deutsche Oper am Rhein in Düsseldorf. In an interview, Trimborn said that working with Erede was eminently formative for them both, as at that time they were very young musicians.[304]

Finally, let us not forget that as an adolescent Carlos Kleiber had dealings, in Buenos Aires, with one of Panizza's main collaborators at the Colón, Roberto Kinsky, who taught him to read an orchestral score.[305]

It is also worth mentioning the case of Carlo Maria Giulini. Beginning in 1950, the ex-violist directed a series of operas and concertos in Bergamo, some of which were broadcast by radio. This work drew the positive attention of Arturo Toscanini as well as Victor de Sabata, both of whom contacted him — separately, of course— to offer him their support. Giulini began to work as an assistant to maestro de Sabata at La Scala, made his opera debut there in 1952, and beginning in 1953 took over the music direction of the Teatro for five years. Giulini's temperament and style were at the opposite extreme of the electric Toscanini's, and in every case came closer to Panizza's balanced personality; however, other elements in common triggered the mutual confidence between the young man and the veteran. In a dialogue from the '50s, partially recorded for posterity, Toscanini summarized the way in which one must prepare an opera, and a philosophical Giulini concluded: "With you a new aesthetic of interpretation began. What Paganini did with the violin, what Liszt did with the piano, you did with orchestral conducting."[306]

THE TOSCANINI-PANIZZA LINE TODAY

To this point — with the exceptions of Levine, Conlon, and Muti— the conductors referred to have already died or are at least retired. For this reason, it is time to take a look at those who are still holding the baton, beginning with the "old guard" and proceeding toward newer generations.

Zubin Mehta — particularly the young Mehta— reminds one a great deal of Toscanini and Panizza in his Verdian approach. How can one forget his first recording of *Aïda*, for example, which seems almost Toscanini's version for NBC or Panizza's for the Met, with only a different cast and an astonishing technical quality in the recording? [307]

Furthermore, Mehta's admiration for Toscanini was never a secret and he also studied with the Toscaninian Hans Swarowsky, as Abbado's classmate in Vienna. [308]

Beyond Muti, if we had to assign the moniker of Toscaninian — and therefore, indirectly, also Panizzian—to an Italian conductor who is still active, undoubtedly we would think of the veteran Nello Santi. Santi does not possess either Arturo's magnetic charisma or ardent temperament (nor, indeed, Riccardo's), but neither does he display the excesses, rigidities, tantrums, and aggressions of the great maestro from Parma, which no orchestra would tolerate in our day.

This very experienced conductor — above all of opera and particularly Italian opera— prepares and directs absolutely everything in his vast repertoire from memory, with a method of rehearsing, a specific set of gestures, a knowledge of the mechanisms of instrumental execution, and a capacity for auditory discernment that no doubt go back to the school of the '20s at the Teatro alla Scala, established by the great conductors about whom we have been speaking. Maestro Santi, with his respectful manner, great technical knowledge, and absolute command of the score, generates a working environment that is very focused but at the same time reasonably relaxed, and always obtains what he proposes musically. In this, perhaps without knowing it himself, he seems more like Serafin and Panizza than like his admired Toscanini.

Another illustrious example of this conducting school is the veteran Maurizio Arena. After studying with Franco Ferrara, he took classes of advanced musical training with Tullio Serafin as well as Antonino Votto and Gianandrea Gavazzeni, a *scaligero* trio that revealed to him all the secrets of Italian-style opera conducting.

Donato Renzetti's path is more curious. Son of a timpani player at La Scala (a position for which he was chosen by Cantelli himself), while he was still underage he began to work as a percussionist at the great Milanese opera house, where he played between 1963 and 1979 at the orders of Votto, Gavazzeni, and Abbado — the three music directors of the Teatro who succeeded one another during those sixteen years—and was also conducted by guest maestros like Karajan. In 1980 he won the "Guido Cantelli" contest, the same one (curious coincidences) that years before had triggered Muti's international career.

Bruno Campanella, an outstanding student of Hans Swarowsky, great specialist in the repertoire of the *bel canto*, possibly the greatest Rossinian conductor of the moment, and a guest maestro at La Scala, is another name we can mention in this context.

Gianluigi Gelmetti, a student of Swarowsky as well as of Franco Ferrara, declared for his part — with a metaphor that is perhaps somewhat elemental, but very clear— that if for him Ferrara was a father, Toscanini was a grandfather. For many years Gelmetti gave the course of advanced musical training in conducting that had belonged to Ferrara at the Accademia Musicale Chigiana in Siena. There he abandoned himself to violent verbal attacks against every student whose work on the podium seemed to him lacking; curiously, in a time in which it is impossible to treat orchestras as badly as Toscanini did, Gelmetti opted to do so with his students.

Another case worthy of mentioning is that of the Milanese conductor Riccardo Chailly, who studied with Ferrara and was assistant to Abbado at La Scala, the house where he is currently music director and where he has displayed talent that has made him one of the best in his profession. For his part, Pier Giorgio Morandi was assistant to Muti as well as Patanè — in addition to ex-member of the Teatro alla Scala orchestra— and also places himself in their tradition.

Among the current well-known conductors of Italian works who follow, in greater or lesser measure, the profession of *maestro concertatore* and orchestra conductor in the Toscanini and Panizza line — though with very personal styles and therefore very different amongst themselves— we can cite the names of Stefano Ranzani, Fabio Luisi, Antonio Pappano, Carlo Rizzi, Daniele Gatti and Gianandrea Noseda, all born between 1959 and 1964.

Among the maestros of other nationalities, three Israelis deserve a mention: the veteran Eliahu Inbal, Ferrara's disciple and Toscanini's ardent admirer; the already mentioned Pinchas Steinberg, a direct student of Votto; and the temperamental Daniel Oren, who in his youth was an assistant to Karajan and Ferrara, and is today one of the main exponents of Italian romantic and veristic opera interpretation.

TOWARD A MORE BALANCED ACCOUNT

For reasons that would be too long to analyze, more political than artistic (already researched by other authors) toward the end of his career and beginning with a press campaign launched from the United States during the Second World War, the name of Toscanini became absolutely exclusive: he transformed into being, simply, the greatest orchestra conductor on the planet and the supreme moral authority in the musical world. There could be no discussion or possible nuance, almost like saying *après lui, le déluge.*[309]

Once it has been clarified that Toscanini absolutely merits all the admiration given to him, one must admit that reality is complex by definition and that one cannot be restricted by simple slogans, however convincing they seem. Precisely due to the process of marketing just mentioned, many excellent conductors from the past and present are followers of Panizza almost as much as of the great Toscanini... without knowing it.

In most cases these maestros are not conscious of the legacy of which Panizza is a vital part because they have grown up and been formed by listening to talk about Toscanini's musical feats as something unique and isolated, outside of any context. But everything human always needs a context and the extraordinary labor of the great Arturo is no exception.

Panizza is a central element in this context, but beginning from the '40s his name passed completely to a second rank in international public artistic opinion, and later went about disappearing completely from collective memory. It is true that if something was not stated by the Italian-Argentine during the course of his life, it was the desire to be a world celebrity or put himself in the spotlight of the media by means of high-flown declarations, nor much less to be a symbol of libertarian ideals or an endorsement artist of the "American dream." In these affirmations, let us clarify, there is neither a value judgment nor, much less, a polemical intention: only the description of a reality.

In any case, Panizza's ideal was perhaps that of being recognized in life as a composer of importance and, if possible, seeing his most important works regularly performed, even after his death. This of course was a dream destined not to be fulfilled. What's more, toward the end of his days he himself declared, with great simplicity, "I only sought in my life to be an honest person and an honest artist."[310] It is not by chance then — and with this, one is not trying to frivolously feed vacuous conspiracy theories— that there exist so many books and documentaries about the career of Arturo Toscanini, or that his studio recordings and the majority of his live recordings are available on the commercial circuit (to mention only two examples), while none of this happened with Héctor Panizza — a conductor of a level objectively comparable with that of Toscanini— either in his native Argentina, or in the Italy of his parents and children, or in the rest of the world.[311]

In harmony with these concepts, an Argentine critic expressed in an article very appropriately titled "By Arturo Toscanini's Side" (that is, "on the same level" as the great maestro of Parma): "To state today that Héctor Panizza's was the great baton born from the soil of America is not the consequence of an emotional state or local position, which in artistic matters would seem particularly inappropriate [...] It is the recognition or the affirmation of an indisputable matter of fact, which at some point we have pretended to ignore."[312]

PART THREE

APPENDICES

Chapter 11

Anecdotes

There is no doubt that Héctor Panizza's primary professional referent was Arturo Toscanini and that many traits of the legendary conductor's artistic preferences molded Panizza's musical identity; he was also a worker as untiring and detail-oriented as his mentor. Yet Héctor's personality had few traits in common with that of Toscanini.

Panizza, due to his two nationalities, his birth in a great capital like Buenos Aires, and his childhood within a family of musicians, was a man of the world from a very young age, which cannot be said of Arturo, who acquired a certain culture and some fluency with languages only with the passing of the years.

In addition, the behavior of the Italian-Argentine toward colleagues, soloists, choirs, and orchestras was always marked by the greatest respect. Héctor is universally remembered as a gentleman who never lost his temper in public. The shouts and insults Toscanini addressed to his musicians (which can still be heard today, for they were recorded without his authorization during rehearsals at the NBC studio in New York) are unimaginable on Panizza's lips.[313]

Even if in private Toscanini knew how to be a charming, amusing, and even a seductive man (he showed boundless enthusiasm for the opposite sex), these aspects of his personality did not often make themselves apparent at the moment of making music, when he exhibited a very singular mixture of dramatic seriousness and harsh charisma.

In contrast, Panizza –above all the mature Panizza– seemed to restrain his temperament as much in his private life as in his professional one. When working he undoubtedly displayed a personality less dominating than that of his mentor, but on the other hand he did know how to display a good sense of humor, a fine irony, and an enviable calm even when something unusual happened during a rehearsal or performance.

The following, then, provides some interesting examples of this, though two curiosities must be pointed out. The first: the majority of the anecdotes were recounted by Héctor himself, but upon doing so, out of respectful modesty he often avoided mentioning names, titles, places, and dates. The second: for some reason, none of the anecdotes refer to his time at the Teatro Colón.

UNFUNNY OPERA

The 19th century was nearing its end when a very young Héctor found himself in Savona to conduct Ponchielli's *La Gioconda* at the Teatro Chiabrera. The improvised manager in charge of the modest opera season, called Salomone (a wholesale greengrocer by profession) was, it seems, as ignorant as he was unscrupulous, and had put together the cast, chorus, and orchestra with a single priority in mind: economizing money.

Thus Mr. Salomone had hired singers with no experience for the secondary roles in anopera, a reduced group of amateurs to sing in the choir, and an authentic "Armata Brancaleone" of amateur instrumentalists —among whom were found a butcher, a shopkeeper, and a post office's employee— for the orchestra.

During rehearsals Panizza found himself obliged to expel from the cast the bass in the minor role of Zuane, a rustic man who earned a living singing popular songs at restaurants. As a consequence of this situation, when leaving a night rehearsal, to his surprise the conductor received a tremendous blow to the head, delivered by this singer with a thick piece of wood. The maestro's skull was unharmed, thanks to the particularly stiff hat he was wearing at that moment.

The issues of the production did not stop there. *La Gioconda*'s Prelude includes a well-known and prominent passage for four soloist cellos... but the orchestra of the wise Salomone included only three performers of the instrument; to top it off, only the first was able to play his part with skill. The twenty-three-year-old conductor, taking a deep breath, saw himself obliged to add a pair of violas to the row, and thanks to this the section seemed to work reasonably well during rehearsals.

However, the biggest problem happened when Alcibiade Ponchielli, the son of Panizza's composer friend, appeared in person to listen to the performance. Informed of the news, the musicians began to panic and the first cello declared himself ill. There was no one to play his part, so Héctor refused to conduct: without this instrumentalist not even the prelude to the opera could be performed.

Salomone insisted that the young man be obliged to conduct the performance regardless; the discussion rose in volume until the young maestro ended by telling off the impresario, calling him ill-mannered and shameless. At Salomone's request, peace officers intervened, who first ordered Panizza to conduct the show (with another viola sight-reading the part of first cello!) before accompanying him to spend the night in jail.

Nothing else was known of Alcibiade Ponchielli, and perhaps it was better this way. Héctor Panizza, for his part, never forgot the opera that brought him into acquaintance with prison. His sharp reaction toward Salomone was perhaps the only one in his career.[314]

AN UNFORTUNATE DRIVER

As an interpreter, Panizza was always curious and open to the new musical trends, even if he did not share them (as we have seen, musical atonality was foreign to him). On one occasion, however, he immediately realized that certain experiments with sound had no greater future and would only provoke the laughter of the public.

In 1910, the Argentine took charge of the musical preparations at the Teatro Dal Verme for a new opera —set in the 20th century, somewhat unusual for that time— in which the music publisher Tito Ricordi served as stage director: Pavanelli's *Vanna*.

At a certain moment a secondary tenor, who had a ruddy figure and was dressed as a driver, advanced with a decided step toward the proscenium; in the meantime, the orchestra insistently repeated a mechanical sequence of sounds that descended from high to low notes, a sequence only interrupted by a few moments of inexplicable silence.

The combination of what was seen with what was heard was truly grotesque, and Panizza had not hesitated to issue a warning about this during rehearsals.

Héctor's musical and theatrical intuition did not fail: at the premiere, during the moments of silence between the different sequences of the descending sounds, a very sharp whistle proceeded from the upper seats of the auditorium performing an imitation of the passage, generating such hilarity in the spectators that the performance had to be interrupted and the production canceled.

Everything indicates that after that Panizza tried to avoid opera composers who dressed their tenors like drivers.[315]

NAPLES VERSUS SYDNEY

During his long stay in London, Panizza conducted a good part of the Italian operatic repertoire, taking under his baton two of the artists who were most admired by the British public: the Italian Enrico Caruso and the Australian Nellie Melba. The diva was initially somewhat resistant to working with a conductor whom she did not know, but later she could verify and would praise his qualities.

These two singers, whose voices were as explosive as their temperaments, did not often act together in London; their psychological incompatability was likely not the only inconvenience, and Covent Garden preferred not to pay two salaries as sizeable as theirs for the same show. After all, with the presence of just one of the two stars, success at the box office for the evening was assured.

The fact is that in 1914, King George V expressed his desire to listen to a performance of Puccini's *La bohème* in which both singers were featured. Naturally the Royal Opera House management had no option but to consent to the monarch's request and programmed the evening, assigning the conducting to Panizza. And so the day of the debut arrived.

Let us imagine the maestro's reaction when Caruso, seconds before ripping into a memorable interpretation of "Che gelida manina," addressed Melba in his booming Neapolitan dialect, saying "Mo' sta' a sentì comme se canta!" ("Now you'll hear how it must be sung!").

A good part of the very elegant British audience did not understand the significance of this unusual "ad-lib," but Héctor took a few seconds to recover his composure after such a surprise. Fortunately, everything ended with a thunderous ovation.[316]

PUCCINIAN TEACHING

In 1915, Panizza found himself on tour through Spain, and on a certain occasion it fell to him to conduct *Tosca* before the public in a small city in the provinces. Possibly people there were listening to Puccini's masterpiece for the first time, or for the first time in a long time.

The work arrived at the passage assigned to four cellos at the beginning of the third act, with a sharp tessitura and difficult pitch. Upon hearing the chromatic descent led by the first cello —which, Héctor recounted, was played by an excellent performer— the spectators burst into shouts of protest: evidently this line descending toward the lower register in semitones was shocking and unpleasant for an audience that knew little about the repertoire.

The maestro had to stop the performance. From the pit he addressed himself toward the audience without losing his calm, to say the following: "Ladies and gentlemen, the soloist [...] has admirably played this very difficult passage. The impression you have had was not correct, and you must allow me to repeat it." The spectators, surprised by the interruption and perfect Spanish of a conductor whom they considered Italian, applauded Panizza and permitted him to resume the section.

The cellos, as can be imagined, put all their effort into the passage, and it sounded even better than the first time. Héctor —who considering his low profile, it seems was experiencing an evening of particular verbosity — sealed the achievement with a resounding "Very good, magnificent!" and made the soloist in the row stand up. He received a strong ovation from the audience. (Apparently in this case maintaining the dramatic continuity of the performance, as important at La Scala for Panizza as it was for Toscanini, did not seem pressing.)

In the performance of *Tosca*'s final act it is known that some tenors have repeated the moving romanza "E lucevan le stelle" at the public's request. (The case of Plácido Domingo at the Teatro Colón might be mentioned.) But to give an "encore" to this passage with the cellos... for that there is no other historical case on record.[317]

ROYAL INTERVENTION AT THE REAL

Sometime after his Spanish *Tosca*, in 1916, another Iberian adventure awaited the Italian-Argentine conductor, when he arrived in Madrid to take over two opera productions at the Teatro Real.

Let us imagine his surprise when, prepared to begin a rehearsal, King Alfonso XIII appeared in the hall. The sovereign approached the pit, gave his hand to Panizza, greeted the musicians and gestured for them to begin their work, while he took a seat on the orchestra's first row, just behind the conductor. As Panizza had made conscientious preparations (according to the working method applied with Toscanini in Milan), everything proceeded perfectly, almost as if it were a dress rehearsal; the king's presence as a spectator undoubtedly also made the participants give the best of themselves. But the problem lay precisely in this.

Don Alfonso gently touched Panizza's back and said to him: "No, no, this is going too well; I want to see a rehearsal." To please the monarch, Héctor had no choice but to interrupt the performance with superfluous commentaries and redundant advice, which logically made the admonished musicians feel uncomfortable.

The situation returned to normal shortly afterward, when the king, apparently satisfied that he had witnessed "a rehearsal," finally left the hall and Panizza could continue his work.[318]

DONIZETTI RETURNS FROM THE GRAVE

Although a composer himself, Panizza felt very uneasy with a habitual behavior in his colleagues. When a composer attended rehearsals for an opera of his own authorship, he often interrupted the conductor during his work of musical preparation to verbally indicate how he preferred a specific passage to be interpreted: more quickly, more slowly, with more or less sound, etcetera.

This had already recently happened with Umberto Giordano and *Siberia*, and with Giacomo Puccini and *Tosca*, and would later happen with Victor de Sabata and *Il macigno*. The knowledge and good intentions of these artists were of course beyond all doubt; even so, to see onself interrupted and in some way deprived of authority before the orchestra during a rehearsal did not exactly please the conductor.

Shortly after these experiences with Giordano and Puccini, in 1917, came the day Héctor had to conduct Donizetti's *Lucrezia Borgia* at La Scala. On the occasion that he began to rehearse, the following exclamation escaped from the maestro's lips, who was in general very sparing with his expressions: "Ah, at last I am conducting an opera by a composer who died a long time ago, so he will not show up to bother me!"

However, a few weeks later, in the middle of a rehearsal, the conductor felt a hand rest on his back as if to call his attention; when he turned around Panizza saw Gaetano Donizetti, who kindly requested him: "A little slower, maestro."

What had happened? The stage manager Napoleone Carottini (who would later embark on a worthy career as opera stage director) had heard Panizza's phrase and dressed up as the venerable maestro of Bergamo, to play a joke on the conductor in front of the orchestra and the singers.

Laughter took hold of all those present and the rehearsal had to be suspended for a few minutes. Panizza, far from being offended, joined in with the general hilarity.

No doubt Héctor never forgot the only time a great composer seemed to have returned from the grave to make a well-intentioned interpretative suggestion.[319]

FROM THE VISUAL TO THE PERFORMING ARTS

In Turin Héctor was in charge of many fortunate productions and also a few that were not so successful, as when in 1920, it fell to him to oversee the city's premiere of Pietro Canonica's *La sposa di Corinto*, a lyrical drama in three acts over a libretto by Carlo Bernardi which had premiered at the Teatro Argentina in Rome two years before.

Canonica, more than a composer, was a sculptor and painter who had by then achieved a great deal of renown in his profession. Evidently the artist had studied music sufficiently to be able to compose an opera in a professional form, but his attempt to pass from the visual to the performing arts did not seem fated for very happy results.

The fact is that this multifaceted creator taught sculpture at an academy of fine arts in Turin where he had been a very severe teacher, failing many students in their exams.

As Panizza recounted, during the inaugural performance, upon finishing the first act and having received a largely positive reaction, the composer came out to greet the audience. When he appeared onstage, however, a thundering mix of whistles, bugle calls, metallic noises produced by shaking a bunch of keys and other sonic interferences overwhelmed Canonica.

It was easy to deduce what had happened: the numerous students of the academy failed by professor Canonica had gained access to the upper seats, converging with all the "instruments" necessary to make the debut an unforgettable event.

Apparently the composer-sculptor-teacher took events with quite a bit of philosophy. As far as one knows, never again did he present an opera under his name... at least not in the same city where he taught.[320]

LAUDING LUCULLUS

While in Turin, another opera was entrusted to Panizza for its world premiere, but the maestro —after having read the script— refused to conduct it: the text and music seemed to him below the minimum professional standard. One scene in particular seemed to him so outlandish (without this being the librettist's and the composer's intention, apparently) that Héctor immediately imagined a reaction of hilarity on the part of the audience.

His refusal to take on the debut did not please the impresario in charge of the season, but entrusting the podium to another experienced conductor solved the problem. (In his version of the story, Panizza tactfully omitted the name of the composer as well as the title of the opera and identity of the colleague hired to conduct it instead of him.)

The work was set in ancient Rome, and based on the character of Lucio Licinio Lucullus, the politician and soldier who passed into history as a great organizer of nocturnal banquets.

One day Panizza sat on the main floor, attending the rehearsal, when the scene that had most attracted his attention was being arranged. In it a soloist tenor sings the words "Lucullo lodate!" (May Lucullus be praised!), to which the different voices of the choir successively respond "Lucullo lodiamo!" (We praise Lucullus!).

The procedure described was repeated several times, with the same verbal exchange around "Lucullus" and childish music whose pulse accelerated little by little until reaching paroxysm, generating what Panizza called —very diplomatically indeed— an "imitative harmony," which during the rehearsal made the performers, choir, and orchestra burst into such laughter the work had to be interrupted.

It could have been no other way: in many dialects of the peninsula —dialects today en route to extinction, but in that time spoken by all Italians— "lu culo" means exactly what the reader imagines (the ass). Ettore was right: such an insistent expression of esteem for the "hindquarters," in the context of a Roman banquet and over such a musical framework could supply no other effect.

This operatic Lucullus and its culinary banquets disappeared from the history of music with notable rapidity.[321]

PARSIFAL WITH A SURPRISE

Panizza found himself conducting a rehearsal for *Parsifal*, the second work of the inaugural season of Toscanini's La Scala. It was the scene of the sacred feast and the chorus singers were located as the composer indicates: a first group was onstage (the knights of the Grail), a second group was at an elevation to the left, and a third group was at an elevation to the right (the two celestial phalanxes). Four maestros oversaw the choral display: Antonino Votto and Mario Frigerio occupied themselves with the first group, Ferruccio Calusio with the second, and Vittore Veneziani with the third.

Still without access to the technology of monitors currently used, it was truly difficult to achieve a perfect coordination of the two celestial choirs with what was happening onstage and in the pit. The rehearsal dragged on without achieving the desired result, while Toscanini listened with growing impatience from the main floor.

So it was that Arturo, without saying anything to anybody, made for the stage, climbed to the place where the left choral flank was found, and relieved Calusio of his responsibility, personally taking charge of the singers. The moment came to repeat the passage; Panizza stopped the performance once again, believing his friend and compatriot Ferruccio was still in his place, and indicated at the top of his lungs, clearly annoyed, "The right flank is fine, but the left is not working!"

It was the first and only time that Panizza publicly undermined, without wishing or knowing it, his illustrious colleague and mentor.[322]

TOSCANINIAN TURMOIL

With evident pleasure, Antonino Votto recounted this story from his first season at the Teatro alla Scala. Ferrucio Calusio, Toscanini's and Panizza' principal assistant, was a shy man who always lived in fear of the Parmesan's sudden explosions of rage. Votto had become Calusio's friend and tried to help him avoid the storms of the irritable maestro or at least calm them.

One evening, Toscanini was scheduled to conduct *Die Meistersinger von Nürnberg*. While in a dressing room next to that of the conductor, Panizza happened to be rehearsing *Gianni Schicchi* on the piano with the soprano Cesarina Valobra in the role of Lauretta and the librettist-stage director Giovacchino Forzano. When he arrived at his dressing room to prepare to conduct, Toscanini heard the lines "oh mio babbino caro" and asked Votto: "Who is singing?" to which the substitute answered: "Valobra." Toscanini let out a kind of grunt and went down to the pit to start the performance.

Returning after the first act, the maestro once again heard the romanza by Lauretta, and from under his breath there escaped an incomprehensible but evidently insulting comment. Immediately afterward, he shut himself in his dressing room, slamming the door. At that moment Calusio and Votto knew that the problem was on the point of explosion, but in contrast to what usually happened, Ferruccio said to Antonino: "Leave them, let them sort it out..."

After the second act, Toscanini returned to the dressing room and began to change his shirt, and upon hearing the soprano once again the storm was unleashed. Arturo came out running, and with his shirt open and suspenders hanging he erupted into the room furiously shouting: "Can I know who these donkeys are? Do they understand or not that the *tempo* is off?!" Panizza stopped playing, Valobra went silent and Forzano remained petrified at the sight of such an apparition. The rehearsal was immediately suspended. In the hallway, the friends Votto and Calusio could not hold back their complicit smiles.[323]

MAESTRO PANIZZA AS LEONORA

It is well-known that few performances can be more hazardous than those of the opera: so many and so various are the elements which must harmoniously converge for an opera performance to be succesful that disaster (or at least a major problem) is always lurking nearby. The same can be said of a dress rehearsal, which must "work" as well as the subsequent premiere that it precedes, with an uninterrupted and impeccable development.

In 1933 our maestro found himself in Berlin, preparing *Il trovatore* with an excellent Italian cast. Everything was proceeding correctly, until the dress rehearsal arrived and the soprano Giannina Arangi-Lombardi, who would take on the role of Leonora, fell ill and could not sing. To top it off, journalists from the most important newspapers in the city had previously been invited to the rehearsal, and were hoping to see something like the live performance.

There was no one who could take the place of Arangi-Lombardi, but Panizza did not lose his calm (in his place, Toscanini would certainly have vanished uttering unrepeatable curses): he knew that up to that moment the opera had been prepared with seriousness down to the last details, so that even in a dress rehearsal without a soprano, he could safely bring the premiere through all the same.

Onstage everything was arranged as best as possible and, for the musical part, Héctor sang the role of Leonora from the pit, as he conducted. His voice had no technical training whatsoever, but his pitch and musicality while singing were apparently irreproachable.

The following day, one of the newspapers with the largest print runs in Berlin published a caricature in which Panizza was seen conducting while wearing a woman's dress, as large tears fell from his eyes, under the headline "Maestro Panizza als Leonore" (Maestro Panizza as Leonora). Evidently for the Berlin journalists his vocal interpretation of the soprano role had been as surprising as it was moving.[324]

AN APOCRYPHAL INTERVIEW

Here we have a curious episode that was very funny for the one who orchestrated it, but did not awaken the least sympathy in Panizza. While Héctor was rehearsing in Berlin, a journalist presented himself at the Hotel Esplanade in the city with the intention of interviewing the conductor. A member of the Italian cast not involved in the rehearsal intercepted the reporter in the lobby and introduced himself as maestro Panizza.

With absolute serenity, the singer answered the interviewer's questions, even commenting on an anecdote entirely invented by himself: that the conductor had once arranged a performance in Parma, in which some spectators were so upset by the tenor protagonist that they threw chicken bones at him, the remains of the dinner they had consumed in the box seats.

A horrified Panizza read the interview in the newspaper the following day and immediately asked for the wrong to be corrected. The same reporter who had interviewed the false Héctor took on the responsibility.

The maestro does not reveal what transpired during his subsequent meeting with the singer who had taken the liberty of playing this joke, but it is easy to imagine that the exchange was not a pleasant moment for either of them. What is certain is that after this, Panizza, already an artist who liked to maintain quite a low profile, tried to concede the least number of interviews possible.[325]

THE CONSTANT RING

Marcos de Estrada, member of an eminent Argentine family, met Héctor Panizza in Buenos Aires during the winter of 1944. Marcos was the grandson of Ángel de Estrada, a writer and poet, and great admirer of Rubén Darío and Gabriele D'Annunzio. Strongly connected with the personalities of the Argentine culture of his time, he invited them to the crowded Sunday lunches he offered at his house.

Among his guests was Giovanni Grazioso, Héctor's father, who had taught music to Santiago, one of Ángel's sons. Santiago de Estrada died unexpectedly at twenty years old, and in a single night an emotional Giovanni composed a *Memento fúnebre* to be played at his funeral. As a sign of gratitude, the relatives gave Santiago's ring to Giovanni.

Nothing more was known of the gift until, half a century later, Marcos saw that Héctor was wearing his uncle's ring. It moved him that the artist remembered the episode and the attention that Panizza granted to him, despite the fact that Panizza's wife was ill and he was afraid his apartment in Milan had caught fire, the manuscript of the *Memento fúnebre* his father had composed along with it.

In the deeply felt account of this meeting, Marcos de Estrada accurately described Héctor Panizza as "a man of good will, frank manners and lively, spontaneous feelings, a simple and kind-hearted spirit." [326]

CHAPTER 12

COMPOSITIONS

Héctor Panizza's artistic path is a more arduous task to trace than one might imagine. In his day Panizza was undoubtedly a public personality, very well-known, and no less admired, but today the sources available to reconstruct some aspects of his existence —such as his private life and his work as composer— are scarcer and less precise than would be desirable.

In his book *Medio siglo de vida musical* (*Half a Century of Musical Life*), Héctor presented a partial and incomplete panorama of his creative output, omitting works, making mistakes upon mentioning his respective publishing houses, and economizing detailed information about many of his works. Even the list of compositions the artist himself included as an appendix to his memoirs is incomplete and inaccurate.

It is for this reason that it seems to us of practical use to gather in a single section the true details of the catalogue of compositions and instrumental arrangements by our musician; there is no certainty that the current list is complete, but it is the most exhaustive of those published to date. The works are presented separated by genre and, within each subsection, by the order in which their premiere took place.

To this summary the wish of the authors is added to one day see a complete critical edition of Héctor Panizza's published works.

STAGE WORKS

El autor del crimen, zarzuela (ca. 1895)

El último invento, zarzuela (ca. 1895)

Il fidanzato del mare, lyrical story, opera (1897)

Medio Evo latino, trilogy, opera (1900)

Aurora, opera (1908, rev. 1945)

Bizancio (Bisanzio), musical poem (1939)

Gavota for strings (1892)

Bodas campestres for orchestra (1892) *Suite* in four movements (1893) [327]

Minué for strings (1893)

Tema y variaciones for orchestra (1919)

Nocturno for orchestra in G flat major (ca. 1923)

El rey y la floresta (Il re e la foresta), symphonic poem for soprano,

baritone, choir and orchestra (1923)

INSTRUMENTAL CHAMBER MUSIC

Cinco piezas for piano (Five Pieces for Piano) (ca. 1895)

Canto de octubre (October Song) for two pianos (1895)

Scherzo for two pianos (1895)

Quartet in C minor for two violins, viola and cello (1898)

Sonata for cello and piano (1899)

Trio in G minor for violin, cello and piano (1902)

Sonata for violin and piano in A minor (undated)

Réverie for violin and piano (undated)

VOCAL CHAMBER MUSIC

Fiori primaverili (Spring Flowers) for voice and piano (1887)
Ave Maria for canto, violin or cello, and piano (1895)
Nueve romanzas sobre Verlaine (Nine Romanzas upon Verlaine)
for high voice and piano (1899)

—Chanson d'automne

—Green

—Colloque sentimental

—En sourdine

—Sérénade

—Mon réve familier

—Ariettes oubliées

—Clymène

—Sagesse

Chanson galante for voice and piano (1915)

D'une prison for voice and piano (1915)

Dos melodías sobre Silvestre (Two melodies upon Silvestre) for voice and piano (1915)

—Je porte sur moi ton image

—Quand tu passes

Escape for voice and piano (1926)

Guitare for voice and piano (1926)

INSTRUMENTAL ARRANGEMENTS

Héctor Panizza: *Minué*

Henry Ketten: *La castagnette*

Louis Moreau Gottschalk: *Pasquinade*

Edvard Grieg: *Lyric Pieces*

Giacomo Puccini: *Madama Butterfly*

Giacomo Puccini: *La fanciulla del West*

Giacomo Puccini: *Il trittico (Il tabarro, Suor Angelica, Gianni Schicchi)*

Blas Parera: *Himno Nacional Argentino* (Argentine National Anthem)

Héctor Panizza: *Tema y variaciones* (Theme and Variations)

CHAPTER 13

CHRONOLOGIES

WORLD OPERA PREMIERES CONDUCTED BY PANIZZA

The following list makes note of the operas whose first world performance appears as conducted by Panizza, with the corresponding detail of the title of the work, author, theater, city where the performance took place, date of the premiere and surname of the principal vocalists who participated. The order is chronological.

Frédéric Alfred d'Erlanger: *Tess*
Teatro di San Carlo, Naples (April 7, 1906)
Giachetti, Bassi, Trentini, Sammarco

Ubaldo Pacchierotti: *Eidelberga mia!*
Teatro Carlo Felice, Genoa (February 27, 1908)
Bruschini, Palet, Quercia, Federici

Héctor Panizza: *Aurora*
Teatro Colón, Buenos Aires (September 5, 1908)
Farneti, Bassi, Ruffo, Clasenti, Nicoletti, La Puma

Franco Alfano: *Il principe Zilah*
Teatro Carlo Felice, Genoa (February 3, 1909)

Kaftal, Dygas, Challis, Giacomelio

Lamberto Pavanelli: *Vanna*
Teatro dal Verme, Milan (November 23, 1910)
Remondini, Rotondi, Costantini, Ricceri

Francesco Santoliquido: *La favola di Helga*
Teatro dal Verme, Milan (November 23, 1910)
Caprile, Rocca, Cigada

Riccardo Zandonai: *Conchita*
Teatro dal Verme, Milan (October 14, 1911)
Tarquini, Schiavazzi, Zinoldi, Lucca-Cannetti

Riccardo Zandonai: *Melenis*
Teatro dal Verme, Milán (November 13, 1912)
Muzio, Beinat, Martinelli, Bettoni

Riccardo Zandonai: *Francesca da Rimini*
Teatro Regio, Turin (February 19, 1914)
Cannetti, Crimi, Cigada, Paltrinieri

Elmerico Fracassi: *Finlandia*
Teatro Regio, Turin (March 25, 1914)
Besanzoni, Crimi, Gandolfi

Victor de Sabata: *Il macigno*
Teatro alla Scala, Milan (March 31, 1917)
Melis, Lappas, Danise, Dentale

Vincenzo Michetti: *Maria di Magdala*
Teatro Costanzi, Roma (March 5, 1918)
Rakowska, Di Giovanni, Danise

Edoardo Berlendis: *Il pastore*
Teatro Donizetti, Bérgamo (September 7, 1920)
Labia, De Voltri, Alabiso, Franci

Attilio Parelli: *Fanfulla*
Teatro Verdi, Trieste (February 11, 1921)

Solari, Genzardi, Zaleswki

Luigi Ferrari Trecate: *La bella e il mostro*
Teatro alla Scala, Milan (March 20, 1926)
Aimaro, Gardino, Carlin, Mercuriali, Taddei, Campi

Arrigo Pedrollo: *Delitto e castigo*
Teatro alla Scala, Milan (November 16, 1926)
Pampanini, Cravcenco, Mirassou, Parvis

Ermanno Wolf-Ferrari: *Sly*
Teatro alla Scala, Milan (December 29, 1927)
Pertile, Llopart / Rasa, Rossi-Morelli / Damiani, Badini, Ferrani,
Conti / Adami-Corradetti

Guido Bianchini: *Thien-Hoa*
Teatro alla Scala, Milan (April 9, 1928)
Pampanini, Melandri, Damiani, Bettoni

Vincenzo Michetti: *La Maddalena* [second version of *Maria di
Magdala*]
Teatro alla Scala, Milan (November 22, 1928)
Rasa, Morelli, Vanelli

Felipe Boero: *El matrero*
Teatro Colón, Buenos Aires (July 12, 1929)
Mirassou, Juárez, Granforte

Giuseppe Pietri: *Maristella*
Teatro di San Carlo, Naples (March 22, 1934)
Saraceni, Rowacewa, Marcato, Santiago

John Laurence Seymour: *In the Pasha's Garden*
Metropolitan Opera, New York (January 24, 1935)
Tibbett, Jagel, Jepson

Raúl Espoile: *La ciudad roja*
Teatro Colón, Buenos Aires (July 17, 1936)
Marengo, Mirassou, Damiani, Romito

Héctor Panizza: *Bizancio*
Teatro Colón, Buenos Aires (July 25, 1939)
Cigna, César, Mirassou, De Svéd, Baronti

Gian Carlo Menotti: *The Island God* [*Ilo e Zeus*]
Metropolitan Opera, New York (February 20, 1942)
Warren, Cordon, Varnay, Jobin, Carter

SEASONS AT THE TEATRO COLÓN

It is of practical interest to bring together crossing sources in a revised chronology of the operatic repertoire and concerts Héctor Panizza had the opportunity of conducting at the foremost opera house of his native city, the Teatro Colón of Buenos Aires.

The list is revealing because —even if it affirms the enormous variety of Panizza's repertoire— it demonstrates what was mentioned by Héctor himself on more than one occasion: the progressive pigeonholing to which the artistic management of the Colón submitted him, assigning him above all the conducting of Italian and Argentine operas (including of course his own compositions), with a good number of premieres.

Within each season the operas are mentioned in the order they were presented, while the concerts are listed by genre at the end of each annual list, without this implying that they were performed after the opera performances.

1908

Panizza: *Aurora* (world premiere)

1921

Massenet: *Manon*

Rossini: *Il barbiere di Siviglia*

Wagner: *Götterdämmerung*

Donizetti: *Don Pasquale*

Meyerbeer: *Les Huguenots*

Gounod: *Faust*

Rabaud: *Marouf*

Verdi: *Un ballo in maschera*

Bellini: *I puritani*

Massenet: *Grisélidis* (first performance at the Teatro Colón)

Bellini: *La sonnambula*

1927

Verdi: *Il trovatore*

Wolf-Ferrari: *I quatro rusteghi* (first performance at the Teatro Colón)
Puccini: *Tosca*

Rossini: *Il barbiere di Siviglia*

Massenet: *Manon*

Rimski-Korsakov: *Tha Tale of the Tsar Saltan*

Massenet: *Thaïs*

Puccini: *La bohème*

1929

Puccini: *Turandot*

Puccini: *Madama Butterfly*

Verdi: *Falstaff*

Giordano: *Andrea Chénier*

Verdi: *La traviata* Massenet: *Thaïs*

Verdi: *Il trovatore*

Rabaud: *Marouf*

Boero: *El matrero* (world premiere)

Saint-Saëns: *Samson et Dalila*

Verdi: *Aïda*

Puccini: *La bohème*

Donizetti: *Lucia di Lammermoor*

Mussorgsky: *Khovanshchina*

1930

Verdi: *Don Carlo*

Wagner: *Götterdämmerung*

Verdi: *Aïda*

Donizetti: *L'elisir d'amore*

Pizzetti: *Lo straniero* (first performance at the Teatro Colón) Gluck: *Orfeo ed Euridice*

Rimsky-Korsakov: *Sadkó* (first performance at the Teatro Colón)

Verdi: *Il trovatore*

Boero: *El matrero*

Puccini: *La bohème*

1934

Dukas: *Ariane et Barbebleue*

Verdi: *La traviata*

Verdi: *Falstaff*

Gluck: *Alceste* (first performance at the Teatro Colón)

Donizetti: *L'elisir d'amore*

Rossini: *Il barbiere di Siviglia*

Bellini: *La sonnambula* Symphonic concerts

1935

Gluck: *Alceste*

Bizet: *Carmen* Puccini: *La bohème*

Verdi: *Simon Boccanegra* (first performance at the Teatro Colón)

Verdi: *Falstaff*

Rabaud: *Marouf*

Weinberger: *Svanda the Bagpiper* (first performance at the Teatro Colón)

1936

Puccini: *La bohème*

Malipiero: *Giulio Cesare* (first performance at the Teatro Colón)

Saint-Saëns: *Samson et Dalila*

Verdi: *La traviata*

Verdi: *Rigoletto*

Puccini: *Tosca*

Espoile: *La ciudad roja* (world premiere) Puccini: *Gianni Schicchi*

Rameau: *Castor et Pollux*

Gluck: *Alcest*

1939

Moussorgsky: *Boris Godunov*

Verdi: *La traviata* Massenet: *Mignon* Puccini: *La bohème*

Verdi: *Macbeth* (first performance at the Teatro Colón)

Zandonai: *Conchita* (first performance at the Teatro Colón) Puccini: *Tosca*

Puccini: *Turandot*

Verdi: *Aïda*

Panizza: *Bizancio* (world premiere) Opera gala

1942

Verdi: *Aïda*

Bizet: *Carmen*

Verdi: *Simon Boccanegra*

Bellini: *Norma*

1943

Verdi: *La traviata*

Verdi: *Rigoletto* Verdi: *Falstaff*

Gluck: *Armide* (first performance at the Teatro Colón) Symphonic concert

1944

Panizza: *Bizancio*

Puccini: *La bohème*

Puccini: *Il tabarro*

Puccini: *Suor Angelica*

Puccini: *Gianni Schicchi*

Verdi: *La traviata*

Montemezzi: *L'amore dei tre re*

Verdi: *Otello*

1945

Verdi: *Rigoletto*

Puccini: *La bohème*

Gluck: *Armide*

Panizza: *Aurora*

Verdi: *La traviata*

Moussorgsky: *Khovanshchina*

1946

Puccini: *Manon Lescaut*

Verdi: *Simon Boccanegra*

Massenet: *Mignon*

Puccini: *La bohème*

Verdi: *Un ballo in maschera*

Gluck: *Iphigénie en Tauride*

Symphonic concerts

1947

Giordano: *Fedora* (first performance at the Teatro Colón)

Verdi: *Aïda*

Puccini: *Tosca*

Giordano: *Andrea Chénier*

Bellini: *Norma*

Mascagni: *Cavalleria rusticana*

1948

Cilea: *Adriana Lecouvreur* (first performance at the Teatro Colón)

Puccini: *La bohème*

Puccini: *Manon Lescaut*

Verdi: *Il trovatore*

Boero: *El matrero*

Gluck: *Armide*

1949

Donizetti: *Lucia di Lammermoor*

Puccini: *Suor Angelica*

Puccini: *Gianni Schicchi*

Puccini: *Madama Butterfly*

Verdi: *La traviata*

Gluck: *Iphigénie en Aulide* (first performance at the Teatro Colón)

1951

Gluck: *Orfeo ed Euridice*

Cilea: *Adriana Lecouvreur*

Puccini: *La fanciulla del West*

1952

Verdi: *Falstaff*

Puccini: *Madama Butterfly*

Gluck: *Armide*

Puccini: *La bohème*

1954

Gluck: *Alceste*

Verdi: *Otello*

1955

Montemezzi: *L'amore dei tre re*

Panizza: *Aurora*

Symphonic concert

CHAPTER 14

DISCOGRAPHY

With respect to the existing discography, it is necessary before all else to separate the part that reflects Héctor Panizza's work as a composer from the part dedicated to his performances as a conductor.

The first consists of only four historical recordings that took place during his lifetime, while the second is substantial, in fact much more prolific than could at first be imagined; the problem is that many of these recordings were not reedited on compact discs with commercial distribution and therefore today are unattainable.

Within the discography as a conductor the "official" registers (made in a studio and published during Panizza's life with his explicit authorization) have been distinguished from the "pirate" recordings (in general corresponding to radio broadcasts edited after the artist's death). These latter are in general circulation today and can be acquired by those interested.

A curiosity: apparently only a single film in which one can see Panizza exists. This consists of a few minutes of footage (possibly a cinematographic newsreel) filmed in New York in 1938, where Panizza can be seen first preparing himself in his dressing room—adjusting his bowtie in front of the mirror and testing batons— and later conducting in the

Met's pit. His gestures are very similar to those of Toscanini, but his facial expression appears relaxed and he is even smiling, in contrast to the expression often found on Arturo's face. It is worth clarifying that the recording is mute and that the music superimposed does not correspond to what he was conducting at the moment of the filming.[328]

There is no proof that Panizza appears in Carmine Gallone's *La signora dalle camelie* (1947), a film whose soundtrack he conducted, as has been said. In contrast, as has also been said, there is a single and very brief recording of his voice in a brief phrase he spoke in *El canto del hornero*, from the first act of Boero's *El matrero*.[329]

The discography that follows, even if it is plausibly the most complete and detailed one published to this date, does not claim to be exhaustive. In fact, to give some examples, we have not considered compilations of arias by famous singers in which an accompaniment is include that is conducted by Panizza. Also not included are the unofficial recordings of operas like *Aurora* or *Bizancio*, taken from the seasons of the Teatro Colón described in other parts of this book, nor the several songs whose recordings (live or in digital captures) are accessible on the Internet but whose rights situation is unknown.

There is also proof that the aria "L'elogio della bocca" from *Medio Evo latino* was broadcast by radio in 1937 during the orchestra cycle of the well-known André Kostelanetz, sung by tenor Nino Martini, but it is unknown if a recording of the *broadcast* has been conserved.[330] In all cases, the information is in chronological order.

Historical Studio Recordings as a Composer

As we have mentioned, Panizza's historical discography as a composer reduces to four recordings during his lilfetime. Ironically, none of them were conducted by Héctor (not even in the case of the romanza on verses by Verlaine, specially orchestrated for his recording).

When listing the following information, we have corrected several slips that Panizza himself made in the list he published in his memoirs.

Panizza: "Alta pel cielo un'aquila guerriera" from *Aurora*
Amedeo Bassi, tenor
Pathé, 1908

Panizza: "Alta pel cielo un'aquila guerriera" from *Aurora*
Florencio Constantino, tenor
Columbia, 1910

Panizza: *Colloque sentimental*
Maria Farneti, soprano
Columbia, 1931

Panizza: *Quartet in C minor*
Pessina Quartet
Odeón, 1958

OTHER STUDIO RECORDINGS OF HIS WORKS

After Panizza' s death, and in recent times, some studio recordings of his works were produced and deserve to be mentioned:

Panizza: From Nine Romanzas over Verlaine (as Op. 24): Chanson d' automne, Green, Colloque sentimental, En sourdine, Sérénade, Il pleure dans mon Coeur [*sic*], A Clymène, Sagesse.

Chanson Galante (A. Silvestre)

From "Puentes. Nineteenth and twentieth centry Argentinian Composers influenced by European music." Gabriela de Gyldenfeldt, soprano. Henning Lucius, piano. Astor VR8009 Telos Music, 2012

Panizza: Guitarra [*sic*] (Upon Autre guitar de Victor Hugo). World premiere recording.

From "Paris – Buenos Aires. Poésie francaise - Musique argentine."
Anahí Scharovsky, soprano. Fernando Albinarrate, piano. Editions
de L' Attrape Science, 2011

Panizza: Canción a la Bandera (sic). Intermezzo épico

From "Aurora. Arias." José Cura. Sinfonia Varsovia, Avie.
B00007EA3N, 2004

STUDIO RECORDINGS AS A CONDUCTOR

These studio recordings were made in the early days of the technology,
between 1926 and 1930. Because of this, their sound is of very poor
quality. In addition, due to the limitations of the format (78 rpm discs),
the repertoire consists primarily of opera highlights and brief pieces
in general.

Contrary to what happened with Toscanini's records, which were
issued in complete editions in which all of his studio recordings were
neatly gathered as the official recordings of the great Toscanini, Panizza
did not receive the same interest, and are therefore generally inaccessible
to the current listener. The very rare compact discs that contain some
of this material have not enjoyed a genuine international commercial
distribution. For that reason, in this list only the discographic label of
the original edition is mentioned. The discs are listed in chronological
order according to the year they were recorded (or, in some specific
cases, according to the year that everything leads one to believe they
were recorded); within each year, the material is ordered according to
the date of birth of the respective composer.

Puccini: "Gravi, enormi ed imponenti" from *Turandot*
Choir of the Teatro alla Scala / Vittore Veneziani
Orchestra of the Teatro alla Scala, Milan
Grammofono, 1926

Alfano: "oh divina! nella luce mattutina" from Puccini's *Turandot*
Choir of the Teatro alla Scala / Vittore Veneziani
Orchestra of the Teatro alla Scala, Milan
Grammofono, 1926

Berlioz: Dance of the Sylphs from *La damnation de Faust*
Orchestra of the Teatro alla Scala, Milan
Odeon, 1928

Berlioz: Hungarian March from *La damnation de Faust*
Orchestra of the Teatro alla Scala, Milan
Odeon, 1928

Wagner: "Nun sei bedankt, mein lieber Schwan" from *Lohengrin*
Fernando Ciniselli, tenor
Choir of the Teatro alla Scala / Vittore Veneziani Orchestra of
the Teatro alla Scala
Milan *Fonotipia*, 1928

Verdi: Trio from the first act of *Il trovatore*
Tina Poli-Randaccio, soprano; Sante Montelauri, tenor; Giovanni
Inghilleri, baritone
Orchestra of the Teatro alla Scala, Milan
Fonotipia, 1928

Verdi: "Vedi! le fosche notturne spoglie" from *Il trovatore*
Choir of the Teatro alla Scala / Vittore Veneziani
Orchestra of the Teatro alla Scala, Milan *Grammofono*, 1928

Verdi: "Squilli, echeggi la tromba guerriera" from *Il trovatore*
Choir of the Teatro alla Scala / Vittore Veneziani
Orchestra of the Teatro alla Scala, Milan
Grammofono, 1928

Verdi: Final scene of the second act of *Aïda*
Tina Poli-Randaccio, soprano; Irene Minghini-Cattaneo, mezzoso-
prano; Sante Montelauri, tenor; Giulio Fregosi, baritone; Antonio
Righetti, bass
Choir of the Teatro alla Scala / Vittore Veneziani

Orchestra of the Teatro alla Scala, Milan
Fonotipia, 1928

Verdi: Opening scene of *Otello*
Giuseppe Nessi, tenor; Emilio Venturini, tenor; Aristide Baracchi,
baritone; Giovanni Inghilleri, baritone
Choir of the Teatro alla Scala / Vittore Veneziani
Orchestra of the Teatro alla Scala, Milan
Fonotipia, 1928

Verdi: Brindisi from *Otello*
Giuseppe Nessi, tenor; Emili Venturini, tenor; Giovanni Inghilleri,
baritone
Choir of the Teatro alla Scala / Vittore Veneziani
Orchestra of the Teatro alla Scala, Milan
Fonotipia, 1928

Ponchielli: Furlana from *La Gioconda*
Grande Orchestra Sinfonica di Milano
Odeon, 1928

Ponchielli: Dance of the Hours from *La Gioconda*
Grande orchestra Sinfonica di Milano
Odeon, 1928

Bizet: Seguidilla from *Carmen*
Irene Minghini-Cattaneo, mezzosoprano; Sante Montelauri, tenor
Grande Orchestra Sinfonica di Milano
Odeon, 1928

Bizet: Interludes to the second and fourth act of *Carmen*
Grande Orchestra Sinfonica di Milano
Odeon, 1928

Bizet: Interlude to the third act of *Carmen*
Grande Orchestra Sinfonica di Milano
Odeon, 1928

Bizet: Scene of the cards from *Carmen*

Ines Maria Ferrari, soprano; Anita Apolloni, mezzosoprano; Irene
Minghini-Cattaneo, mezzosoprano
Grande Orchestra Sinfonica di Milano
Fonotipia, 1928

Boito: Garden scene from *Mefistofele*
Augusta Concato, soprano; Bruna Castagna, mezzosoprano;
Fernando Ciniselli, tenor; Antonio Righetti, bass
Orchestra of the Teatro alla Scala, Milan
Fonotipia, 1928

Boito: Night of the classic sabbath from *Mefistofele*
Augusta Concato, soprano; Bruna Castagna, mezzosoprano;
Fernando Ciniselli, tenor; Giuseppe Nessi, tenor; Antonio Righetti,
bass
Choir of the Teatro alla Scala / Vittore Veneziani
Orchestra of the Teatro alla Scala, Milan
Fonotipia, 1928

Puccini: Quartet from the third act of *La bohème*
Augusta Concato, soprano; Assunta Gargiulo, soprano; Ferdinando
Ciniselli, tenor; Ernesto Badini, baritone
Grande Orchestra Sinfonica di Milano
Fonotipia, 1928

Puccini: "Bimba, non piangere" from *Madama Butterfly*
Rosetta Pampanini, soprano; Fernando Ciniselli, tenor
Grande Orchestra Sinfonica di Milano
Fonotipia, 1928

Mascagni: "Gli aranci olezzano" from *Cavalleria rustican*
Coro del Teatro alla Scala / Vittore Veneziani
Orchestra of the Teatro alla Scala, Milan
Fonotipia, 1928

Giordano: Choir of the little shepherdesses
from *Andrea Chénier*
Choir of the Teatro alla Scala / Vittore Veneziani
Orchestra of the Teatro alla Scala, Milan

Fonotipia, 1928

Respighi: *Pinos de Roma*
Orchestra of the Teatro alla Scala, Milan
Odeon, 1928

Rimsky-Korsakov: Interlude to the second act of *The Tale of the Tsar Saltan*
Choir of the Teatro alla Scala / Vittore Veneziani
Orchestra of the Teatro alla Scala, Milan
Grammofono, 1929

Rimsky-Korsakov: Coronation scene from *The Tale of the Tsar Saltan*
Choir of the Teatro alla Scala / Vittore Veneziani
Orchestra of the Teatro alla Scala, Milan
Grammofono, 1929

Rimsky-Korsakov: Interlude to the fourth act of *The Tale of the Tsar Saltan*
Choir of the Teatro alla Scala / Vittore Veneziani
Orchestra of the Teatro alla Scala, Milan
Grammofono, 1929

Boero: Fragments from *El matrero*
Nena Juárez, mezzosoprano Pedro Mirassou, tenor Apollo Granforte, baritone
Stable Choir of the Teatro Colón / Rafael Terragnolo
Stable Orchestra of the Teatro Colón, Buenos Aires
Victor, 1929

Cherubini: Overture from *Anacreonte*
Orchestra of the Teatro alla Scala, Milan
La Voce del Padrone, 1930

Parera: *Himno Nacional Argentino (Argentine National Anthem)*
Pedro Mirassou, tenor
Stable Orchestra of the Teatro Colón, Buenos Aires
Victor, 1930

Rossini: Overture from *Guillaume Tell*
Orchestra of the Teatro alla Scala, Milan
Grammofono, 1930

Mendelssohn: Overture from The Hebryds (Fingal' s Cave)
Orchestra of the Teatro alla Scala, Milán
Grammofono, 1930

Mendelssohn: *Fourth Symphony*
Orchestra of the Teatro alla Scala, Milan
Grammofono, 1930

Mendelssohn: Wedding March from *A Midsummer Night' s Dream*
Orchestra of the Teatro alla Scala, Milan
Grammofono, 1930

Nápravník: Song of the Nightingale from *Don Juan*
Orchestra of the Teatro alla Scala, Milan
Grammofono, 1930

Casella: Two fragments from *Il convento veneziano*
Orchestra of the Teatro alla Scala, Milan
La Voce del Padrone, 1930

Mancinelli: Andante barcarola from *Cleopatra*
Orchestra of the Teatro alla Scala, Milan
Grammofono, 1930

Mancinelli: Flight of the Lovers by Chioggia from *Scene veneziane*
Orchestra of the Teatro alla Scala, Milan
Grammofono, 1930

Martucci: *Notturno*
Orchestra of the Teatro alla Scala, Milan
Grammofono, 1930

Imbroisi: *Mi bandera*
Pedro Mirassou, tenor
Stable Orchestra of the Teatro Colón, Buenos Aires

Victor, 1930

Sinigaglia: Overture from *Le baruffe chiozzotte*
Orchestra of the Teatro alla Scala, Milan
Grammofono, 1930

Wolf-Ferrari: Overture from *Il segreto di Susanna*
Orchestra of the Teatro alla Scala, Milan
Grammofono, 1930

Pick-Mangiagalli: *La danza di Olaf*
Orchestra del Teatro alla Scala, Milán
La Voce del Padrone, 1930

Pick-Mangiagalli: *Notturno*
Orchestra of the Teatro alla Scala, Milan
Grammofono, 1930

Pick-Mangiagalli: Overture from *I piccoli soldati*
Orchestra of the Teatro alla Scala, Milan
Grammofono, 1930

Pick-Mangiagalli: *Rondo fantastico*
Orchestra of the Teatro alla Scala, Milan
Grammofono, 1930

LIVE RECORDINGS AS A CONDUCTOR

Panizza's radio recordings are later in date –the majority are situated between 1935 and 1942– and come from the tapes the stations used to record his opera broadcasts live. The sound quality of these recordings is reasonable and allows one to appreciate the musical value of their content. They are generally opera performances (complete, in the great majority) made by the New York Metropolitan Opera House.

Today, thanks above all to different labels specializing in remastering old recordings, most of this material can be acquired on compact discs relatively easily.

As far as the wide discography from the Met years, it is important to clarify: according to the Met's official chronologies one can deduce that some of these radio recordings were not made in New York but during tours throughout the United States. Whenever possible, this detail has been specified.

It must also be clarified that in some cases the casts noted differ slightly from those that appear in the official chronologies. This is due to two factors: in the case of productions with a double or triple cast, we are not certain which of the performances was transmitted, recorded, and later edited; in addition —as occurs at any opera house and even more so at one that performs several different operas the same week— unforeseen changes were made to the casts due to illness or other reasons, which was not noted in the playbills.

A final clarification: as can be seen, editions circulate on compact disc of many of Panizza's performances before the New York company; the same cannot be said of the radio broadcasts of the performances that he conducted at the Teatro Colón. However, there are certainly recordings of at least his final ten seasons at the Colón. Unfortunately, they still have not been commercialized in a formal and legal way.

After the details about the artist and recording, the detail of the labels that edited the material on compact discs is noted. As will be seen, contrary to what happened with the studio recordings, there are numerous contemporary editions of these materials, though some have better distribution than others.

Just as in the previous cases, the recordings are listed chronologically.

Verdi: *La traviata*
Rosa Ponselle (Violetta), Frederick Jagel (Alfredo), Lawrence Tibbett (Germont), Elda Vettori (Flora), Paolo Ananian (Grenvil), Alfredo Gandolfi (Douphol), Angelo Badà (Gastone), Millo Picco (Obigny), Henriette Wakefield (Annina)
Metropolitan Opera Chorus / Fausto Cleva
Metropolitan Opera Orchestra

Metropolitan Opera, New York, January 5, 1935
The Fourties
Naxos Pearl

Verdi: *Simon Boccanegra* (selection)
Lawrence Tibbett (Simone), Elisabeth Rethberg (Maria), Giovanni
Martinelli (Gabriele), Alfredo Gandolfi (Paolo)
Metropolitan Opera Chorus / Fausto Cleva
Metropolitan Opera Orchestra
Metropolitan Opera, New York, Feb. 16, 1935
Myto

Verdi: *Rigoletto*
Lawrence Tibbett (Rigoletto), Lily Pons (Gilda), Frederick Jagel
(Duke), Virgilio Lazzari (Sparafucile), Helen Olheim (Maddalena),
Alfredo Gandolfi (Monterone), Thelma Votipka (Giovanna), Gior-
dano Paltrinieri (Borsa), George Cehanovsky (Marullo), Hubert
Raidich (Ceprano), Charlotte Symons (Countess), Paolina Tomisani
(Page)
Metropolitan Opera Chorus / Fausto Cleva
Metropolitan Opera Orchestra
Metropolitan Opera, New York, Dec. 28, 1935
Naxos

Verdi: *Aïda*
Gina Cigna (Aida), Giovanni Martinelli (Radamès), Bruna Castagna
(Amneris), Carlo Morelli (Amonasro), Ezio Pinza (Ramfis), Norman
Cordon (King), Giordano Paltrinieri (Messenger), Thelma Votipka
(Priestess)
Metropolitan Opera Chorus / Fausto Cleva
Metropolitan Opera Orchestra
Metropolitan Opera, New York, Feb. 6, 1937
Immortal Performances
The Fourties Melodram

Bellini: *Norma*
Gina Cigna (Norma), Giovanni Martinelli (Pollione), Bruna
Castagna (Adalgisa), Ezio Pinza (Oroveso), Thelma Votipka
(Clotilde), Giordano Paltrinieri (Flavio)

Metropolitan Opera Chorus / Fausto Cleva
Metropolitan Opera Orchestra
Metropolitan Opera, New York, Feb. 20, 1937
Great Opera Performances Cantus Classics
The Fourties AS Disc
Arkadia

Verdi: *Otello*
Giovanni Martinelli (Othello), Elisabeth Rethberg (Desdemona),
Lawrence Tibbett (Iago), Nicholas Massue (Cassio), Nicola
Moscona (Lodovico), Thelma Votipka (Emilia), Giordano Paltrinieri
(Roderigo), George Cehanovsky (Montano), Wilfred Engelman
(Heraldo)
Metropolitan Opera Chorus / Fausto Cleva
Metropolitan Opera Orchestra
Metropolitan Opera, New York, Feb. 12, 1938
Music & Arts
Fourties Naxos
Myto

Verdi: *Otello*
Giovanni Martinelli (Othello), Maria Caniglia (Desdemona),
Lawrence Tibbett (Iago), Alessio De Paolis (Cassio), Nicola
Moscona (Lodovico), Thelma Votipka (Emilia), Giordano Paltrinieri
(Roderigo), George Cehanovsky (Montano), Wilfred Engelman
(Heraldo)
Metropolitan Opera Chorus / Fausto Cleva
Metropolitan Opera Orchestra
Metropolitan Opera, New York, March 12, 1938
Great Opera Performances

Verdi: *Simon Boccanegra*
Lawrence Tibbett (Simone), Elisabeth Rethberg (Maria), Giovanni
Martinelli (Gabriele), Ezio Pinza (Fiesco), Leonard Warren (Paolo),
Louis D'Angelo (Pietro), Giordano Paltrinieri (Capitán), Pearl
Besuner (Sierva)
Metropolitan Opera Chorus / Fausto Cleva
Metropolitan Opera Orchestra
Metropolitan Opera, New York, Jan. 21, 1939

Immortal Performances Melodram
Arkadia Myto

Verdi: *Aïda* (selection)
Zinka Milanov (Aida), Arthur Carron (Radamès), Bruna Castagna
(Amneris), Richard Bonelli (Amonasro), Norman Cordon (Ramfis)
Metropolitan Opera Chorus / Fausto Cleva
Metropolitan Opera Orchestra
Metropolitan Opera, New York, Dec. 2, 1939
EJS Lyric Distribution

Mussorgsky: *Boris Godunov*
Ezio Pinza (Boris), Charles Kullman (Grigori), Nicola Moscona
(Pimen), Kerstin Thorborg (Marina), Leonard Warren (Rangoni),
Norman Cordon (Varlaam), Giordano Paltrinieri (Missail), Irra
Petina (Fiodor), Marita Farell (Xenia), Anna Kaskas (Nodriza),
Alessio De Paolis (Shuiski), George Cehanovsky (Shelkalov),
Doris Doe (Posadera), Nicholas Massue (Inocente/ Boyardo), John
Gurner (official), Wilfred Engelman (Lavitski), Arnold Gabor
(Chernikovski)
Metropolitan Opera Chorus / Fausto Cleva
Metropolitan Opera Orchestra
Metropolitan Opera, New York, Dec. 9, 1939
The Fourties Arkadia Naxos

Ponchielli: *La Gioconda*
Zinka Milanov (Gioconda), Giovanni Martinelli (Enzo), Carlo
Morelli (Barnaba), Bruna Castagna (Laura), Nicola Moscona
(Alvise), Anna Kastas (Ciega), Wilfred Engelman (Zuane/Cantor),
Giordano Paltrinieri (Isepo), Carlo Coscia (Piloto), Louis D'Angelo
(Monje)
Metropolitan Opera Chorus / Fausto Cleva
Metropolitan Opera Orchestra
Metropolitan Opera, New York, Dec. 30, 1939
Great Opera Performances Immortal Performances Symposium
Arkadia
Myto

Mozart: *Le Nozze di Figaro*

Ezio Pinza (Figaro), Bidu Sayão (Susanna), John Brownlee (Almaviva), Elisabeth Rethberg (Rosina), Jarmila Novotná (Cherubino), Virginio Lazzari (Bartolo), Irra Petina (Marcellina), Alessio De Paolis (Basilio), Giordano Paltrinieri (Curzio), Louis D'Angelo (Antonio), Lucille Browning (Woman I), Maxine Stellman (Woman II)
Metropolitan Opera Chorus / Fausto Cleva
Metropolitan Opera Orchestra
Metropolitan Opera, New York, March 8, 1940
Cantus Classic
Music & Arts Arkadia

Verdi: *Un ballo in maschera*
Jussi Björling (Riccardo), Zinka Milanov (Amelia), Alexander De Svéd (Renato), Bruna Castagna (Ulrica), Stella Andreva (Oscar), Norman Cordon (Samuel), Nicola Moscona (Tom), Arthur Kent (Silvano), John Carter (Judge), Lodovico Oliviero (Servant)
Metropolitan Opera Chorus / Fausto Cleva
Metropolitan Opera Orchestra
Metropolitan Opera, New York, Dec. 14, 1940
Great Opera Performances Inmortal Performances Myto Historical Cantus Classics
The Fourties Line Music Arkadia
Myto

Verdi: *Otello*
Giovanni Martinelli (Othello), Stella Roman (Desdemona), Lawrence Tibbett (Iago), Alessio De Paolis (Cassio), Nicola Moscona (Lodovico), Thelma Votipka (Emilia), John Dudley (Roderigo), George Cehanovsky (Montano), Wilfred Engelman (Heraldo)
Metropolitan Opera Chorus / Fausto Cleva Metropolitan Opera Orchestra
Metropolitan Opera, New York, Jan. 18, 1941
Arkadia Pearl

Gluck: *Alceste*
Rose Bampton (Alceste), René Maison (Admète), Leonard Warren (Priest), Alessio De Paolis (Évandre), George Cehanovsky

(Heraldo), Arthur Kent (Oracle), Marita Farell (Coryphaeus I),
Maxine Stellman (Coryphaeus II), Helen olheim (Coryphaeus III),
Wilfred Engelman (Coryphaeus)
Metropolitan Opera Chorus / Fausto Cleva
Metropolitan Opera Orchestra
Metropolitan Opera, New York, March 8, 1941
Naxos

Verdi: *Aïda*
Stella Roman (Aida), Giovanni Martinelli (Radamès), Bruna
Castagna (Amneris), Leonard Warren (Amonasro), Ezio Pinza
(Ramfis), Norman Cordon (Rey), Lodovico Oliviero (Mensajero),
Maxine Stellman (Priestess)
Metropolitan Opera Chorus / Fausto Cleva Metropolitan Opera
Orchestra
Metropolitan Opera, New York, March 22, 1941
The Fourties Arkadia Walhall

Puccini: *Madama Butterfly*
Licia Albanese (Butterfly), Charles Kullman (Pinkerton), Irra Petina
(Suzuki), John Brownlee (Sharpless)
Metropolitan Opera Chorus / Fausto Cleva
Metropolitan Opera Orchestra
Municipal Auditorium, New Orleans, April 21, 1941
The Record Collector

Verdi: *Il trovatore*
Arthur Carron (Manrico), Stella Roman (Leonora), Richard Bonelli
(Luna), Bruna Castagna (Azucena), Norman Cordon (Ferrando)
Metropolitan Opera Chorus / Fausto Cleva Metropolitan Opera
Orchestra Auditorium, Dallas, April 24, 1941
The Record Collector

Verdi: *La traviata*
Jarmila Novotná (Violetta), Jan Peerce (Alfredo), Lawrence Tibbett
(Germont), Thelma Votipka (Flora), Louis D'Angelo (Grenvil),
Arthur Kent (Douphol), Alessio De Paolis (Gastone), George
Cehanovsky (Obigny), Helen Olheim (Annina)
Metropolitan Opera Chorus / Fausto Cleva

Metropolitan Opera Orchestra
Metropolitan Opera, New York, Nov. 29, 1941
Myto

Verdi: *Rigoletto* (selection)
Robert Weede (Rigoletto), Hilde Reggiani (Gilda), Bruno
Landi (Duque), Nicola Moscona (Sparafucile), Bruna Castagna
(Maddalena), Lansing Hatfield (Monterone), Helen Olheim
(Giovanna), Alessio De Paolis (Borsa), George Cehanovsky
(Marullo), Wilfred Engelman (Ceprano), Maxine Stellman
(Countess), Edith Herlick (Page)
Metropolitan Opera Chorus / Fausto Cleva
Metropolitan Opera Orchestra
Metropolitan Opera, New York, Jan. 31, 1942
Bongiovanni

Puccini: *Tosca* (selection)
Grace Moore (Tosca), Frederick Jagel (Cavaradossi), Alexander
De Svéd (Scarpia), Alessio De Paolis (Spoletta), John Gurney
(Sciarrone)
Metropolitan Opera Chorus / Fausto Cleva
Metropolitan Opera Orchestra
Metropolitan Opera, New York, Feb. 7, 1942
Walhall

Verdi: *Un ballo in maschera*
Giovanni Martinelli (Riccardo), Stella Roman (Amelia), Richard
Bonelli (Riccardo), Bruna Castagna (Ulrica), Josephine Antoine
(Oscar), Norman Cordon (Samuel), Nicola Moscona (Tom), George
Cehanovsky (Silvano), John Carter (Judge), Lodovico Oliviero
(Servant)
Metropolitan Opera Chorus / Fausto Cleva
Metropolitan Opera Orchestra
Metropolitan Opera, New York, Feb. 28, 1942
Eklipse

Verdi: *La traviata*
Bidu Sayão (Violetta), Bruno Landi (Alfredo), Richard Bonelli
(Germont), Thelma Votipka (Flora), Alessio De Paolis (Gastone)

Metropolitan Opera Chorus / Fausto Cleva
Metropolitan Opera Orchestra
Lyric Theater, Baltimore, April 18, 1942
The Record Collector

Verdi: *La traviata*
Helen Jepson (Violetta), Jan Peerce (Alfredo), Richard Bonelli
(Germont), Thelma Votipka (Flora), Alessio De Paolis (Gastone)
Metropolitan Opera Chorus / Fausto Cleva
Metropolitan Opera Orchestra
Auditorium, Birmingham, April 20, 1942
The Record Collector

ENDNOTES

1. Vicente Gesualdo, *Pablo Rosquellas y los orígenes de la ópera en Buenos Aires* (Buenos Aires: Editorial Artes en América, 1962), 15.

2. Vicente Gesualdo, *Breve historia de la música en la Argentina* (Buenos Aires: Editorial Claridad, 1998), 96.

3. Chronology according to Norma Lucía Lisio, *Divina Tani y el inicio de la ópera en Buenos Aires 1824-1830* (Buenos Aires: author's edition, 1996), quoted and glossed in Claudio Ratier, "Escenarios de la historia I. Temas atrapados por el rabo," in *Cantabile* no. 79, July/August 2015.

4. Vera Wolkowicz, "La recepción de la ópera italiana en Buenos Aires a fines del período rosista: una polémica entre el *Diario de la Tarde* y el *Diario de Avisos* (1848-1851)" in Silvina Luz Mansilla, ed., *Dar la nota. El rol de la prensa en la historia musical argentina* (Buenos Aires: Gourmet Musical Ediciones, 2012), 27.

5. Jorge Waddell, "Desvíos y empalmes," in *Revista Teatro Colón* no. 100, Buenos Aires, November / December 2011, 64.

6. Roberto Caamaño, *La historia del Teatro Colón, 1908-1968* (Buenos Aires: Editorial Cinetea, 1969), vol. 1, 45.

7. Paul Groussac, *Críticas sobre música* (Buenos Aires: Biblioteca Nacional, 2007). The French writer affirms, among other similar assertions: "I do not utter the blasphemy of putting Verdi on a par with Meyerbeer: the latter has five extraordinary operas, the entire colonnade of the musical temple" (*Sudamérica*, June 23, 1884, 85).

8. Aníbal Enrique Cetrangolo, Doctoral thesis, *Ópera e identidad en el encuentro migratorio. El melodrama italiano en Argentina entre 1880 y 1920* (Valladolid: Universidad de Valladolid, 2010). Published as Aníbal Enrique

Cetrangolo, *Ópera, barcos y banderas: El melodrama y la migración en Argentina 1880-1920* (Madrid: Biblioteca Nueva, 2015).

9. Daniel Muchnik, Inmigrantes 1860-1914: La historia de los míos y de los tuyos (Buenos Aires: Sudamericana, 2015), 19.

10. Rodolfo Arizaga, *Enciclopedia de la música argentina* (Buenos Aires: Fondo Nacional de las Artes, 1972). One can view images and read more at http://teatrosdebuenosairesdelsigloxviialxxi.blogspot.com.ar/2012_11_01_archive.html

11. César Dillon and Juan Andrés Sala, *El teatro musical en Buenos Aires. Teatro Doria – Teatro Marconi* (Buenos Aires: Ediciones de Arte Gaglianone, 1997), Introduction, X.

12. Harvey Sachs, *Toscanini* (New York: Harper Collins, 1988), 350.

13. César Dillon and Juan Andrés Sala, *El teatro musical en Buenos Aires: Teatro Coliseo* (Buenos Aires: Ediciones de Arte Gaglianone, 1999), 95, 319.

14. Roberto Caamaño, *La historia del Teatro Colón, 1908-1968*, vol. 3 (Buenos Aires: Editorial Cinetea, 1969), 73.

15. According to the *Diccionario biográfico ítalo-argentino* compiled by Dionisio Petriella and Sara Sosa Miatello (Buenos Aires: Asociación Dante Alighieri, 1976).

16. Aníbal Enrique Cetrangolo, "Aida Times Two: How Italian Veterans of Two Historic Aida Productions Shaped Argentina's Music History," *Cambridge Opera Journal* 1, no. 28 (Cambridge, 2016): 79–105.

17. Mary Jane Phillips-Matz, *Puccini. A Biography* (Lebanon: Northeastern University Press, 2002), 44. Considers Achille Panizza to be a "member of another musical dynasty" when he mentions him as conductor of the world premiere of *Le Villi*.

18. Giovanni Masutto, *I maestri di musica italiani del secolo XIX. Notizie biografiche* (Venice: Stabilimento tipografico Giovanni Cecchini, 1884),

130. Other sources point to 1804 as his year of birth, but those who are quoted here are contemporaries and are therefore more reliable.

19. Philip Gossett, *Divas and Scholars: Performing Italian Opera* (Chicago: University of Chicago Press, 2006), 592.

20. Masutto, I maestri di musica.

21. From a Panizza wiki, you can find a photograph of his gravestone: rete.comuni italiani.it/wiki/Frascati/lapide_ad_augusto_panizza.

22. Dieter Schickling, *Giacomo Puccini: Catalogue of the Works* (Kassel: Bärenreiter, 2003). This book describes Arturo Panizza as the conductor of the primeire of *Le Villi* based on contemporary journalistic accounts. The author affirms he does not know any other detail about the musician (personal communication with the authors from March 2, 2017). Julian Budden, *Puccini: His Life and Works* (New York: Oxford University Press, 2002), 44. Unusually mentions one so-called Alfredo Panizza, but later corrects the evident error in the Italian edition, where Arturo is mentioned: Julian Budden, *Puccini* (Rome: Carocci Editore, 2005).

23. Giuseppe Barigazzi, *La Scala Racconta* (Milán: Ulrico Hoepli Editore, 2014), 221. "Scapigliati" (literally "messy haired") is the word used to refer to members of a movement of political and artistic rebellion against backwardness in nineteenth-century Italian culture. Daniel Cotton, *International Bohemia: Scenes of Nineteenth-Century Life* (Philadelphia: University of Pennsylvania Press, 2013), 194, refers to an unidentified source, which describes Achille Panizza as "the greatest *scapigliato* in Italy." Mosco Carner, *Puccini* (Buenos Aires: Javier Vergara Editor, 1987), 67. Colin Kendell, *The Complete Puccini* (Stroud: Amberley Publishing, 2012), and other sources give him credit for the premiere of *Le Villi.*

24. Ibid., *Diccionario biográfico ítalo-argentino*, Arizaga, among several other sources, attributes the work to Giovanni Grazioso. See also "Achille Panizza" in *Opening Night! Opera & Oratorio Premieres*, operadata.stanford.edu.

25.Cetrangolo, "Aida Times Two."

26. Personal communication to the authors by Professor Nora Hebe Sforza (February 8, 2017).

27. The pianist Alexander Panizza, born in Canada to Argentine parents and living in Rosario, confirms that he has no link to Héctor Panizza (query by the authors, June 3, 2016).

28. Opening Night! Opera & Oratorio Premieres, operadata.stanford.edu.

29. Héctor Panizza, *Medio siglo de vida musical. Ensayo autobiográfico* (Buenos Aires: Ricordi americana, 1952), 18. There is therefore a contradiction between the maternal surname attributed by Ettore to his grandmother and the second surname added by his father.

30. Ibid.

31. According to the chronology in Susana Salgado, *The Teatro Solís: 150 Years of Opera, Concert and Ballet in Montevideo* (Middletown: Wesleyan University Press, 2003).

32. Copy of the magazine *El Monitor de la Educación Común* (Buenos Aires: Consejo Nacional de Educación, 1890), 323, digitized at www.bnm.me.gov.ar/. Also available at repositorio.educacion.gov.ar/dspace/handle/123456789/97346/discover. (Last visit: 26 August 2015).

33. Carlos Manso, *Del Teatro de la Ópera a Carmen Piazzini* (Buenos Aires: De los Cuatro Vientos, 2012). See also: Roberto Caamaño, *La historia del Teatro Colón, 1908-1968* (Buenos Aires: Editorial Cinetea, 1969).

34. Panizza, *Medio siglo.*

35. Romina Dezillio, "El ojo de la cerradura: mujeres, música y feminismos en La Mujer Álbum – Revista (1899-1902)," Silvina Luz Mansillaz, ed., *Dar la nota. El rol de la prensa en la historia musical argentina* (Buenos Aires: Gourmet Musical Ediciones, 2012), 122.

36. Ibid., *Diccionario biográfico ítalo-argentino*. The publication contains his signature on the *Nuevo método teórico-práctico de lectura musical y solfeo* in several editions (printed by Andrés Carrano and Breyer Hermanos). One of them was adapted for schools (edited by F. G. Hartmann). Also recorded in Gordon Cox and Robin Stevens, eds., *The Origins and Foundations of Music Education. International Perspectives* (New York: Bloomsbury, 2017), 157.

37. Charles Barber, *Corresponding with Carlos: A Biography of Carlos Kleiber* (Lanham: Scarecrow Press, 2001), 9.

38. Copy of the magazine *El Monitor de la Educación Común* (Buenos Aires: National Council of Education, 1895), 286. Digitized at repositorio.educacion.gov.ar/dspace/bitstream/handle/123456789/101852/Monitor_3083.pdf?sequence=1.

39. The *art nouveau*-style building belonged to the Italian community and still survives, though in a derelict condition (2016), on 1374 Sarmiento Street, in downtown Buenos Aires, with a possibility of restoration as it has recently been acquired by a private institution (the Church of Scientology). A block away was the Prince George Hall, another historical venue for symphonic music, today gone.

40. José Ignacio Weber, "¿Ópera o música sinfónica? El interés de la crítica musical en la modernización del gusto porteño (1891-1895)" in Silvina Luz Mansilla, ed., *Dar la nota, El rol de la prensa en la historia musical argentina* (Buenos Aires: Gourmet Musical Ediciones, 2012), 96.

41. *El Mundo del Arte*, Buenos Aires; copies from the National Library, digitalized in the archive of Gourmet Musical Ediciones.

42. Paul Groussac, *Paradojas sobre música* (Buenos Aires: Biblioteca Nacional, 2008), 149.

43. Groussac, *Paradojas sobre música*.

44. Panizza, *Medio siglo*, 22.

45. Héctor Panizza, *La fanciulla del West de Puccini. Partitura* (Milán: Ricordi, 1911), personal archive of Sebastiano De Filippi, with handwritten annotations by Panizza himself.

46. Carlos Manso, *Del Teatro de la Ópera a Carmen Piazzini* (Buenos Aires: De los Cuatro Vientos, 2012).

47. Act No. 129 was passed on June 5, 1865, and declared enrollment in the active National Guard of the Republic obligatory for "every Argentine citizen, from the age of 17 years until 45, if unmarried."

48. Panizza, *Medio siglo*, 25.

49. Act No. 3318 decreed the first military draft on November 23, 1895, and went into effect on March 12, 1896, with a expedition to Cura Malal in the province of Buenos Aires where conscripts had to face harsh conditions of climate and subsistence. This was the direct antecedent of Act No. 4301, the so-called "Riccheri Law" of 1901 which established obligatory military service in the Armed Forces and definitively concluded with the National Guard and local militias.

50. *Casa Ricordi* (1945), an Italian-French co-production directed by Carmine Gallone, with Paolo Stoppa, Renzo Giovampietro, and Marcello Mastroianni.

51. It is interesting to note how the archive of the Casa Ricordi itself characterizes the great members of the family: Giovanni is "the founder," Tito is "the good-natured one," Giulio is "the genius," and Tito II –more curtly– is "the cosmopolitan"; see www.ricordicompany.com/it/ page/25.

52. Panizza, *Medio siglo*, 34.

53. See the "Anecdotes" section in the appendices of this work.

54. Alan Mallach, "The autumn of Italian opera from verismo to modernism, 1890-1915," 2007: 58; and Samuele Schaerf, "I cognomi degli ebrei d'Italia: con un'appendice su le famiglie nobili ebree," s.v. "Franchetti," quoted in: en.wikipedia.org/wiki/alberto_Franchetti (last visit: July 26, 2015).

55. Gustavo Gabriel Otero and Daniel Varacalli Costas, *Puccini en la Argentina* (Buenos Aires: Instituto Italiano de Cultura, 2006), 17.

56. Harvey Sachs, *Toscanini* (New York: Harper Collins, 1988), 79.

57. Panizza reproduces this anecdote in *Medio siglo*, 49, and repeats it in "Arturo Toscanini. Una evocación en su centenario," *Polifonía* magazine, 133/4, Buenos Aires, second trimester of 1967, 12, though in this account the embrace includes his father and younger brother. The presence of his mother is not mentioned.

58. *Caras y Caretas*, no. 147, Buenos Aires, January 27, 1901.

59. The document bears the number 267 and is titled "Héctor Panizza requests that a pension be accorded to him to be able to continue his musical studies in Europe." It was admitted to the Honorable Chamber of National Deputies on August 17, 1901. A digital reproduction of the original can be found at docs.google.com/gview?url=http://apym.hcdn.gob.ar/pdf/expedientes/267-p-1901. pdf&embedded=true.

60. In accordance with the document cited in the previous note, on June 20, 1902, a consignment was approved in the budget for the applicant with the sum requested, following recommendation from the respective commision on August 27, 1901. However, on September 9, 1902, a revision was advised regarding all pensions granted, according to Act No. 3195, which would have resulted in the loss of the benefit.

61. Panizza, *Medio siglo*, 52.

62. Panizza, *Medio siglo*, 54.

63. Authors like Vicente Gesualdo in the Argentine edition of the *Diccionario de la música* compiled by Eric Blom (Buenos Aires: Editorial Claridad, 1958); Rodolfo Arizaga, *Enciclopedia de la música argentina* (Buenos Aires: Fondo Nacional de las Artes, 1971); and Aníbal Enrique Cetrangolo, *Ópera, barcos y banderas. El melodrama y la migración en Argentina (1880-1920)* (Madrid: Biblioteca Nueva, 2015), in addition to sources from the internet, repeat erroneously that Giovanni Grazioso died

in 1898. The clear reference by Panizza in *Medio siglo* that he received the news while he was conducting a single performance of *Tosca* in Palermo, crossed with the chronology published by Carlo Marinelli Roscioni in *Grandi maestri alla Scala: Héctor Panizza* by Sergio Rossi and Michele Selvini (Milán: Edizioni MC Musica Classica, 2000), confirms it was in 1903. Only the *Diccionario de la música española e hispanoamericana* edited by Emilio Casares Rodicio (Madrid: Sociedad Generales de Autores y Editores, 2002), V. VIII, 439, in the entry signed by Pola Suárez Urtubey specifies that Panizza's father died in Buenos Aires on October 8, 1903. Furthermore, in his memoirs Panizza states that his father died at fifty-two years of age, so that having been born in 1851, he could not have died before that year. Finally, the year is confirmed by the brief obituary published in *Caras y Caretas*, October 24, 1903, 41, which does not specify the date of death.

64. Panizza, *Medio siglo*, 57. There the facsimile of the complete original is reproduced, dated November 20, 1904.

65. Letter from January 29, 1906, in *Carteggi pucciniani*, edited by Eugenio Gara (Milán: Ricordi, 1958), no. 463, 317. The facsimile is reproduced in Panizza, *Medio siglo*, 59-60. On the second day of the same month, Puccini had written to Panizza exchanging ideas about cuts in the score (see facsimile at giacomopucciniatravesdesuscartas.blogspot.com.ar/2009/05/anima-sybil-seguir-buscando-un-tema.html), which clearly indicates the enormous regard in which he held him.

66. Sachs, *Toscanini*, 102.

67. Program from May 14, 1908, at La Scala, according to the chronology of Carlo Marinelli Roscioni in *Grandi maestri alla Scala: Héctor Panizza*. From this, one can infer that it was Panizza's first presentation with the *scaligera* orchestra.

68. *Grande trattato di strumentazione e d'orchestrazione moderne di Hector Berlioz* (Milán: Ricordi, 1912).

69. The frequent denomination "Canción a la bandera" is incorrect.

70. Conf. Roberto Caamaño, *La historia del Teatro Colón, 1908-1968* (Buenos Aires: Editorial Cinetea, 1969).

71. The name shared by Quesada the father with his son has led numerous sources to attribute the idea of the opera and participation in the original libretto to the latter.

72. Panizza states in *Medio siglo*, 72, that the commission came from the government of the province of Buenos Aires, but this statement has no documentary confirmation. In the majority of the indirect sources the commission is attributed, more logically, to the national government (for example, *Aurora*, playbill from the Teatro Colón, 1965 season, or *La Nación*, Buenos Aires, March 3, 1921).

73. Budden, *Puccini*, 290.

74. Panizza, *Medio siglo*, 73.

75. *Revista Artística y Teatral de Buenos Aires*, Buenos Aires, January 10, 1908.

76. *La Nación*, Buenos Aires, September 6, 1908.

77. *Caras y Caretas* no. 517, Buenos Aires, August 29, 1908, 56.

78. Aníbal Enrique Cetrangolo, Doctoral thesis *Ópera e identidad en el encuentro migratorio. El melodrama italiano en Argentina entre 1880 y 1920*, supervised by Enrique Cámara de Landa (Valladolid: Universidad de Valladolid, 2010). Digital edition at uvadoc.uva.es/bitstream/ 10324/3783/1/teSiS381-131024.pdf, 513, 539. Published as Aníbal Enrique Cetrangolo, *Ópera, barcos y banderas. El melodrama y la migración en Argentina (1880-1920)* (Madrid: Biblioteca Nueva, 2015). This pagination corresponds to the digital version.

79. *La Nación*, Buenos Aires, September 6, 1908.

80. Cetrangolo, *Ópera, barcos y banderas*, 518.

81. *La Nación*, Buenos Aires, September 6, 1908.

82. *La Razón*, Buenos Aires, September 7, 1908.

83. *El Diario*, Buenos Aires, June 7, 1908, quoted by Francis Korn and Silvia Sigal, *Buenos Aires antes del Centenario. 1904-1909* (Buenos Aires: Sudamericana, 2010), 210.

84. Ibid., *La Patria degli Italiani*, Buenos Aires, September 6, 1908, quoted by Korn and Sigal.

85. According to Arturo Lagorio in *Caras y Caretas*, Buenos Aires, May 5, 1934.

86. Henry Saxe Wyndham, *Stories of the Operas and the Singers* (London: John Long, 1910).

87. Stanley Sadie, *The New Grove Dictionary of Music and Musicians*, vol. 14 (London: Macmillan, 1980), 155. The chronology drawn up by Carlo Marinelli Roscioni for *Grandi maestri alla Scala: Héctor Panizza* as well as the other editions of the *Grove* confirm the same information. The 1945 edition states that Panizza "usually awoke admiration for his musicality and firm rhythmic pulse" (entry signed by H. K.).

88. Panizza, *Medio siglo*, 77.

89. César Dillon and Juan Andrés Sala, *El teatro musical en Buenos Aires: Teatro Coliseo* (Buenos Aires: Ediciones de Arte Gaglianone, 1999), 67.

90. At last the Argentine debut of *Parsifal* took place in Buenos Aires at the Teatro Coliseo, with Gino Marinuzzi on the podium, on June 20, 1913, breaking the Wagnerian veto that prevented it from being represented in any place but Bayreuth before January 1, 1914. This milestone is often overlooked in the histories of the performance of *Parsifal*. See Dillon, 114.

91. Ulderico Tegani, *La Scala: Nella sua storia e nella sua grandezza* (Milán: Valsecchi Editore, 1946), 88.

92. Walter Mocchi (Turin, 1870 – Rio de Janeiro, 1955) was an impresario with an enormous influence in the first decades of the current Teatro

Colón. He came to create the Società Teatrale Italo-Argentina (S.T.I.A.) with the aim of establishing a permanent commercial link between Argentina and the great Italian artists. He was also an adherent of fascism. Toscanini criticized him harshly and it is probable that his distancing from the Colón, after taking responsibility for the 1912 season, was due to his poor opinion of the impresario. See the letter from Toscanini to Modrone (1916) in Harvey Sachs, *Reflections on Toscanini* (Rocklin: Prima Publishing, 1993), 54.

93. Héctor Panizza, "Arturo Toscanini. Una evocación en su centenario," Magazine *Polifonía* 133/4 (Buenos Aires, second trimester of 1967).

94. See Panizza, *Medio siglo*, 109, and Sachs, *Toscanini*, 144.

95. Ulderico Tegani, *La Scala*, 91.

96. In "Arturo Toscanini. Una evocación en su centenario," Magazine *Polifonía*, no. 133/4 (Buenos Aires, second trimester of 1967), 12.

97. Ibid.

98. Sachs, *Toscanini*, 148.

99. Quoted by Sachs, *Toscanini*, 156. In the text, when he declares "Remember *Butterfly*," Puccini is referring to the fiasco of *Madama Butterfly*'s debut at La Scala.

100. Ulderico Tegani, *La Scala*, 118, describes the complete team of Toscanini and Scandiani at La Scala as an autonomous entity: the secretary Anita Colombo, the secretary Giovanni Binetti, the librettist and lawyer Giovacchino Forzano, Luigi Sapelli (the designer known by the pseudonym "Caramba"), the scene-shifter Giovanni Ansaldo, Giuseppe Pisoni, and Giovannino Beretta. As far as the conductors that accompanied them, he mentions seventeen, without respecting alphabetical order. Panizza appears in the first place; in the tenth is another Argentine: Ferruccio Calusio.

101. Panizza, "Arturo Toscanini. Una evocación." Toscanini would finally conduct *Parsifal* with Isidoro Fagoaga in the lead and Panizza would direct *Lohengrin* with Aureliano Pertile.

102. Panizza, "Arturo Toscanini. Una evocación."

103. Panizza., "Arturo Toscanini. Una evocación."

104. *La Quena*, magazine of the Conservatory of Music in Buenos Aires (Buenos Aires, June 1922).

105. *La Época*, May 16, 1921 ed. (Buenos Aires).

106. The opera company operated at the Auditorium until 1929, when the hall began to face hard times. Currently the property of Roosevelt University, it is now completely restored and continues to be active.

107. Sachs, *Toscanini*, 154.

108. "Chicago Adds a Conductor," *The New York Times*, October 25, 1922.

109. *The Christian Science Monitor*, November 24, 1923.

110. The musical quotation is dated May 30, 1921, when all information indicates that the interview took place. It was published in *Caras y Caretas*, June 11, 1921 (Buenos Aires).

111. *Musical Courier*, Chicago, January 10, 1924, 40.

112. Ferruccio Cattelani, *Actividades musicales en la Argentina* (Buenos Aires: printer of Luis Veggia, 1927), 101, 141. More information about the work is found in the second part of this book.

113. In accordance with the list of first auditions in the United States by the Symphonic Ochestra of Chicago, at cso.org/uploadedFiles/8_about/History_-_Rosenthal_archives/US_premieres.pdf.

114. *La Época*, Buenos Aires, May 16, 1921.

115. Testimony from 1920 quoted *Clarín*, August 12, 1965, and November 30, 1967 (Buenos Aires).

116. "Un gran compositor argentino: el maestro Panizza," Interview with Adolfo Lanús, *Caras y Caretas*, June 11, 1921 (Buenos Aires).

117. Ibid.

118. Panizza, "Arturo Toscanini. Una evocación."

119. Sachs, *Toscanini*, 179.

120. According to John Steane in www.gramophone.co.uk/feature/ puccinis-turandot-a-survey-of-recordings, published in *Grammophon collection*, July 2008.

121. Conf. Mark Overt-Thorn, edition restored from fragments in *El matrero*. See www.pristine- classical.com/pasc189.html.

122. The recording of Panizza's voice is mentioned on the insert of the compilation compact disc on which one can hear him, published in the collection *Grandi maestri alla Scala: Héctor Panizza,*.

123. *Caras y Caretas*, Buenos Aires, September 20, 1930.

124. A recording was made only a few months after Panizza's: on April 10, 1931, the Hallé Orchestra of Manchester conducted by Hamilton Harty made a recording for Columbia.

125. Testimony of Gianandrea Gavazzeni taken by Harvey Sachs and published in *Music in Fascist Italy* (London: Weidenfeld & Nicolson, 1987), 161, where there is evidence of the anger of Toscanini about Adolf Busch's new wedding. Panizza's testimony about Toscanini's reaction to his second wedding is more discreet: see *Medio siglo*, 129.

126. The most complete work on the theme is *Music in Fascist Italy* by Harvey Sachs (London: Weidenfeld & Nicolson, 1987).

127. Panizza, *Medio siglo*, 156.

128. Omar Corrado, *Música y modernidad en Buenos Aires. 1920-1940* (Buenos Aires: Gourmet Musical Ediciones, 2010), ch. 7, 225.

129. According to Panizza, in *Medio siglo.*

130. During these preparations, in 1934 Giordano finally obtained a place on the board of directors of the National Radio in Italy (Unione Radiofonica Italiana, today's RAI) and, even if his adherence to Mussolini was weaker than that of Mascagni, he was the author of *L´Inno del Decennale*, which the dictator used to celebrate the tenth anniversary of the March on Rome, and of *Cesare*, a piece of music incidental to the drama of the same name by Giovacchino Forzano, on whose composition the Fascist leader himself claimed to have collaborated (see Sachs, *Toscanini*, 121).

131. The situation is commented on in Tegani, *La Scala* and particularly in Sachs, *Toscanini*, 81.

132. Sachs, *Toscanini*, 81.

133. "Héctor Panizza ha sido designado director del [*sic*] Scala de Milán," *La Nación*, Buenos Aires, September 17, 1931.

134. Sachs, *Toscanini*, 81.

135. Sergio Rossi and Michele Selvini, *Grandi maestri alla Scala: Héctor Panizza* (Milán: Edizioni Mc Musica Classica, 2000), 60.

136. Harvey Sachs, *Music in Fascist Italy* (London: Weidenfeld & Nicolson, 1987), 189, records this exchange beginning in 1935: de Sabata and Lualdi in Berlin; Marinuzzi in Munich (1935-1935), La Scala with de Sabata on tour through Germany and the Orchestra of the Academia de Santa Cecilia with Molinari (1937), the trip of Lauri-Volpi and Votto (1938), Molinari with the Berlin Philharmonic (1940), the *troupe* of the Teatro dell'Opera of Rome in Berlin (1941), and a new tour of La Scala, this time with Marinuzzi (1941), Gui and Casella, conductors in Vienna (1941-1942).

137. *La Nación*, Buenos Aires, October 11, 1933.

138. Panizza, "Arturo Toscanini. Una evocación en su centenario."

139. Interview by Harvey Sachs with Gianandrea Gavazzeni, published in Sachs, *Music in Fascist Italy*, 160-61.

140. Letter to Ada Mainardi, dated in London, on May 6, 1939; published in *Nel mio cuore troppo d'assoluto. Le lettere di Arturo Toscanini*, edited by Harvey Sachs (Milán: Garzanti Libri, 2003), 488-89. Edition in English: *The Letters of Arturo Toscanini* (Chicago: University of Chicago Press, 2006), 354. In his commentary on the letter, the editor also suggests that the harsh reaction by Toscanini can be attributed to the fact that Panizza agreed to conduct in Berlin in 1938, so close to the war and contemporary with racial laws.

141. *Caras y Caretas*, Buenos Aires, May 5, 1924.

142. In accordance with the database of facts from the Metropolitan Opera in New York; see complete timeline of the performances at archives.metoperafamily.org/archives/frame.htm.

143. Charles Barber, *Corresponding with Carlos: A Biography of Carlos Kleiber* (Lanham: Scarecrow Press, 2001), 18. Apparently, the six maestros have in common their double nationality; Argentine and Italian, except in the case of Kleiber (Argentine and German).

144. Panizza, *Medio siglo*, 145. However, despite what Panizza claims, there is no proof that he conducted at the Paris Opera—the Palais Garnier —but only at the Opéra Comique and the Théâtre des Champs Élysées.

145. "Panizza New Conductor. Noted Argentine Musician to Replace Serafin," *The New York Times*, June 23, 1934.

146. Serafin had been practically ordered by Mussolini to direct the Teatro dell'Opera in Rome. See César Dillon and Michele Selvini, *Grandi maestri alla Scala: Tullio Serafin* (Milán: Edizioni MC Musica Classica, 1998), 26.

147. *Musical America*, New York, December 25, 1934.

148. *La Nación*, Buenos Aires, December 24, 1934, contains the title "En su debut en la ópera de Nueva York fue aclamado Panizza" and quotes

highly complimentary criticism from the *The New York Times* and *The New York Herald Tribune.*

149. *La Nación*, Buenos Aires, December 17, 1934.

150. *The New York Times*, November 30, 1934.

Dennis McGovern and Deborah Grace Winer, *Mis recuerdos de la ópera* (Buenos Aires: Javier Vergara Editor; 1992), 278.

152. *La Nación*, Buenos Aires, December 18, 1935, contains the title: "Panizza dirigió *La traviata* en la ópera de nueva York" and takes note of this new success for the Argentine maestro, reproducing the praiseworthy criticism in *The New York Times.*

153. Currently the Ansonia in New York survives, very well conserved and transformed into a block of apartments. It is located on Broadway between 73rd and 74th Streets. Today a plaque notes that many artists lived there from the performing groups at the Met, among them Toscanini and Caruso.

154. *The New York Times*, December 2, 1937. Even the real estate agency is mentioned: Madison Realty Company.

155. *The New York Times*, December 9, 1934.

156. *La Nación*, Buenos Aires, December 18, 1934. Panizza knew Martinelli from his seasons at the Teatro Dal Verme.

157. *La Nación*, Buenos Aires, December 18, 1934.

158. *The New York Times*, February 10, 1935.

159. The musical material for this opera was destroyed by Menotti after the debut, but the libretto has been conserved and published by the Metropolitan Opera (see wikipedia.org/wiki/Gian_carlo_ Menotti). At archives.metoperafamily.org/ a review appears by Oscar Thompson, which gives an account of the enthusiasm of the debut, though it criticizes Panizza for the raised volume permitted to the brasses, which he characterizes as a "sin."

160. Igor Stravinski and Robert Craft, *Memorias y comentarios* (Barcelona: Acantilado, 2013), 301.

161. Panizza, *Medio siglo*, 158.

162. Panizza, *Medio siglo*, 162.

163. Carlos Manso, *Delia Rigal* (Buenos Aires: El Francotirador Ediciones, 1998), 16.

164. Arthur Bloomfield, *More than the Notes*, chapter 29 from the digital edition: www.morethanthenotes. com/read-the-book/ettore-panizza.

165. Chronology organized by Carlo Marinelli Roscioni in Sergio Rossi and Michele Selvini, *Grandi maestri alla Scala: Héctor Panizza* (Milán: Edizioni Mc Musica Classica, 2000).

166. *The New York Times*, September 18, 1942.

167. Cetrangolo, *Ópera, barcos y banderas*, 521.

168. Juan Sasturain, "Allora, parliemo di Aurora" in *Página/12*, Buenos Aires, November 10, 2008. In the second part of this book, the authors are more precise.

169. Personal testimony of Carlos Manso to the authors (Buenos Aires, August 10, 2015).

170. Various authors, *Historia general de la danza en la Argentina* (Buenos Aires: Fondo Nacional de las Artes, 2008), 95.

171. According to the testimony of José Soler in Manso, *Delia Rigal*, 33.

172. Information taken from www.imdb.com/title/tt0143881/. The film was released on December 22, 1947, and subtitled "Versione cine-matografica della *Traviata* di Giuseppe Verdi." The technical sheet includes Nelly Corradi (Violetta Valéry), Gino Mattera (Alfredo Germont), Manfredi Polverosi (Giorgio Germont), Flora Marino (Flora Bervoix), Carlo Lombardi (Douphol), Massimo Serato (Alexandre Dumas the son, in the prologue) and Nerio Bernardi (Giuseppe Verdi, in the prologue).

Vocal performers: Onelia Fineschi, Francesco Albanese, Tito Gobbi, Arturo La Porta. Héctor Panizza, conductor. Grande Opera Roma. Luigi Ricci, musical supervisor.

173. Susana Salgado, *The Teatro Solís,* 187. International chronologies omit this performance at the main opera theater in Montevideo.

174. Pablo Bardin, *La Sinfónica Nacional cumple medio siglo,* March 20, 2007. Published at http://historiasinfonica.blogspot.com.ar/2007/03/la-sinfnica-nacional-cumple-medio-siglo.html. (Last visit: Aug. 9, 2015) and playbills from the State Radio Symphony (personal archive of Daniel Varacalli Costas).

175. Conf. playbills from the Symphonic Orchestra of the State Radio (personal archive of Daniel Varacalli Costas).

176. Silvina Luz Mansilla, *La obra musical de Carlos Guastavino: Circulación, recepción, mediaciones* (Buenos Aires: Gourmet Musical Ediciones, 2011), 282.

177. Mansilla, *La obra musical,* 234, footnote 121.

178. Personal testimony of José Luis Sáenz to the authors (Buenos Aires, September 15, 2015).

179. *La Prensa,* Buenos Aires, August 8, 1955.

180. Roberto Caamaño, *La historia del Teatro Colón, 1908-1968* (Buenos Aires: Editorial Cinetea, 1969), t. ii, 432 and *La Prensa,* Buenos Aires, August 15, 1955.

181. Letter dated in Nervi, on January 29, 1957, reproduced—without mention of the recipient— in Osvaldo Barrios and Edmundo Piccioni, *Teatro Colón. Orquesta Estable: Historia y anécdotas* (Buenos Aires: Ediciones Nuevos Tiempos, 2006), 191.

182. The letters to Faustino del Hoyo reproduced below are deposited and digitized at the Institute of Ethnomusicology in Buenos Aires.

183. *La Nación* and *La Prensa,* Buenos Aires, August 12, 1965.

184. *La Nación*, Buenos Aires, August 14, 1965. One understands this to mean academic corresponding member, since Panizza did not reside in the country.

185. Note sent to Del Hoyo on November 15, 1965.

186. *Clarín*, Buenos Aires, September 30, 1967.

187. *La Prensa*, Buenos Aires, November 30, 1967.

188. Juan Emilio Martini, *Semblanza de Héctor Panizza*, August 6, 1968; published by Ricordi Americana in the form of a leaflet. (Copy consulted at the archive of *La Nación*).

189. Currently there are no traces of said copy at the Teatro Colón.

190. Leonor Plate, *Óperas Teatro Colón. Esperando el Centenario* (Buenos Aires: Editorial Dunken, 2006).

191. Plate, Óperas Teatro Colón.

192. Daniel Varacalli Costas, Interview with Darío Volonté in *Revista Teatro Colón* number 54 (Buenos Aires: Teatro Colón, July 1999).

193. *Revista Teatro Colón* number 53 (Buenos Aires: Teatro Colón, May 1999). *La Prensa*, Buenos Aires, short article from the year 1923, found in envelope number 20.896 of the Archive of the morning edition. Reproduced in the edition of August 12, 1965.

194. See video on YouTube: www.youtube.com/watch?v=zxk43lwo9_k.

195. *La Prensa*, Buenos Aires, short article from the year 1923, found in envelope number 20.896 of the Archive of the morning edition. Reproduced in the edition from August 12, 1965.

196. Carmen García, Muñoz and Guillermo Stamponi, *Orquesta Filarmónica de Buenos Aires, 1946- 2006* (Buenos Aires: Philharmonic Association of Buenos Aires, 2007), 23.

197. Dillon, César / Selvini, Michele. *Grandi maestri alla Scala. Tullio Serafin* (Milán: Edizioni MC Musica Classica, 1998), 45.

198. Panizza, *Medio siglo*, 28.

199. Mildonian, Paola. *Libretti italiani alle origini dell'opera argentina.* Digital edition at MundoClásico: www.mundoclasico.com/ed/documentos/doc-ver.aspx?id=0013289. Published on September 26, 2003.

200. Valenti Ferro, Enzo. *Historia de la ópera argentina* (Buenos Aires: Ediciones de Arte Gaglianone, 1997), 174. Valenti's work does not in any case include the vocal registers of the characters, which were extracted, according to the operas, by comparing the existing material or cast lists, in accordance with the corresponding programs and playbills.

201. Notably, it does not appear in the Appendix respective to *Medio siglo.*

202. Enzo Valenti Ferro, *Historia de la ópera argentina* (Buenos Aires: Ediciones de Arte Gaglianone, 1997), 224. The vocal registers emerge from comparing the casts.

203. See the reproduction of a few reviews in the first part of this work.

204. Conf. Alberto David Leiva, "Mito patriótico y paradigma en *Aurora,*" *Revista Teatro Colón* no. 53 (Buenos Aires: Teatro Colón, May 1999).

205. For a musical analysis of this opera, see Pola Suárez Urtubey, "*Aurora,* desde la música," *Revista Teatro Colón* no. 53 (Buenos Aires: Teatro Colón, May 1999).

206. Ibid.; Juan Sasturain.

207. *Los Andes,* Mendoza, December 14, 2010 ("Clarificar la *Aurora*").

208. In the successful feature film *Garage Olimpo* (1999), an Italian-Argentine co-production directed by the Italian-Chilean Marco Bechis, the "Canción de la bandera" was chosen to accompany the throwing of prisoners from airplanes into the Río de la Plata during the last Argentine military dictatorship.

209. See on YouTube: www.youtube.com/watch?v=x4S39CpQgeg. Pathé Recordings, 1912.

210. See on YouTube: www.youtube.com/watch?v=2IpG5Lv0o4E.

211. The detail of the interpreters of *Aurora* at the Colón comes from: Ángel Fumagalli, "Aurora. *Un título profético para la ópera argentina"* in *Aurora: Programa de mano del Teatro Colón* (Buenos Aires: Teatro Colón, May 1999), 62, 64.

212. Christian Lauria, *Adelaida Negri: Vida, arte y talento* (Buenos Aires: Editorial Dunken, 2014), 179.

213. Enzo Valenti Ferro, *Historia de la ópera argentina* (Buenos Aires: Ediciones de Arte Gaglianone, Buenos Aires; 1997), 130. Once more, this source has been put together by comparing the vocal recordings of the singers who interpreted the opera.

214. A complete audio recording of the performance from November 7, 1975, can be found at: www.youtube. com/watch?v=axUG_flmoLI.

215. The version of *Madama Butterfly* circulates in an edition by Kalmus. The pit of the Teatro Avenida of Buenos Aires is characterized by a very reduced capacity and only the efficient reductions of Panizza have allowed for a quality performance there, played by the companies Buenos Aires Lírica and Juventus Lyrica.

216. Ferruccio Cattelani, *Actividades musicales en la Argentina* (Buenos Aires: Imprenta de Luis Veggia, 1927), 101, 141.

217. Cattelani, *Actividades musicales en la Argentina*, 41.

218. Caamaño, *La historia del Teatro Colón*, 1908-1968.

219. Information compared with the handbill, which includes a commentary on the music, sent in digital form by the Rosenthal Archives of the Chicago Symphony Orchestra, directed by Frank Vilella (electronic communication to the authors from June 24, 2015).

220. Julian Budden, *Puccini* (Roma: Carocci Editore, 2005), 433.

221. A photocopy of the script dedicated and signed by Panizza is in the personal archive of Sebastiano De Filippi.

222. The dedication and list of performers during the premiere are written in the score of the work, a copy of which is in the personal archive of Sebastiano De Filippi.

223. Héctor Panizza, ed., *Grande trattato di strumentazione e d'orchestrazione moderne di Hector Berlioz* (Milan: Ricordi, 1912).

224. *Digest of Primary Instruction.* Document 14.4, January 29, 1935 from June 2, 1935.

225. *El Monitor de la Educación Común*, Buenos Aires, October 31, 1920.

226. Zulema Manuela Noli, "Thesis Los actos patrios escolares y el cancionero del nivel primario como aporte a la construcción de la identidad nacional durante el peronismo (1946-1955)." Thesis supervisor: Silvia Rivera. From the "José María Rosa" Institutional Digital Repository in the "Rodolfo Puiggrós" Library of the National University of Lanús, published at www.repositoriojmr. unla.edu.ar/descarga/Tesis/MAMIC/032288_Noli.pdf.

227. Carlos Escudé, *La educación patriótica, respuesta a la nueva crisis identitaria de la comunidad imaginada de los argentinos*, published at www.argentina-rree.com/documentos/cultura_escu- de.htm.

228. *El Monitor de la Educación Común*, Buenos Aires, July 31, 1911, 128.

229. Enrique Banchs, "Las canciones escolares," *El Monitor de la Educación Común*, Buenos Aires, July 31, 1909, 29-35.

230. Gustavo Gabriel Otero and Daniel Varacalli Costas, *Puccini en la Argentina* (Buenos Aires: Instituto Italiano de Cultura, 2006), 97.

231. Ibid.; Escudé, La educación patriótica.

232. *Enciclopedia de la música argentina.* Compiled by Rodolfo Arizaga (Buenos Aires: Fondo Nacional de las Artes, 1972), 236.

233. Ibid., Noli, Zulema Manuela.

234. Ibid., Noli, Zulema Manuela.

235. "Message from his excellency the Minister of Culture and Education, Doctor Oscar Ivanissevich. September 1, 1974" (Buenos Aires: National Center of Educational Documentation and Information, 1974).

236. Resolution number 158 of September 18, 1974, from the Ministry of Education of the Nation, published at www.bnm.me.gov.ar/giga1/normas/7973.pdf.

237. See his statements reproduced in the first part of this book, particularly those whose source is indicated in note 115.

238. Michele Selvini and Antonino Votto, *Grandi maestri alla Scala: Antonino Votto* (Milan: Edizioni MC Musica Classica, 1999), 39.

239. *La Prensa*, Buenos Aires, June 13, 1942. The cast from that production included Warren, Milanov (alternating with Rigal), Jagel, Vaghi, and Romito.

240. *La Razón*, Buenos Aires, May 24, 1947. The cast from that performance included Rigal, Gigli (alternating with Vela), Barbieri, Damiani (alternating with Mattiello) and Neri (alternating with Vaghi).

241. Arthur Bloomfield, *More than the Notes*, digital edition, cap. 29 (translation by the authors).

242. The letter from Giacomo Puccini to Maurice Kufferath, dated January 10, 1910, is reproduced in Eugenio Gara, editor, *Carteggi pucciniani* (Milan: Ricordi, 1958), number 557, 374.

243. The letter is reproduced in facsimile in Panizza, *Medio siglo*, 139, and the date in Garmisch is listed as April 11, 1932 (translation by the authors).

244. Sergio Rossi and Michele Selvini, *Grandi maestri alla Scala: Héctor Panizza* (Milan: Edizioni MC Musica Classica, 2000), 44.

245. Authors taken from the chronology organized by Carlo Marinelli Roscioni, in Rossi and Selvini, *Grandi maestri alla Scala: Héctor Panizza*. The same procedure was followed with the soloists and theaters mentioned in what follows, always comparing them with other sources.

246. According to personal testimony to the authors (Buenos Aires, August 15, 2015) by Horacio Sanguinetti, who listened to that radio broadcast.

247. Quoted in Manso, *Delia Rigal*, 30.

248. Enzo Valenti Ferro, *Los directores. Teatro Colón: 1908-1984* (Buenos Aires: Ediciones de Arte Gaglianone, 1985), 24-25.

249. Bloomfield, *More than the notes*, digital edition, cap. 29.

250. Excerpt of a letter from Panizza to a member of the Teatro Colón Resident Orchestra, dated in Milan on Sept. 27, 1963, and reproduced in Osvaldo Barrios and Edmundo Piccioni, *Teatro Colón. Orquesta Estable: Historia y anécdotas* (Buenos Aires: Ediciones Nuevos Tiempos, 2006).

251. Mendelssohn: *Fourth Symphony*. Orchestra of the Teatro alla Scala, Milan. Grammofono, 1930.

252. Wagner: "Nun sei bedankt, mein lieber Schwan" from *Lohengrin*. Fernando Ciniselli, tenor. Choir of the Teatro alla Scala, Vittore Veneziani. Orchestra of the Teatro alla Scala, Milan. Fonotipia, 1928.

253. Bellini: *Norma*. Gina Cigna (Norma), Giovanni Martinelli (Pollione), Bruna Castagna (Adalgisa), Ezio Pinza (oroveso), Thelma Votipka (Clotilde), Giordano Paltrinieri (Flavio). Metropolitan Opera Chorus / Fausto Cleva. Metropolitan Opera Orchestra. Metropolitan Opera, Nueva York, 20-2-1937. Great Opera Performances, Cantus Classics, The Fourties, AS Disc, Arkadia.

254. Pearl Arkadia, Verdi: *Otello*. Giovanni Martinelli (Otello), Stella Roman (Desdemona), Lawrence Tibbett (Jago), Alessio De Paolis (Cassio), Nicola Moscona (Lodovico), Thelma Votipka (Emilia), John Dudley

(Roderigo), George Cehanovsky (Montano), Wilfred Engelman (Heraldo). Metropolitan Opera Chorus, Fausto Cleva. Metropolitan Opera Orchestra. Metropolitan Opera, New York, January 18, 1941.

255. Joseph Horowitz, "The Met's *Otello* when It Sizzled," *The New York Times*, March 9, 2003 (translation by the authors).

256. Cf. Leonor Plate, *Óperas Teatro Colón. Esperando el Centenario* (Buenos Aires: Editorial Dunken, 2006).

257. Alberto Emilio Giménez, "Héctor Panizza, músico argentino de proyección internacional," *Revista Teatro Colón* number 53 (Buenos Aires: Teatro Colón, May 1999).

258. Alberto Williams, in *La Quena*, number 67, Buenos Aires, December 1936.

259. See as examples: "*Aïda* had a mediocre performance last night [...]. The maestro Héctor Panizza demonstrated his great skill," *La Nación*, Buenos Aires, August 24, 1929, and "The brilliant work of the maestro Héctor Panizza must be excepted," *La Nación*, May 25, 1949, among many others from that newspaper. Even in the foreign press, for instance, on the occasion of the debut of the weak *Maddalena de Michetti*, it is left clear that "Panizza conducted with the utmost care and dignity," *La Stampa*, Turin, November 23, 1928, in www.archiviolastampa.it/ component/option,com_lastampa/task,search/mod,libera/ action,viewer/ itemid,3/page,4/articleid,1158_01_1928_0279_0004_24381471/anews,true/ (translation by the authors).

260. See Silvina Luz Mansilla, *El discurso periodístico de Gastón Talamón en torno al nacionalismo musical argentino*, in bdigital.uncu.edu.ar/ objetos_digitales/3282/mansillahuellas7-2010.pdf.

261. Quoted in Juan Emilio Martini, *Semblanza de Héctor Panizza* (Buenos Aires: Ricordi Americana, August 6, 1968).

262. Personal testimony of José Luis Sáenz to the authors (Buenos Aires, September 15, 2015).

263. *El Mundo*, Buenos Aires, August 14, 1936.

264. Mariano Antonio Barrenechea, *Historia estética de la música* (Buenos Aires: Editorial Claridad, 1963), 412.

265. *La Nación*, Buenos Aires, March 3, 1921.

266. *La Época*, Buenos Aires, May 16, 1920.

267. "A great Argentine composer: Maestro Panizza" by Adolfo Lanús in *Caras y Caretas*, Buenos Aires, June 11, 1921.

268. Infographic of the opera seasons 1908–1999. Supplement to *Revista Teatro Colón* (Buenos Aires: Teatro Colón, December 1999).

269. *La Nación*, Buenos Aires, July 13, 1929.

270. *La Nación*, Buenos Aires, January 1, 1930.

271. "Héctor Panizza, argentino al 100 por ciento," by Arturo Lagorio in *Caras y Caretas*, Buenos Aires, May 5, 1934. Some phrases are as significant as the title: "The champion's return home" and "The assurance of his compatriots' recognition as supreme desire."

272. Arturo Lagorio was then general consul in Naples, and in that position had been supported as honorary vice consul by Antonino Malvagni, conductor of the Municipal Symphonic Band. The interview was dated April 1934.

273. Roberto Caamaño, *La historia del Teatro Colón, 1908-1968* (Buenos Aires: Editorial Cinetea, 1969) and Leonor Plate, *Óperas Teatro Colón. Esperando el Centenario* (Buenos Aires: Editorial Dunken, 2006).

274. *La Nación*, Buenos Aires, August 11, 1929.

275. Omar Corrado, *Música y modernidad en Buenos Aires. 1920-1940* (Buenos Aires: Gourmet Musical Ediciones, 2010), 166-171.

276. José Luis Sáenz, "*La Scala y el Colón. Una larga amistad artística,*" *Revista Teatro Colón* no. 88 (Buenos Aires: Teatro Colón, September-October 2009), 22.

277. *El Mercurio Musical,* special number dedicated to the Day of Music February-March 1943. The others consulted were Boero, De Rogatis, Espoile, Gil, Gaito, Gilardi, Ginastera, López Buchardo, Palma, Sammartino, Schiuma, Sofía, Ugarte, Valenti Costa, and Lange.

278. Panizza, *Medio siglo,* 187.

279. Panizza, "Arturo Toscanini. Una evocación," 12.

280. Personal communication from Harvey Sachs to the authors, July 19, 2015 (translation by the authors).

281. Max Rudolf, *The Grammar of Conducting. A Practical Study of Modern Baton Technique* (New York: G. Schirmer, 1950).

282. he conversation can be heard on YouTube: www.youtube.com/watch?v=BegL-02iCEo.

283. Selvini and Votto, *Grandi maestri alla Scala: Antonino Votto,* 37.

284. As we said previously, in 1917 Panizza had debuted his opera *Il macigno* at La Scala; the work was very warmly received. Panizza and De Sabata died within days of one another, in December 1967.

285. See note 140.

286. Erich Leinsdorf, *The Composer's Advocate. A Radical Orthodoxy for Musicians* (New Haven: Yale University Press, 1981), 56-57.

287. Tullio Serafin and Alceo Toni, *Stile, tradizioni e convenzioni del melodramma italiano del Settecento e dell'Ottocento* (Milan: Ricordi, 1958).

288. Juan Emilio Martini, *Convenciones, cortes y transportes en las óperas italianas de repertorio* (Buenos Aires: Ricordi Americana, 1988).

289. Juan Emilio Martini, *Semblanza de Héctor Panizza* (Pamphlet edited by Ricordi Americana, Buenos Aires, 6 August 1968). It is curious that Martini directly connects Panizza with Toscanini but differentiates him markedly from Serafin, who in reality came from the same school.

290. Personal testimony of Jorge Fontenla to the authors (Buenos Aires, September 10, 2016).

291. Personal testimony of Vicente La Ferla to the authors (Buenos Aires, July 10, 2015).

292. See as a good example of this: "Una pasión argentina," the interview given to Miguel Ángel Veltri by G. Maldé (Carlos Ernesto Ure) in Revista *Clásica* 63 (Buenos Aires: Radio Clásica, July 1993), 12-17.

293. Personal testimony of Ronaldo Rosa to the authors (Buenos Aires, Feb. 25, 2010).

294. Notably corroborated by Riccardo Muti in his autobiography *Prima la musica, poi le parole* (Milan: Rizzoli, 2010).

295. Il direttore d'orchestra. Consigli per i giovani che aspirano alla direzione d'orchestra, published in Selvini and Votto, *Grandi maestri alla Scala: Antonino Votto*, 117-135.

296. Hans Swarowsky, *Dirección de orquesta. Defensa de la obra* (Madrid: Real Musical, 1989), 291.

297. *Claudio Abbado. Lux aexterna*, documentary directed in 1985 by Norbert Beilharz and produced by Maran Film for Südfunk Stuttgart, edited in 1986 by ArtHaus Musik on DVD.

298. For some reason, despite his notable pedagogic labor and with Muti fully embarked on his international career, in around 1982 (that is, three years before dying) Votto opined that Toscanini had not left artistic heirs, either direct or indirect, and that there were only some talented youths —whose names he does not mention— who attempted in vain to imitate him. See on YouTube: www.youtube.com/watch?v=XZn0UY3Jkkc.

299. *Verdi: Messa da requiem*, recording produced by Unitel and edited as a DVD in 2005 by Deutsche Grammophon.

300. Fernando Previtali, *Guida allo studio della direzione d'orchestra* (Milan: Ricordi, 1951).

301. Mauro Balestrazzi, *Carlos Kleiber. Angelo o demone?* (Palermo: L'Epos Società Editrice, 2006), 122-24.

302. Harvey Sachs, ed., Nel mio cuore troppo d'assoluto. Le lettere di Arturo Toscanini (Milán: Garzanti Libri, 2003), 180.

303. John Russell, *Erich Kleiber* (Buenos Aires: Editorial Sudamericana, 1958).

304. Carlos Kleiber, *I Am Lost to the World*, documentary directed by Georg Wübbolt, co-produced by BFMI and ZDF/3sat, and edited in 2011 by C Major Entertainment.

305. Alessandro Zignani, *Carlos Kleiber. Il tramonto dell'occidente* (Varese: Zecchini Editore, 2010).

306. See on YouTube: www.youtube.com/watch?v=BegL-02iCEo.

307. Verdi: *Aida*, with Birgit Nilsson, Franco Corelli, Grace Bumbry, Mario Sereni and Bonaldo Giaiotti; Choir and orchestra of the Teatro dell'opera in Rome; EMI, 1967.

308. Zubin Mehta, *La partitura della mia vita* (Milan: Excelsior 1881, 2007), 40.

309. Conf. Joseph Horowitz, *Understanding Toscanini* (New York: Knopf, 1987), whose conclusions in this respect, however, arrive at exaggerated extremes.

310. Giménez, "Héctor Panizza."

311. There seem to have been only a couple of artistic institutions in the world that bear the name of our biographical subject: the "Ettore Panizza" Centro di Documentazione e Produzione Musicale, created in December 1990 in Genoa, which ironically does not pursue objectives directly related to Héctor, and the "Héctor Panizza" Conservatory of Music in Laguna Larga, Río Segundo, Province of Córdoba, Argentina.

312. Alberto Emilio Giménez, Originally published in *La Nación* on November 30, 1967, with the aim of making known the news of the

Argentine director's death; later under the title "A la vera de Toscanini," and afterward on August 10, 1975, under the title "A la vera de Arturo Toscanini," on the occasion of the centenary of his birth.

313. Toscanini's rehearsal of Richard Strauss' symphonic poem *Death and Transfiguration* recorded by NBC is perhaps the most overwhelming example of his poor conduct when working with his musicians; see on YouTube: www.youtube.com/ watch?v=Cxh-o9ENW5o.

314. Panizza, *Medio siglo*, 37. The time and location of this unfortunate performance, which in the chronology is placed as Panizza's first anecdotal memory, was checked by the authors.

315. Panizza, *Medio siglo*, 36. Panizza does not mention either the opera or its author, who have had to be "discovered" by the authors.

316. Panizza, *Medio siglo*, 65. The authors determined the time and location of this performance using the relevant theatrical chronologies, already mentioned.

317. Panizza, *Medio siglo*, 70. It has not been possible to discover the Spanish city where this performance took place.

318. Panizza, *Medio siglo*, 72. The year the performance took place has been incorporated into the story by the authors.

319. Panizza, *Medio siglo*, 141. The authors, who also located the performance in the year mentioned, checked the identity of Carottini, whom Panizza mentions only by his last name.

320. Panizza, *Medio siglo*, 87. Panizza does not mention either the opera or the composer, information that was reconstructed by the authors. Pietro Canonica was a very prolific visual artist, even at the international level; the monumental tomb of the Argentine president José Figueroa Alcorta in the porteño cemetery of Recoleta is his work.

321. Panizza, *Medio siglo*, 88. Several operas about Lucio Licinio Lucullus exist in Italian; none have survived the passage of time and it was not possible to identify which one of them was referred to by Panizza.

322. Selvini and Votto, *Grandi maestri alla Scala: Antonino Votto*, 44. It seems that this episode embarrassed Panizza to the end of his days; perhaps this is why he does not mention it in his memoirs.

323. Selvini, and Votto, *Grandi maestri alla Scala: Antonino Votto*, 43. Panizza does not mention this juicy episode in his memoirs and one can easily understand why.

324. Panizza, *Medio siglo*, 141.

325. Panizza, *Medio siglo*, 142. Panizza erroneously mentions the hotel as Explanada, in some way hispanicizing the original name. It must be said that the scarcity of interviews with Panizza is a fact as true as it is unfortunate for those who propose to research him.

326. Originally from Marcos de Estrada, Typescript, unpublished, in the archive of *La Nación* in Buenos Aires.

327. Unidentified. It could be another name for *Bodas campestres*, or a work of instrumental chamber music. See 33 and 141.

328. See www.criticalpast.com/video/65675041886_Metropolitan-opera_Conductor-Ettore-Panizza_ opera-score, edited by Critical Past. One can also see a fragment of the same footage on YouTube: www.youtube.com/watch?v=LTDEJ3muz5c, edited by Critical Past. (Last visit: August 24, 2015).

329. Recording by Victor, July 1929; edited on the double compact disc that accompanies *Grandi maestri alla Scala: Héctor Panizza*.

330. James North, *André Kostelanetz on Records and on the Air* (Toronto: The Scarecrow Press, 2011), 275.

BIBLIOGRAPHY

The same can be said of Panizza's bibliography that was said about his discography: the attention Toscanini has received over the last half century has been denied to the Italian-Argentine artist. The bibliographic sources that specific comment on Héctor's life and work are thus unfortunately reduced to only two publications.

The first is his autobigraphy, *Medio siglo de vida musical (Half a Century of Musical Life)*, a book as interesting as it is incomplete and imprecise. Written in a dubious Spanish, it went out of print decades ago and was never reedited; Panizza dictated it to his second wife between 1949 and 1950, when the director was already seventy-five years old.

The second is the entry dedicated to Panizza in the series *Grandi maestri alla Scala*, a very brief entry belonging to a collection that only published a few copies, and is thus also difficult to access; a good part of its content, furthermore, is no more than a summary, in Italian, of Héctor's memoirs already mentioned.

No book about Héctor exists in other languages, and the rest of the sources can all be qualified as secondary or minor, without this in any way signifying a judgment of value about them. The majority are, regrettably, difficult to consult.

The *Revista Teatro Colón* magazine, owing to its specific importance as a source for the topic that occupies us and also for possessing a format more assimilable to a volume than a periodical publication, is cited —here as throughout the entire present work— with the method used for books.

The journalistic interviews and electronic sources cited in the notes are not listed here, save for in a few exceptional cases due to their importance.

NEWSPAPERS

Crítica, Buenos Aires

El Mundo, Buenos Aires

La Época, Buenos Aires

La Nación, Buenos Aires

La Prensa, Buenos Aires

La Razón, Buenos Aires

Los Andes, Mendoza

The Christian Science Monitor, Chicago

The New York Times, New York

MAGAZINES

Cantabile, Buenos Aires

Caras y Caretas, Buenos Aires

Clásica, Buenos Aires

Criterio, Buenos Aires

El Mercurio Musical, Buenos Aires

El Monitor de la Educación Común, Buenos Aires

El Mundo del Arte, Buenos Aires

La Gaceta Musical, Buenos Aires *La Quena*, Buenos Aires

Musical America, New York *Musical Courier*, Chicago

Polifonía, Buenos Aires

Revista Artística y Musical de Buenos Aires, Buenos Aires

Revista Teatro Colón, Buenos Aires

GENERAL PUBLICATIONS

Enciclopedia de la música argentina. Compiled by Rodolfo Arizaga. Buenos Aires: Fondo Nacional de las Artes, 1971.

Enciclopedia della musica Ricordi. Edited by Claudio Sartori. Milan: Ricordi, 1964.

Diccionario biográfico ítalo-argentino. Compiled by Dionisio Petriella and Sara Sosa Miatello. Buenos Aires: Asociación Dante Alighieri, 1976.

Diccionario de la música. Compiled by Eric Blom. Buenos Aires: Editorial Claridad, 1958.

Diccionario de la música española e hispanoamericana. Edited by Emilio Casares Rodicio. Madrid: Sociedad Generales de Autores y Editores, 2002.

Dizionario degli interpreti musicali. Musica classica e operistica. Coordinated by Loris Marchetti and Cristina Santarelli. Milan: Editori Associati, 1993.

Grove Dictionary of Music and Musicians. Edited by Eric Blom. London: Macmillan & Company, 1954.

The New Grove Dictionary of Music and Musicians. Edited by Stanley Sadie. London: Macmillan & Company, 1980.

SPECIFIC PUBLICATIONS

Aráoz Badí, Jorge. "De amaneceres y ocasos," *Revista Teatro Colón* number 53 (Buenos Aires: Teatro Colón, May 1999)

Various authors. *Historia general de la danza en la Argentina.* Buenos Aires: Fondo Nacional de las Artes, 2008.

Balestrazzi, Mauro. *Carlos Kleiber: Angelo o demone?* Palermo: L'Epos Società Editrice, 2006.

Balestrazzi, Mauro. *Toscanini secondo me.* Palermo: L'Epos Società Editrice, 2005.

Banchs, Enrique. "Las canciones escolares." *El Monitor de la Educación Común,* Buenos Aires, July 31, 1909.

Barber, Charles. *Corresponding with Carlos. A Biography of Carlos Kleiber.* Lanham: Scarecrow Press, 2001.

Bardin, Pablo. *La Sinfónica Nacional cumple medio siglo.* Published at historia- sinfonica.blogspot.com.ar/2007/03/la-sinfnica-nacional-cumple-medio-siglo. html; 20-III-2007

Barigazzi, Giuseppe. *La Scala racconta.* Milan: Ulrico Hoepli Editore, 2014.

Barrenechea, Mariano Antonio. *Historia estética de la música.* Buenos Aires: Editorial Claridad, 1963.

Barrios, Osvaldo, and Edmundo Piccioni. *Teatro Colón. Orquesta Estable: Historia y anécdotas.* Buenos Aires: Ediciones Nuevos Tiempos, 2006.

Bellucci, Alberto. "*Aurora*: Italiana y argentina." *Revista Teatro Colón* number 53 (Buenos Aires: Teatro Colón, May 1999)

Bloomfield, Arthur. *More than the Notes.* Digital edition (www.morethanthenotes.com/read-the-book/ettore-panizza)

Buch, Esteban. *O juremos con gloria morir. Una historia del Himno Nacional Argentino, de la Asamblea del Año XIII a Charly García.* Buenos Aires: Eterna Cadencia, 2013.

Budden, Julian. *Puccini.* Roma: Carocci Editore, 2005.

Budden, Julian. *Puccini. His Life and Works.* New York: Oxford University Press, 2002.

Caamaño, Roberto. *La historia del Teatro Colón, 1908-1968.* Buenos Aires: Editorial Cinetea, 1969.

Cabrera, Napoleón. "¿Es posible una ópera argentina?" in *Revista Teatro Colón* número 53 (Buenos Aires: Teatro Colón, May 1999)

Carner, Mosco. *Puccini.* Buenos Aires: Javier Vergara Editor, 1987.

Cattelani, Ferruccio. *Actividades musicales en la Argentina.* Buenos Aires: Imprenta de Luis Veggia, 1927.

Cetrangolo, Aníbal Enrique. *Ópera, barcos y banderas. El melodrama y la migración en Argentina (1880-1920)*. Madrid: Biblioteca Nueva, 2015.

Cetrangolo, Aníbal Enrique. Doctoral thesis *Ópera e identidad en el encuentro migratorio. El melodrama italiano en Argentina entre 1880 y 1920*, edited by Enrique Cámara de Landa. Valladolid: Universidad de Valladolid, 2010. Digital edition at uvadoc.uva.es/bitstream/10324/3783/1/ TESIS381-131024.pdf

Corrado, Omar. *Música y modernidad en Buenos Aires. 1920-1940*. Buenos Aires: Gourmet Musical Ediciones, 2010.

Cotton, Daniel. *International Bohemia: Scenes of XIX Century Life*. Philadelphia: University of Pennsylvania Press, 2013.

Cox, Gordon, and Robin Stevens, eds. *The Origins and Foundations of Music Education: International Perspectives*. New York: Bloomsbury, 2017.

D'Amico, Fedele, and Rosanna Paumgartner, eds. *La lezione di Toscanini. Atti del Convegno di studi toscaniniani al XXX Maggio Musicale Fiorentino*. Florence: Vallecchi Editore, 1970.

De la Fuente, Sandra. *"Aurora*: la Argentina como telón de fondo" in *El gran libro del Teatro Colón*. Buenos Aires: Clarín, 2010.

Dezillio, Romina. "El ojo de la cerradura: mujeres, música y feminismos en *La Mujer Álbum — Revista (1899-1902)*" in Silvina Luz Mansilla, director, *Dar la nota. El rol de la prensa en la historia musical argentina*. Buenos Aires: Gourmet Musical Ediciones, 2012.

Dillon, César, and Juan Andrés Sala. *El teatro musical en Buenos Aires. Teatro Doria— Teatro Marconi*. Buenos Aires: Ediciones de Arte Gaglianone, 1997.

Dillon, César, and Juan Andrés Sala. *El teatro musical en Buenos Aires. Teatro Coliseo*. Buenos Aires: Ediciones de Arte Gaglianone, 1999.

Dillon, César, and Michele Selvini. *Grandi maestri alla Scala: Tullio Serafin*. Milán: Edizioni MC Musica Classica, 1998.

D'Urbano, Jorge. *Música en Buenos Aires*. Buenos Aires: Editorial Sudamericana, 1966.

Escudé, Carlos. *La educación patriótica, respuesta a la nueva crisis identitaria de la comunidad imaginada de los argentinos* in www.argentina-rree.com/docu- mentos/cultura_escude.htm

Frassati, Luciana. *Il maestro. Arturo Toscanini e il suo mondo.* Milan: Gruppo Editoriale Fabbri, 1967.

Fumagalli, Ángel. *"Aurora.* Un título profético para la ópera argentina." *Aurora. Programa de mano del Teatro Colón.* Buenos Aires: Teatro Colón, May 1999.

Fumagalli, Ángel. "La historia se dice cantando." *Revista Teatro Colón* number 53 (Buenos Aires: Teatro Colón, May 1999).

Galkin, Elliott. *A History of Orchestral Conducting. In Theory and Practice.* New York: Pendragon Press, 1988.

Gara, Eugenio, ed. *Carteggi pucciniani.* Milán: Ricordi, 1958.

García, Muñoz, Carmen, and Guillermo Stamponi. *Orquesta Filarmónica de Buenos Aires, 1946-2006.* Buenos Aires: Asociación Filarmónica de Buenos Aires, 2007.

Gesualdo, Vicente. *Breve historia de la música en la Argentina.* Buenos Aires: Editorial Claridad, 1998.

Gesualdo, Vicente. *Pablo Rosquellas y los orígenes de la ópera en Buenos Aires.* Buenos Aires: Editorial Artes en América, 1962.

Giménez, Alberto Emilio. "A la vera de Arturo Toscanini." *La Nación,* Buenos Aires, Aug. 10, 1975.

Giménez, Alberto Emilio. "A la vera de Toscanini." *La Nación,* Buenos Aires, Nov. 30, 1967.

Giménez, Alberto Emilio. "Héctor Panizza, músico argentino de proyección internacional." *Revista Teatro Colón* number 53 (Buenos Aires: Teatro Colón, May 1999).

Gossett, Philip. *Divas and Scholars: Performing Italian Opera.* Chicago: The University of Chicago Press, 2006.

Groussac, Paul. *Críticas sobre música.* Buenos Aires: Biblioteca Nacional, 2007.

Groussac, Paul. *Paradojas sobre música*. Buenos Aires: Biblioteca Nacional, 2008.

Horowitz, Joseph. "The Met's *Otello* when It Sizzled," *The New York Times*, March 9, 2003.

Horowitz, Joseph. *Understanding Toscanini*. New York: Knopf, 1987.

Hughes, Spike. *The Toscanini Legacy*. New York: Dover Publications, 1969.

Isotta, Paolo, and Eduardo Rescigno. *Teatro alla Scala*. Milan: RCS Quotidiani, 2004.

Kendell, Colin. *The Complete Puccini*. Stroud: Amberley Publishing, 2012.

Korn, Francis, and Silvia Sigal. *Buenos Aires antes del Centenario, 1904-1909*. Buenos Aires: Sudamericana, 2010.

Lauria, Christian. *Adelaida Negri: Vida, arte y talento*. Buenos Aires: Editorial Dunken, 2014.

Lebrecht, Norman. *El mito del maestro. Los grandes directores de orquesta y su lucha por el poder*. Madrid: Acento Editorial, 1997.

Leinsdorf, Erich. *The Composer's Advocate. A Radical Orthodoxy for Musicians*. New Haven: Yale University Press, 1981.

Leiva, Alberto David. "Mito patriótico y paradigma en *Aurora*." *Revista Teatro Colón* number 53 (Buenos Aires: Teatro Colón, May 1999).

Lisio, Norma Lucía. *Divina Tani y el inicio de la ópera en Buenos Aires (1824- 1830)*. Buenos Aires: author's edition, 1996.

Mansilla, Silvina Luz. *La obra musical de Carlos Guastavino. Circulación, recep- ción, mediaciones*. Buenos Aires: Gourmet Musical Ediciones, 2011.

Manso, Carlos. *Delia Rigal*. Buenos Aires: El Francotirador Ediciones, 1998.

Manso, Carlos. *Del Teatro de la Ópera a Carmen Piazzini*. Buenos Aires: De los Cuatro Vientos, 2012.

Marchesi, Gustavo. *Toscanini*. Milan: Bompiani RCS Libri, 2007.

Martini, Juan Emilio. *Convenciones, cortes y transportes en las óperas italianas de repertorio.* Buenos Aires: Ricordi Americana, 1988.

Martini, Juan Emilio. *Semblanza de Héctor Panizza.* Buenos Aires: Ricordi Americana, 6 August 1968.

Masutto, Giovanni. *I maestri di musica italiani del secolo XIX. Notizie biografiche.* Venecia: Stabilimento Tipografico Giovanni Cecchini, 1884.

Matheopoulos, Helena. *Los grandes directores de orquesta.* Barcelona: Ediciones Robinbook, 2007.

McGovern, Dennis, and Deborah Grace Winer. *Mis recuerdos de la ópera.* Buenos Aires: Javier Vergara Editor, 1992.

Mehta, Zubin. *La partitura della mia vita.* Milan: Excelsior 1881, 2007.

Mildonian, Paola. *Libretti italiani alle origini dell'opera argentina.* Published at www.mundoclasico.com/ed/documentos/doc-ver.aspx?id=0013289; 26-IX-2003

Muchnik, Daniel. *Inmigrantes. 1860-1914. La historia de los míos y de los tuyos.* Buenos Aires: Sudamericana, 2015.

Muti, Riccardo. *Prima la musica, poi le parole. Autobiografia.* Milan: Rizzoli, 2010.

Muti, Riccardo. *Verdi, l'italiano. Ovvero, in musica, le nostre radici.* Milan: Rizzoli, 2012.

Negri, Adelaida. *"María Malibrán: talento y libertad." Revista Teatro Colón* number 80 (Buenos Aires: Teatro Colón, March-April 2008).

Noli, Zulema Manuela. Thesis *Los actos patrios escolares y el cancionero del ni- vel primario como aporte a la construcción de la identidad nacional durante el peronismo (1946-1955),* directed by Silvia Rivera. Institutional Digital Repository "José María Rosa" of the "Rodolfo Puiggrós" Library of the Universidad Nacional de Lanús, published at www.repositoriojmr.unla.edu. ar/descarga/Tesis/MAMIC/032288_Noli.pdf

North, James. *André Kostelanetz on Records and on the Air.* Toronto: The Scarecrow Press, 2011.

Otero, Gustavo Gabriel, and Daniel Varacalli Costas. *Puccini en la Argentina. Junio-agosto 1905*. Buenos Aires: Instituto Italiano de Cultura, 2006.

Panizza, Héctor. "Arturo Toscanini. Una evocación en su centenario." *Revista Polifonía* number 133/4 (Buenos Aires, second trimester of 1967).

Panizza, Héctor. *Aurora. Partitura*. Buenos Aires: Ricordi Americana, 1945.

Panizza, Héctor (in care of). *Grande trattato di strumentazione e d'orchestrazione moderne di Hector Berlioz*. Milan: Ricordi, 1912.

Panizza, Héctor (in care of). *La fanciulla del West* by Puccini. *Partitura*. Milan: Ricordi, 1911.

Panizza, Héctor. *Medio siglo de vida musical. Ensayo autobiográfico*. Buenos Aires: Ricordi Americana, 1952.

Phillips-Matz, Mary Jane. *Puccini. A Biography*. Lebanon: Northeastern University Press, 2002.

Plate, Leonor. *Óperas Teatro Colón. Esperando el Centenario*. Buenos Aires: Editorial Dunken, 2006.

Previtali, Fernando. *Guida allo studio della direzione d'orchestra*. Milan: Ricordi, 1951.

Ratier, Claudio. "Escenarios de la historia I. Temas atrapados por el rabo." *Cantabile* number 79 (Buenos Aires, July-August 2015).

Reale, Giovanni. *L'arte di Riccardo Muti e la musa platonica*. Milan: Bompiani, 2005.

Rigal, Delia. "Mi *Aurora*." *Revista Teatro Colón* number 53 (Buenos Aires: Teatro Colón, May 1999)

Rossi, Sergio, and Michele Selvini. *Grandi maestri alla Scala: Héctor Panizza*. Milan: Edizioni MC Musica Classica, 2000.

Russell, John. *Erich Kleiber*. Buenos Aires: Editorial Sudamericana, 1958.

Sachs, Harvey. *Music in Fascist Italy*. London: Weidenfeld & Nicolson, 1987.

Sachs, Harvey, ed. *Nel mio cuore troppo d'assoluto. Le lettere di Arturo Toscanini*. Milan: Garzanti Libri, 2003.

Sachs, Harvey, ed. *The Letters of Arturo Toscanini.* Chicago: University of Chicago Press, 2006.

Sachs, Harvey. *Toscanini.* New York: Harper Collins, 1988.

Sachs, Harvey. *Reflections on Toscanini.* Rocklin: Prima Publishing, 1993.

Sáenz, José Luis. "La Scala y el Colón. Una larga amistad artística." *Revista Teatro Colón* número 88 (Buenos Aires: Teatro Colón, September-October 2009).

Salgado, Susana. *The Teatro Solís: 150 Years of Opera, Concert and Ballet in Montevideo.* Middletown: Wesleyan University Press, 2003.

Sanguinetti, Horacio. *Los maestros cantores del siglo XX. Los tenores de la era disco- gráfica.* Buenos Aires: Ediciones Lumiere, 2005.

Sasturain, Juan. "Allora, parliemo di *Aurora.*" *Página/12,* Buenos Aires, Nov. 10, 2008.

Schickling, Dieter. *Giacomo Puccini: Catalogue of the Works.* Kassel: Bärenreiter, 2003.

Schoenberg, Harold. *Los grandes directores.* Buenos Aires: Javier Vergara Editor, 1990.

Selvini, Michele, and Antonino Votto. *Grandi maestri alla Scala: Antonino Votto.* Milan: Edizioni MC Musica Classica, 1999.

Serafin, Tullio. *Il direttore d'orchestra. Ai giovani che intendono dedicarsi all'arte direttoriale.* Milan: Ulrico Hoepli Editore, 1940.

Serafin, Tullio, and Alceo Toni. *Stile, tradizioni e convenzioni del melodramma italiano del Settecento e dell'Ottocento.* Milan: Ricordi, 1958.

Stravinski, Igor, and Robert Craft. *Memorias y comentarios.* Barcelona: Acantilado, 2013.

Suárez Urtubey, Pola. "*Aurora,* desde la música." *Revista Teatro Colón* number 53 (Buenos Aires: Teatro Colón, May 1999).

Suárez Urtubey, Pola. "La ópera y la generación del Ochenta." *Revista Teatro Colón* number 53 (Buenos Aires: Teatro Colón, May 1999).

Swarowsky, Hans. *Dirección de orquesta. Defensa de la obra.* Madrid: Real Musical, 1989.

Tegani, Ulderico. *La Scala. Nella sua storia e nella sua grandezza.* Milan: Valsecchi Editore, 1946.

Ure, Carlos Ernesto (G. Maldé). "Una pasión argentina." *Revista Clásica* number 63 (Buenos Aires: Radio Clásica, July 1993).

Valenti Ferro, Enzo. *100 años de música en Buenos Aires.* Buenos Aires: Ediciones de Arte Gaglianone, 1992.

Valenti Ferro, Enzo. *Historia de la ópera argentina.* Buenos Aires: Ediciones de Arte Gaglianone, 1997.

Valenti Ferro, Enzo. *Las voces. Teatro Colón: 1908-1982.* Buenos Aires: Ediciones de Arte Gaglianone, 1983.

Valenti Ferro, Enzo. *Los directores. Teatro Colón: 1908-1984.* Buenos Aires: Ediciones de Arte Gaglianone, 1985.

Varacalli Costas, Daniel. Interview with Darío Volonté in *Revista Teatro Colón* number 54 (Buenos Aires: Teatro Colón, June 1999).

Waddell, Jorge. "Desvíos y empalmes." *Revista Teatro Colón* number 100 (Buenos Aires: Teatro Colón, November-December 2011)

Weber, José Ignacio. "¿Ópera o música sinfónica? El interés de la crítica musical en la modernización del gusto porteño (1891-1895)" in Mansilla, Silvina Luz (editor): *Dar la nota. El rol de la prensa en la historia musical argentina.* Buenos Aires: Gourmet Musical Ediciones, 2012.

Wolkowicz, Vera. "La recepción de la ópera italiana en Buenos Aires a fines del período rosista: una polémica entre el *Diario de la Tarde* y el *Diario de Avisos* (1848-1851)" in Silvina Luz Mansilla, (editor): *Dar la nota. El rol de la prensa en la historia musical argentina.* Buenos Aires: Gourmet Musical Ediciones, 2012.

Wyndham, Henry Saxe. *Stories of the Operas and the Singers.* London: John Long, 1910.

Zignani, Alessandro. *Carlos Kleiber. Il tramonto dell'occidente.* Varese: Zecchini Editore, 2010.

INDEX